# EYEWITNESSES
## TO THE
# RUSSIAN
# REVOLUTION

# EYEWITNESSES
## TO THE
# RUSSIAN
# REVOLUTION

Edited by Todd Chretien

Haymarket Books
Chicago, Illinois

Published in 2017 by
Haymarket Books
P.O. Box 180165
Chicago, IL 60618
773-583-7884
www.haymarketbooks.org
info@haymarketbooks.org

ISBN: 978-1-60846-861-4

Trade distribution:
In the US, Consortium Book Sales and Distribution, www.cbsd.com
In Canada, Publishers Group Canada, www.pgcbooks.ca
In the UK, Turnaround Publisher Services, www.turnaround-uk.com
All other countries, Ingram Publisher Services International, IPS_Intlsales@
ingramcontent.com

This book was published with the generous support of Lannan Foundation and
Wallace Action Fund.

Cover design by Rachel Cohen.

Printed in Canada by union labor.

Library of Congress Cataloging-in-Publication data is available.

10 9 8 7 6 5 4 3 2 1

*To Isabela,*
*Who separates fact from fiction*

# TABLE OF CONTENTS

# ACKNOWLEDGMENTS

Over the years, many people have contributed to my appreciation of the Russian Revolution of 1917 and I owe them all a debt of gratitude. When I was in high school, Jean Souliere and Betsy Sweet made it possible for me to join a youth delegation to travel across the Soviet Union in 1987. A year or so later, Phil Gasper first acquainted me with a revolutionary Marxist analysis of Stalinism. In 1990, while I was renting a room in Colonia Máximo Jerez in Managua, Nicaragua, Mirna Gomez lent me a collection of Lenin's writings *en español* to help me learn vocabulary. Although I still lacked an outline of the revolution's basic narrative, I was intrigued enough to underline evocative words in *State and Revolution* (such as *lucha*) and work my way through sentences like *es más agradable y más provechoso vivir la "experiencia de la revolución" que escribir acerca de ella.* All the same, during those months, I absorbed a degree of skepticism with regard to the Great October Revolution from S., a Soviet cultural attaché on assignment in Managua, over home-cooked dinners with his family.

In 1991, I moved to New York City just as George H.W. Bush invaded Iraq. I joined the Barnard/Columbia Antiwar Coalition. There I had the good fortune to meet a dedicated core of organizers and to be introduced to socialists and communists, who convinced me of the importance of understanding the Russian Revolution as a precondition to making heads or tails of the state of global politics. Leon Trotsky's *My Life, The Revolution Betrayed,* and *The History of the Russian Revolution* burned away my foggy notions of "really existing communism." Sherry Wolf, Eric Fretz, Barbara Kancelbaum, and Pete Gillard teamed up to win me over to Trotskyism with books and pamphlets by writers like Tony Cliff and Chris Harman. Nightly subway rides on the 2 train back to Brooklyn with Lee Sustar and long-running discussions with Tristin Adie dramatically accelerated my learning curve.

Since then, discussions and debates with too many comrades to name have enriched and enhanced my view of the revolution and those exchanges have influenced the choices I have made in this anthology. Special thanks go to: Anthony Arnove for proposing this project and providing kindly, if insistent, encouragement along the way; Jessie Muldoon for insisting on the centrality of the theory of permanent revolution and Lenin's approach to national liberation; Ahmed Shawki for advice on the manuscript; Paul D'Amato for lending hard-to-find books; Eric Blanc for helpful source suggestions; John Riddell for innumerable insights into Bolshevik history; Ragina Johnson for helping me understand this book's audience; Nisha Bolsey for her consummate professionalism; Rachel Cohen for the beautiful book cover; and the tireless staff at Haymarket Books for their second-to-none design, editing, and promotional work.

Specifically, with regard to content, this book would not have been possible without the incredible work of the Marxist Internet Archive and their permission to use online versions of various texts as the starting basis for many of the selections in this book. Special thanks are due to David Walters on this score and to Brian Baggins, whose chronology of 1917 I used as a starting point for my own. I unreservedly encourage anyone reading this book to go to www.marxists.org to browse their invaluable archives and contribute whatever financial support or volunteer efforts you can. Many of the selections in this anthology are in the public domain, but the following publishers graciously granted permission for selections from the following works: Haymarket Books for Trotsky's *History of the Russian Revolution;* Pluto Press for *The Bolsheviks and the October Revolution: Minutes of the Central Committee of the Russian Social-Democratic Labor Party (Bolsheviks), August 1917–February 1918,* translated by Ann Bone; New Park Publications Ltd/Indexreach Ltd (Index Books) for F.F. Raskolnikov, *Kronstadt and Petrograd in 1917;* Princeton University Press for Nikolai Nikolaevich Sukhanov, *The Russian Revolution of 1917: A Personal Record by N.N. Sukhanov,* translated by Joel Carmichael; and Orion Publishing Group for Isaac Nachman Steinberg, *In the Workshop of Revolution.*

# A NOTE ON THE TEXT AND SOURCES

In the early years of the Russian Revolution, English-language sources transliterated unfamiliar places and names unsystematically: Lenine and Trotzky are easy enough to figure out, but names like Nikolay Chkheidze, as you can imagine, went through various derivations. Where it is not confusing or misleading, I have left the original renderings because, I believe, the struggle with nomenclature goes to show how the Revolution took the international movement by surprise. I have left syntactical mashups in their original form for much the same reason, as they demonstrate the haste with which many writers dashed off their accounts. On the other hand, if errors appear to be later editorial concoctions or if they are unduly confusing, I have corrected them. Additionally, I have lightly edited British English to conform to American English as well as other minor corrections for consistency and meaning.

In order to adapt shorter sections of much longer works, I have cut and spliced a great deal of material. My approach has been to maintain the coherence of eyewitness reports while controlling for length and repetition. Unless noted with an italicized subheading, all selections have been made within single articles, interviews, documents, or chapters of books. In order to signal where I have interrupted an author's text, I use ellipses as follows: three dots to indicate missing words within a single sentence; three dots in brackets [ . . . ] to indicate a missing section (that is, a gap consisting of sentences or whole paragraphs or sections that I have cut out); and four dots followed by a space to indicate missing words at the end of a sentence.

I have kept endnotes to a bare minimum, generally using them only to refer to secondary sources. I have decided not to burden the text with explanatory notes, either at the bottom of the page or in the endnotes. My reasoning is that context is usually enough to make the names and places meaningful. Where there is ambiguity or it might lead to confusion, I have inserted editorial comments in brackets [like this].

I have included an extensive chronology and glossary of characters, parties, and events at the end of the book. For those unfamiliar with the general history of 1917, I would suggest reading my introduction and then glancing through the chronology to get a sense of key events.

Some additional things: After the beginning of World War I, the Russian government changed the name of St. Petersburg to Petrograd, as they believed the former sounded too German. I have stuck with the original name, unless an eyewitness uses the name Petrograd. Where the Russian word *soviet* refers to the general phenomena of workers, soldiers, sailors, and peasants setting up "councils," the word is not capitalized. However, when referring to a particular institution, it is capitalized. So, for instance, *soviets were established all over Russia after February 1917, but the St. Petersburg Soviet was the most important of all.* As the word soon also became an adjective, the same formula applies: *Bolsheviks relied on the soviet masses as the key to overthrowing Kerensky, after which the Second All-Russian Congress of Soviets formally established Soviet Russia.* Similarly: *The Bolsheviks argued a revolution was necessary to win socialism, but Lenin argued the February Revolution should not be understood as the final phase of the Revolution, but only its beginning. Tsar* and *Czar* are used interchangeably by many of the authors in this book, but I use Tsar in any editorial comments.

In 1917, Russia used the Julian calendar, which runs thirteen days behind the Gregorian calendar in use today (and was then in use in Western Europe, the United States, and elsewhere). Thus, what was called the February Revolution by the Julian calendar actually occurred in March according to the Gregorian calendar; likewise, the October Revolution (Julian) took place in November (Gregorian). Except where noted, I have rendered all dates in Julian, as this was the calendar then in use in the Russian Empire.

Each section begins with a brief overview of important events and debates and is designated with a Roman numeral. Each selection gives specifics on events and, when needed, the eyewitness themselves and is designated with sequential Arabic numbers. Source references are listed at the end of the book.

# INTRODUCTION TO 1917

## Todd Chretien

In the wake of the October 1917 Bolshevik Revolution, Menshevik leader Julius Martov proclaimed that "before us after all is a victorious uprising of the proletariat—almost the entire proletariat supports Lenin and expects its social liberation from the uprising."[1] The aim of this book is to help prove Martov right—at least in this judgment.

For more than seventy years, October made its presence felt on the global stage. Yet here is where separating fact from fiction with respect to the October Revolution and the Bolshevik Party is paramount. If several generations of twentieth-century communist activists labored honestly (their more compromised leaders notwithstanding) toward the goal of human emancipation, the supreme tragedy of their struggle was that they all too often held aloft the banner of Stalinism (or in later days Maoism), political creeds altogether at odds with the Bolshevik Party in its heyday. Rather than leading toward full liberation, Stalinism led into cul-de-sacs and new tyrannies that often enough masqueraded as "communist." However, as Leon Trotsky, mortal foe of the bureaucratic regime, put it:

> The present purge [1937] draws between Bolshevism and Stalinism not simply a bloody line but a whole river of blood. The annihilation of all the older generation of Bolsheviks, an important part of the middle generation which participated in the civil war, and that part of the youth that took up most seriously the Bolshevik traditions, shows not only a political but a thoroughly physical incompatibility between Bolshevism and Stalinism.[2]

Trotsky's revolutionary opposition to Stalinism, however, remained a minority trend (and a small minority at that) from the late 1920s until the fall of the Berlin Wall and the final collapse of the Soviet Union. And despite many

1

false hopes, Stalinism's implosion gave rise not to democracy, but to a new class of oligarchic capitalists. This long disaster demands an explanation, but in order to know what went wrong, it is first necessary to know what went right.

In many ways, the Bolsheviks entered the maelstrom of 1917 at a distinct disadvantage compared to their main rivals on the left—the Socialist Revolutionary Party (SRs) and the Mensheviks—even as they negotiated a complicated set of unity negotiations with independent socialist factions and an array of socialist parties rooted in the Russian Empire's oppressed national minorities (Finns, Letts, Poles, Jews, etc.). In the end, the Bolsheviks' commitment to three assumptions, each of which had deep roots in the revolutionary socialist movement, allowed them to penetrate deeply into the working class, win over many rank-and-file Menshevik and SR opponents, and serve as a focal point for a unification of various revolutionary socialist currents and organizations.

Karl Marx explained the first of these core conceptions in a letter addressed to President Abraham Lincoln in 1864: "That the emancipation of the working classes must be conquered by the working classes themselves; that, the struggle for the emancipation of the working classes means . . . equal rights and duties, and the abolition of all class rule."[3] Over the course of his long career as an organizer, writer, and theorist, Marx never wavered in his belief that workers must win socialism for themselves through mass struggle, it could not be granted to them from on high. The key distinguishing feature of the Bolshevik Party during 1917 was its faith in and reliance on the energy, intelligence, and courage of ordinary workers, soldiers, and poor peasants to solve their own problems without submitting to their social superiors.

Second, if Marx had always held that people can make history, he also argued that "they do not make it as they please; they do not make it under self-selected circumstances, but under circumstances existing already, given and transmitted from the past."[4] Among other things, this means that objective economic conditions matter a great deal. This belief directed Marx to look, first of all, to the most advanced capitalist countries (Great Britain, Germany, France, the United States) for socialist revolution, not the poorest countries with underdeveloped manufacturing sectors, apparently ruling out Russia—although Marx remained open to the unexpected. The Bolsheviks found a way around this apparent roadblock.

As it turned out, in the late nineteenth century, the Tsar embarked on a crash course of capitalist development, chiefly in order to modernize his army—heavy artillery required heavy machinery. In this way, Russia developed a modern factory system built around some of the largest industrial plants in the world, importing the latest technology and concentrating tens of thousands of skilled workers (and hundreds of thousands of unskilled or semi-skilled workers) in close proximity to his imperial throne. At the same time, the vast majority (approximately 120 million out of 150 million) of Russians worked the land as impoverished, small-scale peasants or agricultural workers, and the Empire lagged far behind its Western rivals in terms of productivity and output. Most Marxists in Russia assumed that socialism was therefore not feasible in the short term.

What *was* possible was overthrowing feudalism and the Tsar and winning a democratic republic that would grant all people the right to vote, workers the right to organize trade unions, peasants the hope of land reform, and oppressed nationalities (Jews, Poles, Finns, Muslims, Ukrainians, Georgians, etc.) the dignity to speak their own languages and practice their own religions. Just how radical (or not) a new constitution turned out to be would depend on the struggle, but most radicals assumed that capitalism would have to grow stronger (and thereby develop the economy) before workers could, perhaps in a decade or two or three, take over.[5]

While the Bolsheviks and Mensheviks broadly accepted these constraints, there was a difference in terms of what class each faction believed must lead the anti-tsarist revolution. Lenin emphasized this distinction, as he had done for more than a decade, in his "Letters from Afar" in the days after the February Revolution:

> Ours is a bourgeois revolution, therefore, the workers must support the bourgeoisie, say the [Menshevik] Potresovs, Gvozdyovs and Chkheidzes, as Plekhanov said yesterday.
>
> Ours is a bourgeois revolution, we Marxists say, therefore the workers must open the eyes of the people to the deception practiced by the bourgeois politicians, teach them to put no faith in words, to depend entirely on their own strength, their own organization, their own unity, and their own weapons.[6]

It fell to Trotsky, however, to explain how this *political* hostility toward the bourgeoisie—and insistence on the revolutionary role of the working class—could be transformed into an *economic* basis for socialist revolution. In summing up the lessons of the 1905 Revolution, he writes:

> The proletariat grows and becomes stronger with the growth of capitalism. In this sense, the development of capitalism is also the development of the proletariat toward dictatorship. But the day and the hour when power will pass into the hands of the working class depends directly not upon the level attained by the productive forces but upon the relations in the class struggle,

*upon the international situation* [emphasis added] and finally, upon a number of subjective factors: the traditions, the initiative, readiness to fight of the workers.

It is possible for the workers to come to power in an economically backward country sooner than in an advanced country. . . . In our view, the Russian Revolution will create conditions in which power can pass into the hands of the workers—and in the event of the victory of the revolution it must do so—before the politicians of bourgeois liberalism get the chance to display to the full their ability to govern.[7]

In 1917, "the international situation" pivoted around advanced capitalist nations bleeding each other dry in a devastating war that was rapidly radicalizing their own working classes. First Lenin and then the Bolsheviks as a whole effectively adopted Trotsky's "permanent revolution" thesis, betting that Russian workers could take power in their own name. Political power—"conquered by the working classes themselves"—would inspire revolution in Germany, France, and beyond, providing the impoverished Russians and oppressed nationalities with the solidarity and concrete economic aid necessary to make their temporary victory permanent.

The third unique attribute of Bolshevik thinking pertains to the scope and role of a revolutionary workers' party. For Lenin and his comrades, rather than attempting to represent all workers, the party should strive to bring together the most class-conscious workers and organizers who understand that

Working-class consciousness cannot be genuine political consciousness unless the workers are trained to respond to all cases of tyranny, oppression, violence, and abuse, no matter what class is affected—unless they are trained, moreover, to respond from a Social Democratic [that is, Marxist] point of view and no other.[8]

While circumscribing their appeal at times—for instance, in the early patriotic period of World War I—the Bolsheviks' insistence on building a principled revolutionary party that did not tolerate pro-war politicians in its midst (as almost all other socialist parties of the day did) meant that they were able to provide a cohesive alternative, even under great duress. Furthermore, the Bolsheviks embodied revolutionary politics not simply as a set of slogans in the mouths of popular leaders, but in the work of some 25,000 party members who stuck it out through the grim days of counterrevolution after 1905 and the early disasters of the war.

Keeping these three factors in mind, the basic story of 1917 is simple enough: the Bolsheviks—armed with the guiding principles of working-class self-emancipation, permanent (and international) revolution, and a clearly defined revolutionary party—argued that only a workers' revolution could deliver "peace, land, and bread," while the Mensheviks and Socialist Revolutionary (SR) parties clung to their erstwhile liberal allies in the Provisional Government, seeking to reform an unreformable situation.

The most important arena for this struggle was the workers', soldiers', and peasants' soviets (the word *soviet* means "council" in Russian). The first of these arose as strike committees during the 1905 revolt; they sprang back to life in the midst of the February Revolution of 1917. Composed of delegates elected at varying ratios in urban workplaces, among rank-and-file soldiers and sailors, and among peasants in the countryside, the soviets quickly became a power all to themselves, commanding the loyalty of all those who sent delegates. Yet there was nothing automatic about scattered soviets becoming the Soviet Union—that is, a working-class state. Perhaps their form lent itself to national coordination, but they could just as easily have remained local movement organizations or perhaps trade-union coordinating bodies. "All power to the soviets," the Bolsheviks' central slogan throughout 1917, was thus a demand that the masses ought to create a government of, by, and for themselves.

In the early months of 1917, from February through June, the Bolsheviks' call for socialist revolution through "all power to the soviets" placed them in a distinct minority. Most workers, soldiers, and peasants were overjoyed at the Tsar's downfall and hoped that their new "democratic" government, the Provisional Government, led as it was by liberals and reform-minded socialists, would find a way to distribute the land, raise wages, and end the war. Fitting this mood, the Mensheviks and SRs won majorities in the major soviets in the spring, promising to pressure, but not replace, the Provisional Government.

But by June, Mensheviks' and SRs' loyalty to the Provisional Government—and their never-ending search for an alliance with the capitalists, who in turn insisted on continuing the war—was driving workers and soldiers over to the Bolsheviks. Radicalization raced ahead in the major cities, even if the millions of soldiers stuck in trenches across the far-flung military front and the tens of millions of peasants scattered across Russia's vast agricultural prairie needed time to catch up. This contradiction almost led to disaster during the July Days, when the Bolshevik rank and file and many of their local leaders—as well as hundreds of thousands of soldiers and workers in St. Petersburg—wanted to take power on their own. The Bolshevik Central Committee tapped the brakes just enough to bring the movement under control and avert what would have been a chaotic and divided uprising; nevertheless, the Menshevik and SR leaders and their capitalist and officer allies brought the Bolsheviks to heel by imprisoning many of their leaders or driving them underground.

Paradoxically, at the height of their power, these reformist socialists froze—or worse. The SR Alexander Kerensky, who was appointed president of the Provisional Government after the July Days, became entangled in a plot led by reactionary General Lavr Kornilov to seize St. Petersburg. With the revolution in danger, its greatest defenders proved to be, naturally enough, the most ardent revolutionaries—the Bolsheviks. Upon defeating the coup, the Bolsheviks grew in stature. Trotsky was released from prison on September 2 and elected president of the Petrograd Soviet three weeks later. Over the late summer and early fall, the Provisional Government hobbled together various ad hoc bodies (a so-called Democratic Conference, followed by a Pre-Parliament—neither of which was based on new elections) as a way to forestall the gathering of the Second All-Russian Congress of Soviets set for late October, in which there was sure to be a Bolshevik majority. This majority gained strength through an alliance with a powerful left-wing current developing within the Socialist Revolutionary Party, as well as pro-Soviet anarchist, nonparty, and Menshevik currents.

During this time, the Bolsheviks debated the strategy and tactics of insurrection. Lenin suggested taking power in the name of the party and then handing it over to the Soviet Congress. Trotsky countered that the soviets themselves should take power using their own fighting infrastructure. He counted on Kerensky trying one more desperate gamble to block the Bolsheviks, now the majority party. Kerensky soon obliged by trying to suppress a Bolshevik newspaper; when he did, the multiparty Military Revolutionary Committee of the Saint Petersburg Soviet overturned the Provisional Government and handed power over to the Second All-Russian Congress of Soviets on October 25. Having finally taken power, the Bolshevik Party, on its very first day in power at the head of the Soviet Congress, granted land to the peasants, ordained workers' control in the factories, and offered a ceasefire to all belligerent nations.

This was high drama and captured the imagination of revolutionaries all over the world, while giving liberals and conservatives alike nightmares. There were no guarantees the gamble would pay off. Even Lenin, usually the most levelheaded of the bunch, wasn't sure they could hang on for long if revolutions didn't spread to Germany and France in short order. In early January 1918 he quipped, "Ten more days and we shall have lived seventy days—as long as the Paris Commune."[9]

For a time, it appeared that the Bolsheviks' wager on international revolution might pay off. Anarchist-Bolshevik Victor Serge recalls: "Riots in Paris, riots in Lyon, revolution in Belgium, revolution in Constantinople, victory of the Soviets in Bulgaria, rioting in Copenhagen. In fact, the whole of Europe is in movement; clandestine or open Soviets are appearing everywhere, even in the Allied armies; everything is possible, everything."[10] Sadly, the center held. Revolution was beaten back everywhere by 1923, largely for want of Bolshevik-type parties of sufficient size, experience, and strength in the main centers of upheaval in Western Europe.

Compounding this isolation, in 1918 the German army seized the Ukraine and Poland and took much of Russia for itself, robbing the infant workers' state of food, fuel, and spare parts. Kerensky and his generals retreated from Saint Petersburg and Moscow, only to receive military supplies, cash, and troops from France, Britain, and the United States (among others) to form a White Army, initiating a long and bloody civil war. In the end, the Red Army rallied the working class and poor peasants. The Bolsheviks survived, but just barely. More than a million deaths (including thousands of the most experienced Bolshevik cadre) were added to the seven million casualties suffered in World War I. One statistic suffices to demonstrate the grim reality: Saint Petersburg, the heart of the revolution, saw its population decline from 2,400,000 in 1917 to just 574,000 by 1920, in the middle of the civil war. "Without a working class and without production," writes Anthony Arnove, "workers' control of production was an impossibility, and the workers' state became unhinged from its social basis."[11] Adding insult to injury, counterrevolutionaries killed dozens of leading Bolsheviks. Lenin himself was shot in the neck in the summer of 1918. He recovered, but suffered a series of debilitating illnesses and strokes starting in late 1921 before dying in January of 1924. Which brings us to Stalin.

Strong enough to defend itself from invasion but too weak to build up democratic, working-class socialism, the Soviet Union turned in on itself. In order to break the impasse, Stalin embarked on a fanatical plan that turned workers' power on its head. Rather than the Soviet state defending the interests of the working class (even if under frightful circumstances), Stalin led a bureaucratic counterrevolution to radically increase the rate of exploitation under the guise of his Five-Year Plans for industrialization. "This led to brutality on an immense scale," Arnove points out. "In essence, Stalin embarked on what Marx had called 'primitive accumulation,' the earliest and bloodiest stage of the development of capitalism."[12] There were instances of heroic resistance, but Stalin prevailed and recast himself in the image of a red Tsar.

Since then, the legacy of the Russian Revolution has been up for grabs. It could never serve as a blueprint for anticapitalist revolutions elsewhere to copy whole, but the lessons and dynamics of class struggles fought at a fever pitch are apparent for anyone willing to study them. History may not repeat itself, but we can recognize recurring patterns and assimilate them into revolutionary political practice. I expect that, one way or the other, these patterns will reemerge in the escalating and intersecting crises of our era. Whether they are provoked by recession, oppression, or exploitation, the people bearing the brunt of union-busting, police brutality, sexual assault, poverty, and climate change will resist, reanimating the dynamics embedded in the drama of 1917. If we aim for a better outcome this time around, we must understand just how close the Bolsheviks came to breaking down the walls guarding capitalist privilege and profit—and integrate those lessons into our theory and practice today.

This text is arranged in roughly chronological order. It relies on eyewitness accounts and documents produced by journalists, accidental observers, and political protagonists alike. I am obviously sympathetic to the Bolshevik voices, but I've included disinterested and even hostile reporters as well, especially when they help to confirm the basic facts of the story. Each section begins with a brief overview (*in italics*) to set the stage for each of the selections contained therein. The selections then feature even briefer introductions with background pertinent to the story. Taken together, they give the reader a solid grasp of the course of 1917. Rather than weighing down the text with explanations and definitions, I have included a glossary of people, places, and things and a chronology. I've also included a small guide to further reading. I hope these accounts spark questions, conversations, polemics, and debates. As for the writers I've chosen to present, they can speak for themselves—so I'll yield the floor to Eugene V. Debs:

> In Russia and Germany our valiant comrades are leading the proletarian revolution, which knows no race, no color, no sex, and no boundary lines. They are setting the heroic example for worldwide emulation. Let us, like them, scorn and repudiate the cowardly compromisers within our own ranks, challenge and defy the robber-class power, and fight it out on that line to victory or death! From the crown of my head to the soles of my feet I am Bolshevik, and proud of it.[13]

Scorn! Repudiate! Challenge! Defy! That is the Russian Revolution summed up.

# I.

# THE FEBRUARY REVOLUTION

*By February 1917, the Russian Empire was in a state of collapse on all fronts: political, economic, military, and social. The German war machine was mowing down whole divisions of the Tsar's pathetically provisioned armies. Millions of casualties piled up and soldiers' families back home suffered from grief and hunger, while bending under the lash of the world's most bloated and reactionary landed aristocracy. Workers in the cities fared little better as wages collapsed, bread became scarce, and strikes were met with brutal repression, often including a ticket to the trenches for trade union and socialist ringleaders. Meanwhile, the Tsar and his dissolute coterie put Marie Antoinette's court to shame in a truly historic orgy of excess and debauchery. It is true that Lenin remarked in January 1917 to a group of students, "We of the older generation may not live to see the decisive battles of this coming revolution." But this line was really nothing more than a well-placed warning against any notion of inevitability. In reality Lenin, and anyone who had eyes to see, understood that mighty forces were on the move. Women workers struck in St. Petersburg beginning on February 23, 1917, International Women's Day by the Julian calendar. Hundreds of thousands soon joined in. Street fighting ensued, and five days later, Tsar Nicholas II, the last in a 300-year line of Romanov monarchs, abdicated.*

# 1.

# The Storm Bursts

*Claude Anet was a French military officer on assignment in Russia. He sympathized with the anti-tsarist revolution of February, enjoyed easy access to the Russian officer corps, despised the Bolsheviks, and became an ardent admirer of Socialist Revolutionary leader Alexander Kerensky. Anet communicated directly with the moderate socialists (Mensheviks and Socialist Revolutionaries—SRs), who dominated the early phase of the revolution as they progressively pushed aside the party of the liberal (and thoroughly capitalist) Constitutional Democrats (Cadets). During these months, Kerensky's star rose—from Minister of Justice in March to Minister of War in May to Minister-Chairman of the Provisional Government in July—before setting just as quickly in October.[1]*

## February 24—A riot? A revolution?

The newspapers continued to observe the most absolute silence about the disorders of yesterday. The Government was more fit to maintain order in the press than in the street. Petrograd was asking itself only one question: "Is it a riot? Is it a revolution?"

And the newspapers, organs of public opinion, appeared without a word which might relieve the universal suspense. It was a beautiful winter's day, wonderfully clear, but bitterly cold. Few people were in the streets, but on the Nevsky [Prospect] a motley crowd of sightseers, workmen and women had assembled. At three o'clock there were no cordons, and I was able to go wherever I pleased. On Nicholas Square, in front of the railway station, at the

11

Kazan Cathedral, and on the Winter Palace Square, I saw soldiers in great force. Detachments of troops passed by, armed. At the head of one section I counted three officers; they wore an anxious air, and it was easy to see that they were not on parade. The police and the Cossacks continued to display great patience towards the demonstrators. Processions of workmen marched along, with the red flag at their head, under the indifferent eye of the authorities, crying: "Down with the Government!" and others—might they not have been provocateurs?—"Down with the war!" But any minute the situation might change and become serious. A woman standing in front of me shouted to the Cossacks: "Are you going to kill me, because I have no bread?"

I went to the Central Telegraph Office to send news to the *Petit Parisien*. But what news would be allowed to go through? When, at five o'clock, I returned to the Nevsky, the first mutterings of the coming storm were audible. Everywhere cordons were to be seen; cavalry and police occupied the roadway. Half of the cavalry had dismounted. I was unable to cross in front of the Kazan; and I passed along the Catherine Canal and the Italianskaya. And when I arrived on Michael Square [Mikhailovskaya], at the corner of the Hotel de l'Europe, I heard the sharp report of rifles, some hundreds of paces distant on Nevsky.

Then, immediately afterwards, debouching from the Mikhailovskaya, came a stream of people and sleighs, flying from the Prospect. The drivers lashed their horses vigorously. In the midst of the route was one of the Court carriages driven by a coachman wearing a two-cornered hat; a sleigh upset at the corner of the street.

The crowd of fugitives hustled me. All the doors, carriage-entrances and others, were at once, and as though by a miracle, shut. With difficulty I made my way against the current and passed along the Mikhailovskaya. It was empty. A squadron of cavalry occupied the end of it. In an adjoining house, in which I took refuge for a moment, I learned what had happened. On a level with the Anitchkoff Palace, where resides, on Nevsky, the Empress-Mother, there was a cordon of cavalry. Five hundred demonstrators arrived, headed by a red flag bearing the inscription: "Down with the war!" The officer commanding the platoon was assisted by a commissary of police, who three times summoned them to disperse. The workmen refused to do so, and the officer gave the order to fire. Some thirty soldiers fired, many of them discharging their rifles in the air; but a few balls whistled by and ricocheted on the frozen snow. At the order "Fire!" the workmen threw themselves on the ground, then, rising to their feet, made off; while the crowd fled, panic-stricken. A few were wounded. A student was hit in the arm. A young woman, who accompanied him, supported him. . . . The young woman placed the student, deadly pale and with blood trickling down his face, in [a] sleigh, and then, instead of going towards the bottom of the Nevsky, which was for the moment empty, directed the driver towards the hedge of soldiers, which half-opened to let him pass. Passing through their midst, and pointing to the wounded student by her side, she cried to them: "What, brothers, you will fire on your own friends?"

At the street corners the students mingled with the groups and carried on an active propaganda, saying to the workmen: "Remain with us, comrades. There is no necessity for disorder during the war. If we fight amongst ourselves, Germany will be our master. Let us wait until it is over, and together settle accounts with our Government."

In the evening, there was sharp firing on the Souvorovski Prospect and on the square in front of the Nicholas Railway Station. The crowd was in a dangerous mood, and orators mounted the hideous equestrian statue of Alexander III and harangued the people. I went so far as Nevsky, at the corner of Litheini. Here there were few people; the roadway was empty, save for some patrols of mounted gendarmes moving about. In the middle of the street a horse, killed during the day, lay on the snow. The police made me retrace my steps. I returned on foot, still on foot. . . .

## February 25—Cossacks disobey orders

It was a beautiful day of bright sunlight, which caused the temperature, which during the night had fallen to fifteen [Fahrenheit], to rise a little. Along Litheini came a crowd making its way towards Nevsky, to which the police and the troops did the best they could to prevent access. At three o'clock, firing began. Panic seized the crowd, but today the number of the revolutionaries was considerable and they offered resistance. On Souvorovski a siege-war was organized. The police themselves built a barricade to prevent the rioters passing. Everywhere, in the crowd, people declared that it was the police alone who were firing at them, and that the soldiers were discharging their rifles in the air. It was also asserted that the Government had dressed some police-agents as soldiers. A young girl related that, on Nevsky, an officer of Cossacks had ordered his men to charge the demonstrators. But at the command: "Forward!" he rode on alone, no one following him.

I had, by chance, confirmation of this fact from three workmen who were in conversation behind me. Said one of them to his companions: "You have seen what has just happened? The officer of Cossacks gave the order: 'Forward!'

but the soldiers did not follow him. The Government must now reckon with us, since even the Cossacks are on our side." It was the most sensible remark that I garnered during the day.

Fighting proceeded all the afternoon, the motor-ambulances passed by unceasingly. In a single hospital 300 wounded were taken in. What was the Government doing? Where was it hiding itself? In the evening, tranquility was entirely restored. The troops of police, the gendarmes, the Army, remained masters of the field of battle. Between ten and eleven o'clock at night I took a walk near Nevsky. The town was deserted, lugubrious, hardly lighted at all. Few people passed me, and they kept close to the wall. . . . I was unable to cross the Prospect at any part. Cordons of troops prevented people passing. I did not hear a single shot. The revolutionaries had not gained the day, and had returned to their homes.

## February 26—A new government

At five o'clock, they telephoned me that great news was going the round of the town. It was to the effect that that same evening a provisional government would be nominated, with General Alexeief as its chief. If this news were true, tranquility would at once be re-established, since the personality of the Commander-in-Chief was universally respected. If not, it was impossible to foresee how far things might not go. I telephoned to the Duma and received from one of the head ushers the following information: The Duma was invaded by a crowd of civilian rioters and soldiers. They were conducting themselves there in an orderly manner and were awaiting the result of the deliberations of the Duma. There also it was said that Alexeief was going to assume the leadership of a new Government, and it was considered that, if the report were true, the situation was saved. I was informed that the Government had already prorogued the Duma and adjourned it until after the Easter recess. This showed the political sense of the Government, the intuition which it possessed of the spirit which animates mobs, and the profound reasons which had brought about what one could no longer call disturbances, but a revolution. [ . . . ]

Twelve police stations were on fire. The people, in destroying the offices of the all-powerful police, whence so many annoyances had come upon them, were exacting a just retribution. At seven o'clock, a student escaped from the Duma [and] telephoned that he had the list of the Committee of Public Order, nominated by the Duma. At its head were: Rodzianko, Lvof, Miliukoff, Tchkeidze, Kerensky, Chidlovski, Chingaref, etc. Was it a Provisional Government? The student informed me that Sheglovitof, President of the Council of the Empire, had been brought to the Duma, with bound hands, and that they had sent to arrest Protopopoff. The Committee and the Duma requested the workmen to appoint their representatives at the evening sitting, as well as a delegate from each regiment which had gone over to the people.

## February 27—Soldiers refuse orders

At the Duma, it was already felt that the moderate parties had been outdistanced and thrust on one side. The Rodziankos, the Lvofs, the Miliukoffs, the Shulgins, who were they beside the Tchkeidzes, the Skobelefs, the Kerenskys, the Bogdanofs, those leaders of the Socialist party, who but yesterday had been scarcely known, but who, today, have been thrust into prominence by the force of the popular tide? The former leaders of the Duma, the Cadets, were all, with slight differences, upholders of order, who would accommodate themselves to a liberal monarchy with a parliamentary regime. Rodzianko had once been an officer in the Army, and the spectacle of the soldiers forgetting all the rules of discipline must have been a very distressing one to him. The following little incident will serve to illustrate the state of mind of the soldiers: Rodzianko, who was in his cabinet [office], was informed that the soldiers had brought General Adrianof, whom they had made prisoner at the Hotel Astoria. He gave directions that the general should be admitted, and he entered between two armed soldiers. Rodzianko said to the soldiers: "Leave the room; I am going to question the general." The soldiers answered bluntly: "No, we shall not leave the room." And they remained.

# 2.

# Five Days: Scenes from the February Revolution

*Trotsky's classic retelling,* The History of the Russian Revolution, *relies on first-hand accounts to paint a blow-by-blow picture of the five days of street fighting that brought down the Tsar in St. Petersburg, while offering insight into the mass psychology of crowds and the powerful but brittle nature of military discipline.[1]*

## Women lead the way

The 23rd of February was International Women's Day. The Social Democratic circles had intended to mark this day in a general manner: by meetings, speeches, leaflets. It had not occurred to anyone that it might become the first day of the revolution. Not a single organization called for strikes on that day. What is more, even a Bolshevik organization, and a most militant one—the Vyborg Borough Committee, all workers—was opposing strikes. The temper of the masses, according to Kayurov, one of the leaders in the workers' district, was very tense; any strike would threaten to turn into an open fight. But since the committee thought the time unripe for militant action—the party not strong enough and the workers having too few contacts with the soldiers—they decided not to call for strikes but to prepare for revolutionary action at some indefinite time in the future. Such was the course followed by the committee on the eve of the 23rd of February, and everyone seemed to accept it. On the following morning, however, in spite of all directives, the women textile workers in several factories went on strike, and sent delegates to the metal workers with an appeal for support. "With reluctance," writes Kayurov, "the

17

Bolsheviks agreed to this, and they were followed by the worker Mensheviks and Social-Revolutionaries. But once there is a mass strike, one must call everybody into the streets and take the lead." Such was Kayurov's decision, and the Vyborg Committee had to agree to it. "The idea of going into the streets had long been ripening among the workers; only at that moment nobody imagined where it would lead." Let us keep in mind this testimony of a participant, important for understanding the mechanics of the events.

It was taken for granted that in case of a demonstration the soldiers would be brought out into the streets against the workers. What would that lead to? This was wartime; the authorities were in no mood for joking. On the other hand, a "reserve" soldier in wartime is nothing like an old soldier of the regular army. Is he really so formidable? In revolutionary circles they had discussed this much, but rather abstractly. For no one, positively no one—we can assert this categorically upon the basis of all the data—then thought that February 23 was to mark the beginning of a decisive drive against absolutism. The talk was of a demonstration which had indefinite, but in any case limited, perspectives.

Thus the fact is that the February Revolution was begun from below, overcoming the resistance of its own revolutionary organizations, the initiative being taken of their own accord by the most oppressed and downtrodden part of the proletariat—the women textile workers, among them no doubt many soldiers' wives. The overgrown breadlines had provided the last stimulus. About 90,000 workers, men and women, were on strike that day. The fighting mood expressed itself in demonstrations, meetings, encounters with the police. The movement began in the Vyborg district with its large industrial establishments; thence it crossed over to the Petersburg side. There were no strikes or demonstrations elsewhere, according to the testimony of the secret police. On that day detachments of troops were called in to assist the police—evidently not many of them—but there were no encounters with them. A mass of women, not all of them workers, flocked to the Municipal Duma demanding bread. It was like demanding milk from a he-goat. Red banners appeared in different parts of the city, and inscriptions on them showed that the workers wanted bread, but neither autocracy nor war. Women's Day passed successfully, with enthusiasm and without victims. But what it concealed in itself, no one had guessed even by nightfall.

On the following day the movement not only fails to diminish, but doubles. About one-half of the industrial workers of Petrograd are on strike on the 24th of February. The workers come to the factories in the morning; instead of going to work they hold meetings; then begin processions toward the center.

New districts and new groups of the population are drawn into the movement. The slogan "Bread!" is crowded out or obscured by louder slogans: "Down with autocracy!" "Down with the war!" Continuous demonstrations on the Nevsky—first compact masses of workmen singing revolutionary songs, later a motley crowd of city folk interspersed with the blue caps of students. "The promenading crowd was sympathetically disposed toward us, and soldiers in some of the war-hospitals greeted us by waving whatever was at hand." How many clearly realized what was being ushered in by this sympathetic waving from sick soldiers to demonstrating workers? But the Cossacks constantly, though without ferocity, kept charging the crowd. Their horses were covered with foam. The mass of demonstrators would part to let them through, and close up again. There was no fear in the crowd. "The Cossacks promise not to shoot," passed from mouth to mouth. Apparently some of the workers had talks with individual Cossacks. Later, however, cursing, half-drunken dragoons appeared on the scene. They plunged into the crowd, began to strike at heads with their lances. The demonstrators summoned all their strength and stood fast. "They won't shoot." And in fact they didn't. . . .

## Under the belly of a Cossack's horse

The workers at the Erikson, one of the foremost mills in the Vyborg district, after a morning meeting came out on the Sampsonievsky Prospect, a whole mass, 2,500 of them, and in a narrow place ran into the Cossacks. Cutting their way with the breasts of their horses, the officers first charged through the crowd. Behind them, filling the whole width of the Prospect galloped the Cossacks. Decisive moment! But the horsemen, cautiously, in a long ribbon, rode through the corridor just made by the officers. "Some of them smiled," Kayurov recalls, "and one of them gave the workers a good wink." This wink was not without meaning. The workers were emboldened with a friendly, not hostile, kind of assurance, and slightly infected the Cossacks with it. The one who winked found imitators. In spite of renewed efforts from the officers, the Cossacks, without openly breaking discipline, failed to force the crowd to disperse, but flowed through it in streams. This was repeated three or four times and brought the two sides even closer together. Individual Cossacks began to reply to the workers' questions and even to enter into momentary conversations with them. Of discipline there remained but a thin transparent shell that threatened to break through any second. The officers hastened to separate their patrol from the workers, and, abandoning the idea of dispersing them, lined the Cossacks out across the street as a barrier to prevent the demonstrators from getting to the center. But even this did not help: standing stock-still in perfect discipline, the Cossacks did not hinder the workers from "diving" under their horses. The revolution does not choose its paths: it made its first steps toward victory under the belly of a Cossack's horse. A remarkable incident! And remarkable the eye of its narrator—an eye which took an impression of every bend in the process. No wonder, for the narrator was a leader; he was at the head of over two thousand men. The eye of a commander watching for enemy whips and bullets looks sharp.

It seems that the break in the army first appeared among the Cossacks, those age-old subduers and punishers. This does not mean, however, that the Cossacks were more revolutionary than others. On the contrary, these solid property owners, riding their own horses, highly valuing their Cossack peculiarities, scorning the plain peasants, mistrustful of the workers, had many elements of conservatism. But just for this reason the changes caused by the war were more sharply noticeable in them. Besides, they were always being pulled around, sent everywhere, driven against the people, kept in suspense — and they were the first to be put to the test. They were sick of it, and wanted to go home. Therefore they winked: "Do it, boys, if you know how—we won't bother you!" All these things, however, were merely very significant symptoms. The army was still the army, it was bound with discipline, and the threads were in the hands of the monarchy. The worker mass was unarmed. The leaders had not yet thought of the decisive crisis. . . .

## Police, Cossacks, army

[Gen.] Khabalov meticulously adhered to the plan he had worked out. On the first day, the 23rd, the police operated alone. On the 24th, for the most part the cavalry was led into the streets, but only to work with whip and lance. The use of infantry and firearms was to depend on the further development of events. But events came thick and fast.

On the 25th, the strike spreads wider. According to the government's figures, 240,000 workers participate that day. The most backward layers are following up the vanguard. Already a good number of small establishments are on strike. The streetcars are at a stand. Business concerns are closed. In the course of the day students of the higher schools join the strike. By noon tens of thousands of people pour into the Kazan Cathedral and the surrounding streets. Attempts are made to organize street meetings; a series of armed encounters with the police occurs. Orators address the crowds around the Alexander III monument. The mounted police open fire. A speaker falls wounded. Shots from the crowd kill a police inspector, wound the chief of police and several other policemen. Bottles, petards and hand grenades are thrown at the gendarmes. The war has taught this art. The soldiers show indifference, at times hostility, to the police. It spreads excitedly through the crowd that when the police opened fire by the Alexander III monument, the Cossacks let go a volley at the horse "Pharaohs" (such was the nickname of the police) and the latter had to gallop off. This apparently was not a legend circulated for self-encouragement, since the incident, although in different versions, is confirmed from several sources.

A worker-Bolshevik, Kayurov, one of the authentic leaders in those days, relates how at one place, within sight of a detachment of Cossacks, the demonstrators scattered under the whips of the mounted police, and how he, Kayurov, and several workers with him, instead of following the fugitives, took off their caps and approached the Cossacks with the words: "Brother Cossacks, help the workers in a struggle for their peaceable demands; you see how the Pharaohs treat us, hungry workers. Help us!" This consciously humble manner, those caps in their hands—what an accurate psychological calculation! Inimitable gesture! The whole history of street fights and revolutionary victories swarms with such improvisations. But they are drowned without a trace in the abyss of great events—the shell remains to the historian, the generalization. "The Cossacks glanced at each other in some special way," Kayurov continues, "and we were hardly out of the way before they rushed into the fight." And a few minutes later, near the station gate, the crowds are tossing in their arms a Cossack who before their eyes had slaughtered a police inspector with his sabre.

Soon the police disappear altogether—that is, begin to act secretly. Then the soldiers appear, bayonets lowered. Anxiously the workers ask them: "Comrades, you haven't come to help the police?" A rude "Move along!" for answer. Another attempt ends the same way. The soldiers are sullen. A worm is gnawing at them, and they cannot stand it when a question hits the very center of the pain.

Meanwhile disarmament of the Pharaohs becomes a universal slogan. The police are fierce, implacable, hated and hating foes. To win them over is out of the question. Beat them up and kill them. It is different with the soldiers: the crowd makes every effort to avoid hostile encounters with them; on the contrary, seeks ways to dispose them in its favor, convince, attract, fraternize, merge them in itself. In spite of the auspicious rumors about the Cossacks, perhaps slightly exaggerated, the crowd's attitude toward the mounted men remains cautious. A horseman sits high above the crowd; his soul is separated from the soul of the demonstrator by the four legs of his beast. A figure at which one must gaze from below always seems more significant, more threatening. The infantry are beside one on the pavement—closer, more accessible. The masses try to get near them, look into their eyes, surround them with their hot breath. A great role is played by women workers in relationship between workers and soldiers. They go up to the cordons more boldly than men, take hold of the rifles, beseech, almost command: "Put down your bayonets—join us." The soldiers are excited, ashamed, exchange anxious glances, waver; someone makes up his mind first, and the bayonets rise guiltily above the shoulders of the advancing crowd. The barrier is opened, a joyous and grateful "Hurrah!" shakes the air. The soldiers are surrounded. Everywhere arguments, reproaches, appeals the revolution makes another forward step. . . .

## Inner logic of the movement

Let us try to get a clearer idea of the inner logic of the movement. On February 23, under the flag of "Women's Day," began the long-ripe and long-withheld uprising of the Petrograd working masses. The first step of the insurrection was the strike. In the course of three days it broadened and became practically general. This alone gave assurance to the masses and carried them forward. Becoming more and more aggressive, the strike merged with the demonstrations, which were bringing the revolutionary mass face to face with the troops. This raised the problem as a whole to the higher level where things are solved by force of arms. The first days brought a number of individual successes, but these were more symptomatic than substantial.

A revolutionary uprising that spreads over a number of days can develop victoriously only in case it ascends step by step, and scores one success after another. A pause in its growth is dangerous; a prolonged marking of time, fatal. But even successes by themselves are not enough; the masses must know about them in time, and have time to understand their value. It is possible to let slip a victory at the very moment when it is within arm's reach. This has happened in history.

The first three days were days of uninterrupted increase in the extent and acuteness of the strife. But for this very reason the movement had arrived at a level where mere symptomatic successes were not enough. The entire active mass of the people had come out on the streets. It was settling accounts with the police successfully and easily. In the last two days the troops had been drawn into the events—on the second day, cavalry, on the third, the infantry too. They barred the way, pushed and crowded back the masses, sometimes connived with them, but almost never resorted to firearms. Those in command were slow to change their plan, partly because they under-estimated what was happening—the faulty vision of the reaction supplemented that of the leaders of the revolution—partly because they lacked confidence in the troops. But exactly on the third day, the force of the developing struggle, as well as the Tsar's command, made it necessary for the government to send the troops into action in dead earnest. The workers understood this, especially their advance ranks; the dragoons had already done some shooting the day before. Both sides now faced the issue unequivocally.

On the night of the 26th about a hundred people were arrested in different parts of the city—people belonging to various revolutionary organizations, and among them five members of the Petrograd Committee of the Bolsheviks. This also meant that the government was taking the offensive. What will happen today? In what mood will the workers wake up after yesterday's shooting? And most important: what will the troops say? The sun of February 26 came up in a fog of uncertainty and acute anxiety. [ . . . ]

## Military discipline: Soldiers and officers

There is no doubt that the fate of every revolution at a certain point is decided by a break in the disposition of the disposition of the army. Against a numerous, disciplined, well-armed and ably led military force, unarmed or almost unarmed masses of the people cannot possibly gain a victory. But no deep national crisis can fail to affect the army to some extent. Thus along with the conditions of a truly popular revolution there develops a possibility—not, of course, a guarantee—of its victory. However, the going over of the army to the insurrection does not happen of itself, nor as a result of mere agitation. The army is heterogeneous, and its antagonistic elements are held together by the terror of discipline. On the very eve of the decisive hour, the revolutionary soldiers do not know how much power they have, or what influence they can exert. The working masses, of course, are also heterogeneous. But they have immeasurably more opportunity for testing their ranks in the process of preparation for the decisive encounter. Strikes, meetings, demonstrations are not only acts in the struggle, but also measures of its force. The whole mass does not participate in the strike. Not all the strikers are ready to fight. In the sharpest moments the most daring appear in the streets. The hesitant, the tired, the conservative, sit at home. Here a revolutionary selection takes place of itself; people are sifted through the sieve of events. It is otherwise with the army. The revolutionary soldiers—sympathetic, wavering or antagonistic—are all tied together by a compulsory discipline whose threads are held, up to the last moment, in the officer's fist. The soldiers are told off daily into first and second files, but how are they to be divided into rebellious and obedient?

The psychological moment when the soldiers go over to the revolution is prepared by a long molecular process, which, like other processes of nature, has its point of climax. But how to determine this point? A military unit may be wholly prepared to join the people, but may not receive the needed stimulus. The revolutionary leadership does not yet believe in the possibility of having the army on its side, and lets slip the victory. After this ripened but unrealized mutiny, a reaction may seize the army. The soldiers lose the hope which flared in their breasts; they bend their necks again to the yoke of discipline, and in a new encounter with the workers, especially at a distance, will stand opposed to the insurrection. In this process there are many elements imponderable or difficult to weigh, many crosscurrents, collective suggestions and autosuggestions. But out of this complicated web of material and psychic forces one conclusion emerges with irrefutable clarity: the more the soldiers in their mass are convinced that the rebels are really rebelling—that this is not a demonstration after which they will have to go back to the barracks and report, that this is a struggle to the death, that the people may win if they join them, and that this winning will not only guarantee impunity, but alleviate the lot of all—the more they realize this, the more willing they are to turn aside their bayonets, or go over with them to the people. In other words, the revolutionaries can create a break in the soldiers' mood only if they themselves are actually ready to seize the victory at any price whatever, even the price of blood. And the highest determination never can, or will, remain unarmed.

The critical hour of contact between the pushing crowd and the soldiers who bar their way has its critical minute. That is when the grey barrier has not yet given way, still holds together shoulder to shoulder, but already wavers, and the officer, gathering his last strength of will, gives the command: "Fire!" The cry of the crowd, the yell of terror and threat, drowns the command, but not wholly. The rifles waver. The crowd pushes. Then the officer points the barrel of his revolver at the most suspicious soldier. From the decisive minute now stands out the decisive second. The death of the boldest soldier, to whom the others have involuntarily looked for guidance, a shot into the crowd by a corporal from the dead man's rifle, and the barrier closes, the guns go off of themselves, scattering the crowd into the alleys and backyards. But how many times since 1905 it has happened otherwise! At the critical moment, when the officer is ready to pull the trigger, a shot from the crowd—which has its [Bolshevik] Kayurovs and Chugurins—forestalls him. This decides not only the fate of the street skirmish, but perhaps the whole day, or the whole insurrection. [ . . . ]

To bring the soldiers from a deep but as yet hidden revolutionary discontent to overt mutinous action—or, at least, first to a mutinous refusal to act—that was the task. On the third day of the struggle the soldiers totally ceased to be able to maintain a benevolent neutrality toward the insurrection. Only accidental fragments of what happened in those hours along the line of contact between workers and soldiers have come down to us. We heard how yesterday the workers complained passionately to the Pavlovsky Regiment about the behavior of its training squad. Such scenes, conversations, reproaches, appeals, were occurring in every corner of the city. The soldiers had no more time for hesitation. They were compelled to shoot yesterday, and they would be again today. The workers will not surrender or retreat; under fire they are still holding their own. And with them their women—wives, mothers, sisters, sweethearts. Yes, and this is the very hour they had so often whispered about: "If only we could all get together . . ." And the moment of supreme agony, in the unbearable fear of the coming day, the choking hatred of those who are imposing upon them the executioner's role, there ring out in the barrack room the first voices of open indignation, and in those voices—to be forever nameless—the whole army with relief and rapture recognizes itself. Thus dawned upon the earth the day of destruction of the Romanov monarchy. [ . . . ]

## Victory

The soldiers of the Volynsky Regiment were the first to revolt. As early as seven o'clock in the morning a battalion commander disturbed [General] Khabalov with a telephone call and this threatening news: the training squad—that is, the unit especially relied on to put down the insurrection—had refused to march out, its commander was killed, or had shot himself in front of the troops. The latter version, by the way, was soon rejected. Having burned their bridges behind them, the Volintzi hastened to broaden the base of the insurrection. In that lay their only salvation. They rushed into the neighboring barracks of the Litovsky and Preobrazhensky Regiments "calling out" the soldiers, as strikers go from factory to factory calling out the workers. Some time after,

Khabalov received a report that the Volynsky Regiment had not only refused to surrender their rifles when ordered by the general, but together with the Litovsky and Preobrazhensky regiments—and what is even more alarming, "having joined the workers"—had wrecked the barracks of the political police. This meant that yesterday's experiment of the Pavlovtsi had not been in vain: the insurrection had found leaders, and at the same time a plan of action.

In the early hours of the 27th, the workers thought the solution of the problem of the insurrection infinitely more distant than it really was. It would be truer to say that they saw the problem as almost entirely ahead of them, when it was really nine-tenths behind. The revolutionary pressure of the workers on the barracks fell in with the existing revolutionary movement of the soldiers to the streets. During the day these two mighty currents united to wash out, clean and carry away the walls, the roof, and later the whole groundwork of the old structure.

Chugurin was among the first to appear at the Bolshevik headquarters, a rifle in his hands, a cartridge belt over his shoulder, all spattered up, but beaming and triumphant. Why shouldn't he beam? Soldiers with rifles in their hands are coming over to us! In some places the workers had succeeded in uniting with the soldiers, penetrating the barracks and receiving rifles and cartridges. The Vyborgtsi [district workers], together with the most daring of the soldiers, outlined a plan of action: seize the police stations where the armed police have entrenched themselves; disarm all policemen; free the workers held in the police stations, and the political prisoners in the jails; rout the government troops in the city proper; unite with the still inactive troops and with the workers of other districts.

The Moscow Regiment joined the uprising not without inner struggle. Amazing that there was so little struggle among the regiments. The monarchist command impotently fell away from the soldier mass, and either hid in the cracks or hastened to change its colors. "At two o'clock," remembers Korôlev, a worker from the Arsenal factory, "when the Moscow Regiment marched out, we armed ourselves. . . . We took a revolver and rifle apiece, picked out a group of soldiers who came up and some of them asked us to take command and tell them what to do, and set out for Tikhvinskaia Street to shoot up the police station." The workers, it seems, did not have a moment's trouble telling the soldiers "what to do."

One after another came the joyful reports of victories. Our own armored cars have appeared! With red flags flying, they are spreading terror through the districts to all who have not yet submitted. Now it will no longer be necessary to crawl under the belly of a Cossack's horse. The revolution is standing up to its full height.

# II.

# A SPRINGTIME OF DUAL POWER

*In place of the Tsar, two competing institutions vied for political supremacy: the Provisional Government and the St. Petersburg Soviet (soviet simply means "council" in Russian), both products of the failed 1905 Revolution. The former was an improvised body composed of political leaders, ranging from the liberal Constitutional Democrats (Cadets) to the Mensheviks and the Socialist Revolutionary Party (SRs), heavily leavened with tsarist politicians and Imperial Army officers. The Bolsheviks refused to join it. The St. Petersburg Soviet's first decree was for soldiers to elect delegates and demand that the Army High Command recognize its authority.*

*In 1917, soviets spread like wildfire across the entire country, reaching beyond the factories into the countryside and trenches. Within months, local soviets coordinated efforts across the cities, provinces, and military fronts and came together in June to convene the First All-Russian Congress of Workers' and Soldiers' Deputies. The struggle between the Provisional Government and the soviets—one basing itself on the framework of the old tsarist state and seeking an alliance between all classes in Russian society, the other representing the power of the oppressed and exploited classes alone by means of direct elections—became known as "dual power." The conflicts within the revolution over the course of 1917 can best be understood as a fight over which institution would win out.*

# 3.

# Political Parties in Russia and the Tasks of the Proletariat

*Within weeks of the February Revolution,* **Lenin** *drafted the "Political Parties in Russia and the Tasks of the Proletariat" as a pamphlet (abridged here) to explain where the major political parties stood on the burning issues of the day. Although it was not distributed until July, the pamphlet accurately describes the various contenders' positions and, to a remarkable degree, anticipates their actions over the course of the entire revolution.[1]*

The following is an attempt to formulate, first, the more important and then the less important questions and answers characterizing the present political situation in Russia and the way it is understood by the various parties.

## 1) What are the political groupings in Russia?

A. Parties and groups to the right of the Constitutional-Democrats.
B. The Constitutional-Democratic Party (Cadets, or the People's Freedom Party) and kindred groups.
C. The Social Democrats [Mensheviks], the Socialist Revolutionaries, and kindred groups.
D. The Bolsheviks. The party which properly should be called the Communist Party, but which at present is named the Russian Social

Democratic Labor Party united under the Central Committee or, popularly, the "Bolsheviks."

## 2) What classes do these parties represent? What class standpoint do they express?

A. The feudalist landowners and the most backward sections of the bourgeoisie (capitalists).

B. The bourgeoisie as a whole, that is, the capitalist class, and the landowners who have become bourgeois, i.e., who have become capitalists.

C. Small proprietors, small and middle peasants, the petit-bourgeoisie, and that section of the workers which has come under the influence of the bourgeoisie.

D. Class-conscious proletarians, wageworkers and the poor peasantry (semi-proletarians) standing close to them.

## 3) What is their attitude towards socialism?

A. and B. Decidedly hostile, since it threatens the profits of the capitalists and landowners.

C. For socialism, but it is too early to think of it or to take any immediate practical steps for its realization.

D. For socialism. The Soviets must immediately take all possible practicable steps for its realization.

## 4) What forms of government do they want at present?

A. A constitutional monarchy, the absolute power of the bureaucracy and the police.

B. A bourgeois parliamentary republic, i.e., the consolidation of the rule of the capitalists, while retaining the old bureaucracy and the police.

C. A bourgeois parliamentary republic, with reforms for the workers and peasants.

D. A republic of Soviets of Workers', Soldiers', Peasants', and other Deputies. Abolition of the standing army and the police, who are to be replaced by the arming of the whole people; officials to be not only elected, but also displaceable; their pay not to exceed that of a competent worker. [. . .]

## 6) What is their attitude towards the seizure of power? What do they regard as order, and what as anarchy?

A. If a tsar or some gallant general seizes power, that is God-given, that is order. All else is anarchy.

B. If the capitalists seize power, even by force, that is order; to seize power against the capitalists would be anarchy.

C. If the Soviets alone seize all the power, that means a threat of anarchy. Let the capitalists keep the power for the time being, and the Soviets keep the "Contact Commission" [a liaison committee between the Soviet and the Provisional Government].

D. All power must be in the hands of the Soviets of Workers', Soldiers', Peasants', Agricultural Laborers' and other Deputies. All propaganda, agitation and the organization of the millions must immediately be directed towards this end. [ . . . ]

## 8) For undivided power or dual power?

A. and B. For the undivided power of the capitalists and landowners.

C. For dual power. The Soviets to exercise "control" over the Provisional Government. It is bad to reflect whether control can be effective without power.

D. For the undivided power of the Soviets from the bottom up all over the country.

## 9) Should a Constituent Assembly be convened?

A. No, for it might prejudice the landowners. You never know—the peasants in the Constituent Assembly may decide that the landowners ought to have their estates taken away from them.

B. Yes, but without fixing a date. As much time as possible should be spent consulting professors of law; first, because, as Bebel said, jurists are the most reactionary people in the world; and, second, because the experience of all revolutions has shown that the cause of popular freedom is lost when it is entrusted to professors.

C. Yes, and as quickly as possible. A date must be fixed; we have already said so two hundred times at the meetings of the Contact Commission, and shall say so again tomorrow, for the last and two-hundred-and-first time.

D. Yes, and as soon as possible. But there is only one way to assure its convocation and success, and that is by increasing the number and strength of the Soviets and organizing and arming the working-class masses. That is the only guarantee.

## 10) Does the state need the usual type of police and standing army?

A. and B. It certainly does, for they are the only firm guarantee of the rule of the capitalists; in case of need, as the experience of all countries has shown, the return from a republic to a monarchy is thus greatly facilitated.

C. On the one hand, they are perhaps not necessary. On the other hand, is not so radical a change premature? However, we shall raise the matter in the Contact Commission.

D. It definitely does not. The arming of the entire people must be proceeded with everywhere immediately and unreservedly, and they must be merged with the militia and the army. The capitalists must pay the workers for days served in the militia. [ . . . ]

## 12) Should officers be elected by the soldiers?

A. and B. No. That would be detrimental to the landowners and capitalists. If the soldiers cannot be pacified otherwise, they must be temporarily promised this reform, but it must be withdrawn at the earliest possible moment.

C. Yes, they should.

D. Not only must they be elected, but every step of every officer and general must be supervised by persons specially elected for the purpose by the soldiers. [ . . . ]

## 14) For or against the present war?

A. and B. Decidedly for, because it yields the capitalists untold profits and promises to consolidate their rule by disuniting the workers and setting them against one another. We shall fool the workers by calling the war a war for national defense, the real object of which is to dethrone Wilhelm.

C.  In general we are opposed to imperialist wars, but we are willing to be fooled, and are prepared to call the support given to the imperialist war waged by the imperialist government of Guchkovs, Milyukov and co. "revolutionary defensism."

D.  We are decidedly against all imperialist wars and all bourgeois governments waging such wars, including our own Provisional Government; we are decidedly against "revolutionary defensism" in Russia. [ . . . ]

## 16) For or against annexations [of foreign territory]?

A. and B.  If it is a question of annexations by the German capitalists and their robber chieftain, Wilhelm, we are against. If by the British, we are not against, for they are "our" Allies. If by our capitalists, who are forcibly keeping within the boundaries of Russia the peoples who were oppressed by the Tsar, we are in favor; we do not call that annexation.

C.  Against annexations, but we still hope it will be possible to secure even from the capitalist government a promise to renounce annexations.

D.  Against annexations. All promises on the part of capitalist governments to renounce annexations are a sheer fraud. There is only one method of exposing it, namely, to demand the liberation of the peoples oppressed by their own capitalists. [ . . . ]

## 20) Shall the peasants take all the landed estates immediately?

A. and B.  By no means. We must wait for the Constituent Assembly [ . . . ]

C.  Better the peasants wait for the Constituent Assembly.

D.  All the land must be taken over immediately. Order must be strictly maintained by the Soviets of Peasants' Deputies. More grain and meat must be produced, and the soldiers better fed. Injury and damage to livestock, implements, etc., must in no case be permitted. [ . . . ]

## 22) Shall the people take over the largest and most powerful capitalist monopolies, the banks, the manufacturers' conglomerates, etc.?

A. and B.  On no account, as this might injure the landowners and capitalists.

C.  Generally speaking, we are in favor of transferring such organizations to the entire people, but it is too early just now to think of this or prepare for it.

D. We must at once start preparing the Soviets of Workers' Deputies, the Councils of Bank Employees' Deputies, etc., for taking practical and practicable steps towards merging all banks into a single national bank, to be followed by the establishment of control by the Soviets of Workers' Deputies over the banks and syndicates, and then by their nationalization, i.e., their transfer to the possession of the whole people. [ . . . ]

## 25) What color banner would be in character with the various political parties?

A. Black, for they are the real Black Hundreds.

B. Yellow, for that is the international banner of workers who serve capitalism willingly, heart and soul.

C. Pink, for their whole policy is a rose-water one.

D. Red, for this is the banner of the international proletarian revolution.

# 4.

# The Provisional Government Prevaricates

*The most immediate demands of the February Revolution were for an end to the war, land reform, workers' rights, and the convocation of nationwide democratic elections to a Constituent Assembly, with the aim of establishing a democratic republic. Although the Provisional Government initially enjoyed enormous support, its moderate leaders worried that granting any of these demands might endanger Russia's war efforts, including commitments to its French and British allies. Faced with an increasingly restive populace, the Government attempted to temporarily appease workers, peasants, and soldiers in hopes, according to* **Claude Anet**, *of gaining control over the revolution as it kept a close eye on the growing power of the soviets.[1]*

## March 23

The Government was granting everything which was asked of it. "We want a Poland, free, united, intact," say the Poles.

"You shall have a Poland, free, united, intact," answers the Government.

The women say: "We want the right to vote."

"You shall have the right to vote."

The different races are agitating: "Equality of all races, of all religions, everyone's right of admission to all offices, abolition of all restrictions."

And the Government replies: "We are decided on equality," etc., etc.

In the dawn of liberty, the Government refuses nothing. All desires are crowned, all prayers receive a favorable hearing. Ask for the moon, it will give it to you by decree; but I am inclined to think that the Government knows very well what it is doing. It understands the Russian mind, which requires fine promises. And, in reality, what does it give it? Lavish promises, and, meanwhile, time passes, and it will be the duty of the Constituent Assembly to put all this in order; to see what is at once realizable and what is not; what is chimerical and what is reasonable. The vote for women for the Constituent Assembly will postpone the elections from three to six months at least. Already, election by the votes of men alone appears impossible before at least six months; we shall pass thus, from material impossibility to material impossibility, to postponing the elections until after the war. That is the only reasonable solution. [ . . . ]

To all these difficulties, the Government, by a stroke of the pen, added that, more formidable still, of the vote for women. There was no electoral list of the illiterate women; and the Kalmuck, Turcoman, Khirgize and Tartar ladies were all demanding their voting-papers. There would be 120 million electors, both male and female.

The elections, then, appeared to me likely to be postponed to the Greek Kalends [that is, indefinitely]. In Russia, as in France, the provisional is made to last. Let us admit that the Government was skillfully playing a pretty game. It was powerless against the extreme parties. And so, it accorded them all that they demanded. Their contradictory exigencies would inevitably bring about a prolongation of the status quo; and the Government, confronted with this impossible situation, would be able to do very much as it wished, without ever coming into collision with the redoubtable Caliban. Yes; but, at Petrograd, the situation, so far from showing any improvement, was growing worse.

I wished to have precise information respecting the constitution and the functions of the famous Council of Workmen's and Soldiers' Delegates. Nothing was more difficult, as the members of the Executive Committee were but little desirous of affording enlightenment on the subject, and for a long time were unwilling to give even the names of the members of the Executive Committee. This is what I knew with some degree of certainty:

The number of delegates was increasing every day. Why? That was still unexplained. But, anyway, there were at present 3,000 of them; of whom two-thirds were soldiers. This amorphous and chaotic mass set its face against every attempt to organize it. And how was it possible to maneuver 3,000 delegates? The Executive Committee formed a plan. The 3,000 delegates were to nominate a little council of 500 members, to which the Committee would refer matters and which would discuss and vote upon them. But the delegates saw that 2,500 among them would sit no more. Why should they allow that? Why should Russia pass out of their hands? They rejected the Committee's plan. They were the masters, and they intended to remain so. I had the impression that already the Executive Committee was no longer listened to, and that it was impotent. The anarchical tendencies of the mass of the workmen were too much for it. Everyone wanted to play an important part; no one considered it consistent with the dignity of an intelligent citizen to follow a leader, even an elected one. In every factory, the workmen wanted to be the masters. In vain, the Committee multiplied appeals. I noticed several of them. It recalled the workmen to their labor; it spoke of national defense; it declared that, without order, they were on the road to ruin; that the time for demonstrations was passed. Vain objurgations! The workman did only what he wished; and the Committee was already no more than a head without a body. Tomorrow, it would be as bourgeois as the Government. Meantime; several factories had decided to close down, and some thousands of workmen would be out of employment.

And the war? The Army of the Southwest had yesterday sustained a check, with heavy losses. But among the soldiers and workmen of Petrograd, who read the communiqués?

# 5.

# Lenin Returns to Russia

*One of the twists of the February Revolution is that the leaders who took power were those who happened to be in Saint Petersburg, the capital city. This presented no particular problem for the Cadets and more conservative politicians, giving them a decided advantage over the left, but literally thousands of revolutionary activists and most of the leaders of radical parties—Bolsheviks, Mensheviks, Mezhraiontsy, Socialist Revolutionaries, and anarchists alike—were exiled, scattered from Siberia to Paris to New York. As weeks went by, not only were the masses growing increasingly impatient with the Provisional Government's delaying tactics, but many of their most tenacious radical critics were figuring out how to get back home, carefully picking their way through German and Allied blockades. One large group of exiles that included Lenin worked out a way to cross the German lines in a sealed train. Obviously the Kaiser hoped these leftists would stir up trouble at home; subsequently, the Bolsheviks' opponents doggedly accused them of being "German agents." Regardless, after seven years of exile, Lenin returned just four weeks after the Tsar's fall to add his voice to those who believed the revolution, far from settling down, had only just begun.*

*After receiving a hero's welcome upon disembarking the sealed train at Saint Petersburg's Finland Station, Lenin attended a large welcome-home gathering that included Bolsheviks as well as many others. **Fyodor Raskolnikov**, a twenty-five-year-old Bolshevik navy officer, describes the scene.*[1]

The train stopped, and at once we perceived, over the crowd of workers, the figure of Comrade Lenin. Lifting Ilyich [Lenin] high above their heads, the

39

Sestroretsk workers conducted him into the station hall. There, all those who had come from Petrograd pushed their way through to him, one after the other, to congratulate him heartily on his return to Russia. All of us who were seeing Ilyich for the first time kissed him just as his old Party comrades did, as though we had known him for a long time. He was somehow serenely cheerful and the smile never left his face for a moment. It was clear that the return to this homeland, now embraced by the flame of revolution, gave him indescribable joy. We had not finished greeting Ilyich when Kamenev, excited and happy, came quickly into the hall, leading by the hand a no less excited Comrade Zinoviev [who had made the trip with Lenin]. Comrade Kamenev introduced us to him and after exchanging a firm handshake we all, surrounding Lenin, made our way into his carriage.

Hardly had he entered the compartment and sat down than Vladimir Ilyich turned on Comrade Kamenev. "What's this you're writing in *Pravda*? We've seen several issues, and we really swore at you . . ." we heard Ilyich say in his tone of fatherly reproof, in which there was never anything offensive.

The comrades from Sestroretsk were asking that Vladimir Ilyich say a few words to them. But he was absorbed in his conversation with Kamenev: there was so much to be learned and even more to be said.

"Let Grigory [Zinoviev] speak to them: you'll have to ask him," said Comrade Lenin, turning back to his interrupted political discussion with Kamenev.

Comrade Zinoviev went out on the platform of the carriage and delivered a brief but ardent speech, his first on the soil of revolutionary Russia.

Then we all went into his compartment where we were introduced to Comrade Lilina [Zinoviev's wife] and to Zinoviev's little son. Comrade Grigory was unusually lively and happy. He told us how the Swiss socialist Fritz Platten had organized their journey, how they had travelled across Germany and how Scheidemann [the leader of the German Social Democratic Party's right wing] had tried to make contact with Lenin, but the latter had categorically refused to meet with him. "We [believed we] were on our way to prison, we were prepared to find ourselves arrested immediately [when] we crossed the frontier," he said, and then recounted to us his impressions of the journey.

The train, meanwhile, had started off again and arrived in Petrograd without our having realized it. Our carriage was now under the awning of the long passenger platforms. Along the platform at which our train had stopped, on both sides of it but leaving a wide passage down the middle, the sailors of the Second Baltic Fleet Depot were drawn up. The depot commander, Maksimov, a young officer from among the fleet's ensign, who was fervently making a career in the revolution, stepped forward, barring Comrade Lenin's path, and delivered a speech of greeting. He ended it with a curious expression of hope that Comrade Lenin would enter the Provisional Government.

Smiles appeared on our faces. "Well, now," I thought, "Lenin will show you what he thinks of participation in the Provisional Government. You won't like it!" And indeed when, the next day, Ilyich publicly expounded his program, Maksimov, an upstart and political infant, published a letter in the bourgeois papers in which he disowned his greeting to Comrade Lenin and explained it by saying that he had not known of Lenin's journey through Germany.

But the mass of the sailors had no reason to repent for they already then saw in Lenin their acknowledged leader. In reply to the wish expressed that he join the Provisional Government, Comrade Lenin loudly hurled forth his battle slogan, "Long live the socialist revolution!"

There were masses of people in the station—mostly workers. Comrade Lenin went to the "ceremonial waiting rooms" of the Finland Station, where he was welcomed by the representatives of the Petrograd Soviet, Chkheidze and Sukhanov. He replied briefly, again ending his remarks with the cry "Long live the socialist revolution!" Finally, he addressed the same slogan to the crowd of thousands who had assembled in the square in front of the station in order to greet the old leader of the Russian proletariat. This speech Lenin delivered standing on an armored car. A row of these steel-clad motorcars stood outside the Finland Station. The beams of their headlamps cut through the darkness of the evening and cast long shafts of light down the streets of the Vyborg Side. [ . . . ]

*[Sometime later, hundreds of Bolshevik activists and others gathered at the Party's headquarters, the requisitioned mansion of the Tsar's favorite ballerina, Mathilde Kshesinskaya, to welcome Lenin, Zinoviev and the others, and to begin a monthlong internal party debate about strategy and tactics.]*

Ilyich sat and listened with a smile to all the speeches, waiting impatiently for them to finish.

When the list of speakers was exhausted, Ilyich at once came to life, got to his feet and set to work. He resolutely assailed the tactics which the leading Party groups and individual comrades had been pursuing before his return. He caustically ridiculed the notorious formula of support for the Provisional Government "in so far as . . . to that extent," and gave out the slogan, "No support whatsoever to the government of capitalists," at the same time calling on the Party to fight for power to be taken over by the Soviets, for a socialist revolution.

Using a few striking examples, Comrade Lenin brilliantly demonstrated the whole falsity of the policy of the Provisional Government, the glaring contradiction between its promises and its actions, between words and deeds, emphasizing that it was our duty to expose ruthlessly its counter-revolutionary and anti-democratic pretensions and conduct. Comrade Lenin's speech lasted nearly an hour. The audience remained fixed in intense, unweakening attention. The most responsible Party workers were represented here, but even for them what Ilyich said constituted a veritable revelation. It laid down a "Rubicon" between the tactics of yesterday and those of today.

Comrade Lenin posed the question clearly and distinctly: "What is to be done?" and summoned us away from half-recognition, half-support of the Government to non-recognition and irreconcilable struggle.

The ultimate triumph of Soviet power, which many saw as something in the hazy distance of a more or less indefinite future, was brought down by Comrade Lenin to the plane of an urgently necessary conquest of the revolution, to be attained within a very short time. This speech of his was in the fullest sense historic. Comrade Lenin here first set forth his political program, which he formulated next day in the famous theses of April 4. This speech produced a complete revolution in the thinking of the Party's leaders, and underlay all the subsequent work of the Bolsheviks. It was not without cause that our Party's tactics did not follow a straight line, but after Lenin's return took a sharp turn to the left.

# 6.

# Horrible Socialist Jargon

*Of course, the "sharp turn to the left" proposed by Lenin was greeted with incredulity and hostility by those who wanted to continue the war against Germany and to limit the aims of the Revolution to (more or less) democratic capitalism.* **Claude Anet**'s *remarks exemplify this point of view and remind us that, in April, Lenin's thesis of "All power to the soviets" remained in a small majority among soldiers, workers, and socialist activists alike.*[1]

## April 4—The reddest of the red

The famous Social Democrat Lenin had arrived yesterday evening at Petrograd, from Switzerland, where he had been living. He is the reddest of the red. And what road had he and the comrades who escorted him taken to regain their fatherland, if I dare employ a word so denuded of sense in speaking of the place which had witnessed the birth of these Social Democrats? They had passed across Germany, which, as one might expect, had opened her doors wide to this ill-omened company. Ah! Germany had made no difficulty about allowing Lenin and his friends to pass. She knew what she was sending us, and the cause which these comrades would serve here. She would have no better allies than they. She introduced the enemy into the fortress. It was a skillful stroke of policy. But, surprising thing! These men, returning from Germany, were very well received here. No one seemed disposed to seek a quarrel with them about the way of return that they had followed. I do not speak, that goes without saying, of the Extremists. But a Kerensky, a Minister, said: "It was difficult to prevent them from passing through Germany. We could scarcely object to that." [ . . . ]

This Lenin is what one calls, in the horrible socialist jargon, a "Defeatist," that is to say, one of those who prefer defeat to the war. He wanted peace, peace at any price, and without delay, and no matter what kind it might be. That was the thesis which he came to defend in the frightful confusion of the present hour in Russia.

Well, Lenin and his acolytes had been received at the Finland Station with the same enthusiasm, and by the same delegates of the Committee, as had Plekhanof and the English and French Socialists. Affecting speeches were delivered, while today there were grand demonstrations in the streets, with red banners, and the citizen Lenin was delivering a speech in the Duma at the very time I was writing these lines. Our French and English Socialist friends were greatly disgusted. They began to understand in what amazing anarchy we were living here: political anarchy, military anarchy, administrative and economic anarchy, which had, as its basis, the anarchy of minds.

# April 5—Badly received

Lenin did not triumph, yesterday evening, at the Congress of the different fractions of the Social Democratic Party. He said that the Government was detestable, that the Executive Committee was not good, that the Government must be thrown out and that the Social Democratic party ought to organize a Commune and assume power. Civil war and force! "The English and French socialist parties," said he, "are rotten with imperialism." [. . .] On the question of peace, he demanded it immediately and without conditions. Anything, rather than war. Russia, besides, owed autonomy to all the diverse peoples who composed her: autonomy to Georgia, to Armenia—and Daghestan?—Turkestan, Poland, the Ukraine, Lithuania, Courland, Estonia, Bessarabia, and I know not what else besides. Russia would be reduced to Grand Muscovy. That was the future which Lenin was preparing for his country. At home, no union between the socialist fractions: "Down with concord. The struggle *à outrance* [to the end] and the victory of the Extremists!"

Lenin was badly received. This visionary, who preached war at home and peace with the enemy abroad, had succeeded today in bringing about unity against himself.

# April 9—A worker and an officer debate Lenin

A discussion began with a workman seated near us, who was listening to the speeches delivered from the tribune and manifesting his disapproval. This comrade was a partisan of Lenin, and the non-commissioned officer attacked him with force and directness: "Comrade," said he, "you ought before everything to explain to me why Germany has sent us Lenin, while she has ignored the other revolutionaries."

The member was unable to parry this direct thrust, and argued about the necessity of concluding the War in agreement with all the democracies, giving to each country its liberty.

"And if Germany does not want this kind of peace?" he was asked.

"Germany cannot make peace with Gutchkoff and Miliukoff. Then we must overthrow them. Once we have a true democracy, the German Socialists will put down William and come to an arrangement with us."

"The German Socialists have, up to the present, supported the Emperor in the war because they saw in it a victorious war and the power which Germany would gain over the whole world. When Lenin has made disorder complete in Russia, nothing will be easier for the Germans than to beat us. Then the Germans will have the peace which they want, and not that which you hope for."

The Leninist was unconvinced, and said: "I do not want to make a war about which I understand nothing. I demand that the secret treaties between Russia, France and England be shown to me."

But the non-commissioned officer replied: "[S]o that Germany may profit by it[?]"

The Leninist, feeling the ground failing under his feet, sought refuge in the question of the classes. "Who is it who governs us? Bourgeois! This Chingaref is a monarchist. We ought to assume power."

"My dear fellow," replied the non-commissioned officer, "I have a great respect for Chingaref. See what he has done. Yesterday, we had no bread. Today, do you want for it? Think only of the position in which we were two months ago, and to what a state of misery Tsarism had reduced us. This Chingaref is a man who knows how to work. If it was you or myself who was in charge of the revictualling of Russia, we should very soon die of hunger."

The fellow took himself off, grumbling more and more. The non-commissioned officer turned towards me and said:

What is it that they have come to do here, these people? Now we have the Revolution; the Old Regime is overthrown; we are happy, we are free, and this wretch Lenin must needs come to create disorder. Ah, no! . . . I will tell you plainly that we soldiers do not want it. We had decided to go and seize this comrade who is stirring up the people . . . Yes, we were going in two companies . . . But our leaders restrained us, explaining to us that, up to the present, he had done nothing but talk, and that people had the right to speak, even to talk absurdities. But let him take care what he is doing! We are keeping an eye on him. Let him try and budge, and we shall settle his account. And that will not take long.

# 7.

# Lenin's April Theses:
# The Tasks of the Proletariat in the Present Revolution

*Two days later, on April 7, 1917, after Lenin had met with a wide range of Bolshevik and other party leaders and spoken at several meetings, he published his views in* Pravda. *Although he does not use the phrase here, the guiding demand of the Bolsheviks for the remainder of the revolution is implicit: "All power to the soviets." Far from proposing a coup, a common slander against Lenin, he suggests that, until they convince the majority of this position, the Bolsheviks should provide a "patient . . . explanation" of the need to overthrow the Provisional Government. In February, the Bolsheviks had roughly 25,000 members and won 10 percent of the seats in workers' soviets and even fewer in the soldiers' and peasants' soviets. However, their cohesion and experience, their significant base among workers in the biggest cities, and **Lenin***'s strategic outlines, charted in his "April Theses," make them a serious force to be reckoned with.[1]*

## THESES

1) In our attitude towards the war, which under the new [Provisional] Government of Lvov and Co. unquestionably remains on Russia's part a predatory imperialist war owing to the capitalist nature of that government, not the slightest concession to "revolutionary defensism" is permissible.

The class-conscious proletariat can give its consent to a revolutionary war, which would really justify revolutionary defensism, only on condition: (a)

47

that the power pass to the proletariat and the poorest sections of the peasants aligned with the proletariat; (b) that all annexations be renounced in deed and not in word; (c) that a complete break be effected in actual fact with all capitalist interests.

In view of the undoubted honesty of those broad sections of the mass believers in revolutionary defensism who accept the war only as a necessity, and not as a means of conquest, in view of the fact that they are being deceived by the bourgeoisie, it is necessary with particular thoroughness, persistence and patience to explain their error to them, to explain the inseparable connection existing between capital and the imperialist war, and to prove that without overthrowing capital it is impossible to end the war by a truly democratic peace, a peace not imposed by violence. The most widespread campaign for this view must be organized in the army at the front. [Including . . . ] fraternization.

2) The specific feature of the present situation in Russia is that the country is passing from the first stage of the revolution—which, owing to the insufficient class-consciousness and organization of the proletariat, placed power in the hands of the bourgeoisie—to its second stage, which must place power in the hands of the proletariat and the poorest sections of the peasants. This transition is characterized, on the one hand, by a maximum of legally recognized rights (Russia is now the freest of all the belligerent countries in the world); on the other, by the absence of violence towards the masses, and, finally, by their unreasoning trust in the government of capitalists, those worst enemies of peace and socialism. This peculiar situation demands of us an ability to adapt ourselves to the special conditions of Party work among unprecedentedly large masses of proletarians who have just awakened to political life.

3) No support for the Provisional Government; the utter falsity of all its promises should be made clear, particularly of those relating to the renunciation of annexations. Exposure in place of the impermissible, illusion-breeding "demand" that this government, a government of capitalists, should cease to be an imperialist government.

4) Recognition of the fact that in most of the Soviets of Workers' Deputies our Party is in a minority, so far a small minority, as against a bloc of all the petty-bourgeois opportunist elements, from the Popular Socialists and the Socialist Revolutionaries down to the Organizing Committee (Chkheidze, Tsereteli, etc.), Steklov, etc., etc., who have yielded to the influence of the bourgeoisie and spread that influence among the proletariat. The masses must be made to see that the Soviets of Workers' Deputies are the only possible form of revolutionary government, and that therefore our task is, as long as this

government yields to the influence of the bourgeoisie, to present a patient, systematic, and persistent explanation of the errors of their tactics, an explanation especially adapted to the practical needs of the masses. As long as we are in the minority we carry on the work of criticizing and exposing errors and at the same time we preach the necessity of transferring the entire state power to the Soviets of Workers' Deputies, so that the people may overcome their mistakes by experience.

5) Not a parliamentary republic—to return to a parliamentary republic from the Soviets of Workers' Deputies would be a retrograde step—but a republic of Soviets of Workers,' Agricultural Laborers,' and Peasants' Deputies throughout the country, from top to bottom. Abolition of the police, the army and the bureaucracy. The salaries of all officials, all of whom are elective and displaceable at any time, not to exceed the average wage of a competent worker.

6) The weight of emphasis in the agrarian program to be shifted to the Soviets of Agricultural Laborers' Deputies. Confiscation of all landed estates. Nationalization of all lands in the country, the land to be disposed of by the local Soviets of Agricultural Laborers' and Peasants' Deputies. The organization of separate Soviets of Deputies of Poor Peasants. The setting up of a model farm on each of the large estates (ranging in size from 100 to 300 dessiatines [a dessiatine is about 2.7 acres], according to local and other conditions, and to the decisions of the local bodies) under the control of the Soviets of Agricultural Laborers' Deputies and for the public account.

7) The immediate union of all banks in the country into a single national bank, and the institution of control over it by the Soviet of Workers' Deputies.

8) It is not our immediate task to "introduce" socialism, but only to bring social production and the distribution of products at once under the control of the Soviets of Workers' Deputies.

9) Party tasks:

    (a) Immediate convocation of a Party Congress;

    (b) Alteration of the Party Program, mainly:

        (1) On the question of imperialism and the imperialist war,

        (2) On our attitude towards the state and our demand for a "commune state";

        (3) Amendment of our out-of-date minimum program;

    (c) Change of the Party's name.

10) A new International.

# 8.

## Tsereteli's April Anti-Theses

*After a month-long debate, including the convening of a national convention, the Bolshevik Party adopted the radical core of Lenin's April Theses and began to put forth their "patient explanation" for handing all power to the soviets. The Mensheviks decided upon a very different approach. Irakli Tsereteli, a Menshevik leader from Georgia, served on the Executive Committee of the St. Petersburg Soviet and as a minister in the Provisional Government between April and July, taking part in a "Coalition" Government between the socialist and liberal capitalist parties (principally the Cadets). During his tenure, he advocated an international agreement to end the war while maintaining that, in the meantime, Russia must continue the war against Germany and keep up its commitments to the Allies. These positions proved popular initially, but as time passed they placed him and his Menshevik comrades increasingly at odds with the war-weary population. **Claude Anet** explains his predicament.*[1]

### April 28

The Social Democrats were still making up their minds. I was under the impression that the moving spirit among the "objectors" [to forming a coalition government] was Tsereteli. He was certainly the most intelligent. This man, who has spent ten years in Siberia, an ex-member of the second Duma, a Georgian with the pale, drawn face of a Greco, seems to have the best head of the whole council [that is, Soviet]. His speeches have a decision and snap about them which is conspicuously absent from the discursive pathos of his colleagues. But even supposing he has character and an instinct of statesmanship, what then? Where has he come from? Siberia, and ten weary years of exile. His experience of life is nil. His knowledge is the bookworm's. He is perfectly familiar with Karl Marx and other writers, but of the knowledge gained by direct contact with men and affairs he has none. What notion of love of country has he? He is a Caucasian and comes from an ancient race which fell on evil days and in the seventeenth century was subject to the Shahs of Persia. Georgia has only been Russian for rather more than fifty years. Tsereteli has no Russian connections. Not that that matters, for your "Internationalist" sees the world and society through formulae. Class warfare is one, the Internationale another.

He was now on the threshold of power. The time for formulae had passed, and fearsome realities had to be faced. Before him was the Russian Empire; 160 million people of different races, still only half welded together under the imperial hammer, a vague mass, practically uneducated and only emerged from serfdom within the last fifty years; a working class only just born, weak in numbers as in influence, without organization or discipline; a peasantry strong in numbers but amorphous, chaotic, and without leaders. And it was this uneducated and inorganic proletariat which formed the congregation of the preachers of class wars and (so ran the formula) must take all power into its own hands. Tsereteli's quick wits told him at once that the peasantry and working classes of Russia were totally incapable of governing the Empire, even if the conditions of the time had been favorable to the experiment, that is, even if Russia had been at peace. But Russia was at war. This was the plain truth, and no Social Democrat in the world could alter the fact. The war! Yes, there was the International and the dream of Universal Brotherhood, the old romance on which the Socialists of all countries have brought up their adherents, though the sound of guns has dispelled it often enough.

There is no question that in the first days of the Revolution the only cry that went up from Russia was a cry for peace. A passionate desire for peace was universal. The fearful suffering, the terrible toll of human life, the appalling internal difficulties which were the direct product of the war, the shortage of supplies, the transport crisis, the amazing rise in price of the most elementary necessities, the semi-starvation of the great cities—all these legacies of the collapse of autocracy made men everywhere hope fervently that the Revolution meant peace.

But Tsereteli, to whom Universal Brotherhood is a dogma, knows quite well that for some time longer this dogma must lie on the shelf with the books which preach it. Russia was invaded. She was allied with the Powers of Western

Europe with whom she had formal agreements, whose money and munitions she had freely received, with whom she could not break without grave danger of finding herself the vassal of Germany. But if he took power and supported the war, who would back him?

In this respect, at least, the policy of the Russian Social Democratic Party [or the Menshevik section thereof], however tentative as to means, must be admitted to have been perfectly decided as to ends. They wanted peace, and as it could not be reached by a separate peace, they mean to obtain it by an understanding with all the countries involved in the struggle. They seriously believed that a lasting peace could be realized by persuasion. A chimerical notion which I cannot think Tsereteli ever shared. But what were his alternatives? Even if he were convinced that peace could only be reached through the defeat of Germany, how could this apostle of Pacifism and Internationalism be expected to advocate an intense and aggressive war against the armies of the Kaiser? Tsereteli was far too intelligent not to know that the very same obstacles that had faced Tsarism would have to be faced and surmounted by the Revolutionary Government which had succeeded it. Order had to be restored in the country.

# 9.

# Kerensky's First Visit to the Army

*If Tsereteli and the Mensheviks hoped for peace, Alexander Kerensky agitated for war. Kerensky belonged to the Trudovik current of the Socialist Revolutionary Party and built up his prerevolutionary reputation as a radical attorney who had defended workers and peasants from tsarist persecution. In mid-April, a diplomatic note from the Provisional Government to the Allies promising Russia's continued participation in the war was leaked to the public. After mass protests, Cadet minister of war Pavel Milyukov was forced to resign and Kerensky took his place. In the shuffle, half the positions in the Provisional Government went to Menshevik and SR leaders, constituting a coalition between the moderate socialists and liberal capitalists of the Cadet Party. The Bolsheviks refused to join. While left-wing factions of the Menshevik and SR Parties began to turn against the war and the generals' authority over their soldiers collapsed, here **Kerensky** himself describes how he attempted to counter Bolshevik antiwar agitation among the troops. In the end, he decided to launch a new offensive, not because he believed the army could defeat Germany but in order to restore order and purge the army of Bolshevik influence.[1]*

After short trips to the Caucasus front at the very beginning of the war and to the Western front in 1915, I again saw the army in May 1917. Having repaired to some extent the ministerial machine and reorganized the administration of the Petrograd military district, I left on May 20 for the Galician front, where General Brusiloff was in command.

This front had remained in a better state of preservation than any other after the revolutionary explosion, but here, too, one beheld a terrible picture of destruction. It seemed as if the army had forgotten the enemy and turned its face towards the interior of the country, its attention riveted on what was going on there. There was neither the crack of machine guns nor the exchange of artillery fire. The trenches were deserted. All preparatory work for offensive operations had been abandoned. With their uniforms in ludicrous disorder, thousands of troops were devoting their time to interminable meetings. Most of the officers seemed completely confused. The local Galician population was looking on in surprise and amusement.

But beneath this discouraging picture of destruction there was already being kindled a new will to action. Like General Brusiloff, the officers who had retained their self-possession and ignored the countless blows to their self-respect continued to toil with immeasurable enthusiasm and self-sacrifice for the creation of new spiritual and human contacts between the commanders and the troops. From morning till night many commanders strove to gain the ear of their soldiers, in an effort to convince them of the necessity of fighting for the preservation of the country and its newly won liberty. The commissars of the War Ministry and the local army committees were working feverishly in the same direction. In general, the Galician army, while not capable of active operations, was rapidly developing the will to action.

I remember the army conference at Kamenetz-Podolsk, General Brusiloff's headquarters. The huge hall was filled with hundreds of soldier delegates, sent from the most remote corners of the front. I beheld weary faces, feverish eyes, extraordinary tension. It was quite clear that before me were people who had experienced a great shock and, having lost the capacity to reason normally, were seeking for some sort of new justification of their continued sojourn in the trenches. In listening to the speeches of the delegates and the representatives of the army committees, of Brusiloff himself, and of the Bolsheviki who were led by the subsequently notorious Krilenko, I felt as if I were putting my hand to the very heart of the army. What the army was experiencing at that time, in the very deepest recesses of its consciousness, was a great, irresistible temptation, too great for human powers to endure. After three years of the cruelest suffering, the millions of soldiers, exhausted to the last degree by the tortures of war, found themselves confronted suddenly with the questions: "What are we dying for? Must we die?"

To put these questions to a man who must be ready and willing to die at any moment, to put before him anew, and in the midst of war, the question of the meaning of his sacrifice implied the paralysis of his will to action. Man can endure war and remain in the trenches under artillery fire only when he does not reason, when he does not think of the aims or, to be more correct, when he is animated by an unshakable, almost automatic conviction of the inevitability and necessity of sacrifice, for the sake of an already clear and established purpose, no longer subject to discussion. It is too late to think of war aims and to build up an "ideology of war" when you are already being called upon to stop the enemy's bullets.

No army can withstand such a temptation without grievous consequences. Everything else which was destroying the army—persecution of the officers, mutinies, the Bolshevization of various units, the interminable meetings, etc.—was only the painful expression of that terrible struggle for life which gripped the soul of every soldier. He suddenly perceived an opportunity to justify morally his human weakness, his well-nigh unconquerable, instinctive desire to run away from those disgusting, horrible trenches. For the army to fight again meant to conquer anew the animal in man, to find anew some sort of unquestionable slogan of war that would make it possible again for everybody to look death in the face calmly and unflinchingly. For the sake of the nation's life it was necessary to restore the army's will to die.

"Forward to the battle for freedom! I summon you not to a feast but to death!" These were the words I used before the conference at Kamenetz-Podolsk. These words were also the keynote of all my addresses before the troops in the front-line positions.

"We call you to social revolution! We summon you not to die for others but to destroy others, to destroy your class enemies in the rear!" This counter-slogan of Lenin carried with it terrible force, for it justified beforehand the animal fear of death which lurks in the heart of even the bravest. It supplied the mind with arguments in support of everything that was dark, cowardly, and selfish in the army. There is nothing remarkable in the fact that in the end, after months of bitter struggle, the most ignorant of the masses preferred murder and rapine and followed the leaders of the Bolshevist counter-revolution. The remarkable thing was the mighty wave of patriotic self-abnegation which swept the army at the front in the summer of 1917.

# 10.

# June 18 Soviet Demonstration and the Rise of the Bolsheviks

*While Kerensky toured the front preparing for a new offensive, Bolshevik influence grew steadily in the capital, especially among the radicalizing soldiers stationed there and the sailors of the Kronstadt fortress nearby. After a complex series of fights, the Bolsheviks agreed to cancel a mass march scheduled for June 10, under threat of repression from both the Provisional Government and the hostile Menshevik and SR majority leadership in the citywide Soviet. Hoping to humiliate the Bolsheviks and demonstrate that they commanded the loyalty of the working masses, the Menshevik and SR leaders called for a "pro-Soviet" march on June 18.* **Nikolai Sukhanov,** *a "nonparty" socialist who eventually joined Julius Martov's left-wing Menshevik Internationalist faction, describes how this maneuver backfired on the moderate socialists and how the Bolsheviks seized the opportunity to display their strength.*[1]

## June 18

I left for [Maxim] Gorky's nearby. He or some literary friend might go with me to watch the demonstration. But there were no literary people around, and Gorky said: "The demonstration's a failure. I've heard from a number of places; only handfuls of people are marching. The streets are empty; there's nothing to see. I'm not going."

Hm! Somewhere someone already had his conclusions ready. At the same time these conclusions, if correct, could be interpreted in two ways. The demonstration was a "failure" because the revolutionary energy of the masses

59

was drying up; they no longer wanted to come out when the Soviet called them and demand peace, etc., but to pass onto peaceful labor and finish the revolution—in spite of the exhortations of Soviet demagogues and loudmouths. It was obvious which circles, thirsting for the reaction, have been anticipating just these conclusions.

But there might be another interpretation: the democracy of the capital remained relatively indifferent to the demonstration because it was official, "Soviet," and its slogans did not correspond to the mood of the masses; the revolutionary energy had perhaps long since definitely rolled past the boundary at which the Star Chamber [the St. Petersburg Soviet Executive Committee] have been trying to stop it.

But one moment! The failure of the demonstration might be utter nonsense. All the Soviet parties, after all, had decided to take part in it, and prepare for it! I went out alone, turning towards the Champ de Mars, through which all the columns were to march. In the Kamenno-Ostrovsky Prospect, near Kshesinskaya's house, near Trinity Bridge, it was really rather deserted. It was only on the other side of the Neva that the detachments of demonstrations were visible. It was a magnificent day, and already hot.

There wasn't a dense crowd blocking the Champ de Mars, but the columns formed moving towards me. "Bolsheviks!" I thought, looking at the slogans on the banners.

I went over to the graves of those who had been killed, where familiar Soviet people were standing in compact groups taking the salute. Apparently the demonstration was rather behind time. The district had started from the assembly points later than scheduled. It was still only the first detachments of the Petersburg Revolutionary Army that were parading through the Champ de Mars. Columns were still on the way from every part of Petersburg. There was nothing, however, to be heard of any excesses, disorders or upset. No arms have been seen amongst the demonstrators.

The columns marched swiftly and in close order. There could be no question of a "failure," but there was something *peculiar* about this demonstration. On the faces, in the movements, in the whole appearance of the demonstrators—there was no sign of lively participation in what they were doing. There was no sign of enthusiasm, or holiday spirits, or a political indignation. The masses had been called and they had come. They all came—to do what was required and then go back. [. . .] Probably some of those called from their homes and private affairs this Sunday were indifferent. Others thought this was a government demonstration, and felt that they were doing not their *own* business but something compulsory and perhaps superfluous. There was a businesslike veneer over the entire demonstration. But it was on a magnificent scale. All worker and soldier Petersburg took part in it.

But what was the political character of the demonstration? "Bolsheviks again," I remarked, looking at slogans, "And there behind them is another Bolshevik column."

"Apparently the next one too." I went on calculating, watching the banners advancing towards me and the endless rows going away towards Michael Castle a long way down the Sadovoy.

"All power to the soviets!" "Down with the Ten Capitalist Ministers!" "Peace to the hovels, war for the palaces!"

In this sturdy and weighty way worker-peasant Petersburg, the vanguard of the Russian and the world revolution, expressed its will. The situation was absolutely unambiguous. Here and there the chain of Bolshevik flags and columns was interrupted by specifically SR and official Soviet slogans. But they were submerged in the mass; they seemed to be exceptions, intentionally confirming the rule. Again and again, like the unchanging summons of the very depths of the revolutionary capital, like fate itself, like the fatal Birnam wood—they advanced towards us: "All power to the soviets!" "Down with the Ten Capitalist Ministers!"

An astonishing, bewitching slogan, this! Embodying a vast program in naive and awkward words, it seemed to emerge directly from the very depths of the nation, reviving the unconscious, spontaneously heroic spirit of the great French Revolution.

At the sight of the measured advance of the fighting columns of the Revolutionary Army, it seemed that the Coalition [Government] was already formally liquidated and that Messrs. the Ministers, in view of the manifest popular mistrust, would quit their places that very day without waiting to be urged by more imposing means.

I remember the purblind Tsereteli's fervor of the night before. Here was the duel in the open arena! Here was the honest legal review of forces in an official Soviet demonstration!

A few steps away from me Kamenev's stocky figure was visible in the thin crowd, rather like a victor acknowledging a parade. But he looked more perplexed than triumphant.

"Well, what now?" I said to him? "What sort of government is there going to be now? Are you going into a Cabinet with Tsereteli, Skobelev and Chernov?"

"We are," Kamenev replied, but somehow without real assurance.

The program of action in the minds of the Bolshevik leaders was evidently completely vague. And Kamenev himself was vacillation incarnate.

The detachment was approaching with an anonymous, heavy, gold-embroidered banner: "The Central Committee of the Russian Social Democratic Workers Party (Bolsheviks)." The leader demanded that, unlike the others, that attachment be allowed to stop and go right up to the graves. Someone who was acting as master of ceremonies tried to argue with them, but yielded at once. Who and what could have stopped the victors from allowing themselves this trifling indulgence, if that was what they wanted?

# 11.

# Bolsheviks on Battleships

*As it turned out, June 18 was also the day of Kerensky's military offensive. Tens of thousands of Russian soldiers perished in the vain attempt to break through the superior German lines. The lesson was simple enough in so far as the masses were concerned: the Provisional Government represented the prolongation of the senseless war. The disaster all but destroyed the last vestiges of discipline in the military and spurred a dramatic lurch to the left among millions of workers, soldiers, and peasants. But it is one thing to refuse orders from illegitimate authority and another to create mechanisms for a new sort of democratic, rank-and-file authority. In June 1917, local Bolshevik leaders from the Kronstadt fortress decided to tour the Russian Fleet, then anchored in the harbor near St. Petersburg. Remarkably, sailors' soviets on each ship invited them aboard and organized political meetings to hear the Bolshevik delegation's point of view. The tsarist officer corps could hardly interfere. Where they did try,* **Fyodor Raskolnikov** *demonstrates how the revolutionary process transgressed the line between protest and power.*[1]

## Late June

Next the entire delegation made a tour of the remaining battleships. Everywhere we met with a joyful reception. The majority of the crews, wholly sympathetic to Kronstadt, expressed readiness to support it in all revolutionary actions and saw us off with even greater enthusiasm. An entire crew, covering the top deck, cheered us for a long time, waving their caps.

On the *Poltava*, as our launch was about to leave, we were asked to wait a few minutes, and when we eventually put off, a band struck up. The comrades from *Poltava* had specially rounded up the ship's band to play as we left. The hardiest reception was given us on the *Petropavlosk*. Among other things, it was here that intense hatred between the officers and the crew was particularly noticeable.

On the *Petropavlosk* we encountered a delegate from the front, a certain second lieutenant. We let him speak first, as we wanted to put ourselves in the most favorable position, expecting as we did a "patriotic" speech from him such as was usual at that time; however, the second lieutenant turned out to be a Bolshevik. He spoke no less sharply than we did against the war, harshly criticized the Provisional Government, and vigorously demanded that power be handed to the Soviets. At the end of the meeting the sailors, delighted to meet officers who were Bolsheviks, such as they evidently had not had the pleasure of meeting on their own vessel, made speeches of welcome and even carried shoulder-high their co-thinkers from the commanding personnel.

We liked the second lieutenant so much that we took them with us when we visited the *Respublika* (formerly the *Pavel I*). Already in the first days of the February Revolution the *Respublika* had won a firm reputation throughout the Baltic Fleet and even beyond, as a floating citadel of Bolshevism, a steadfast bulwark of our Party.

Naturally, we at once felt at home there. After mounting to the bridge, which had been transformed into a tribunal for speakers, we first of all emphasized that it was with particular pleasure that we have come aboard the ship, since *Respublika* had more than once delighted us with the splendid, firm resolutions adopted by her crew and, as we discovered, our Party group on *Respublika* had grown to an unusually large size—600 men.

From there we proceeded to the battleship the *Andrei Pervozvanny*. When we arrived they had just received a wireless message from the First All-Russian Congress of Soviets which was then being held, aimed exclusively against the Bolsheviks. This somewhat dampened the ardor of the crew where we were concerned. But Comrade Kolbin then spoke about this appeal "to all," [and] dissipated the bad impression it had created and restored to the general morale.

The next stage in our journey was to the battleship *Slava*. It has only just returned from action off Oesel Island [near Riga in the Baltic Sea]. Without losing a moment we took our seats in a steam launch and in a few minutes made fast the armored side of *Slava*. As a general rule we went first to the ship's committee in order to tell them we were going to call a general meeting. On this ship, however, the procedure was somewhat strange. We were told to apply for permission for our meeting to the captain of the ship, whose name was Antonov. This delicate diplomatic function was trusted by the Kronstadt comrades to me.

When I entered the captain's cabin I found him sitting there—an officer of middle height, with gray hair, wore a St. Vladimir's Cross, fourth class, on the left breast of his jacket.

"What can I do for you?" Antonov asked suspiciously.

"We want to hold a meeting here," I answered.

"But what do you want to talk about?" the captain muttered in a discontented tone and as though fully on alert for something. Such a question was highly improper. Nevertheless I replied: "We want to convey to the sailors of the ship what our comrades at Kronstadt, whom we represent, have instructed us to convey."

Then I briefly enumerated our main political theses. The captain remained for a short time sunk in thought, as though hesitating whether to permit or forbid our meeting.

Eventually, faced with our resolute attitude, he realized without much delay that he was quite helpless, appreciating that regardless of whether or not he gave permission, we should hold our general meeting in one way or another and report to it everything we have been instructed to report.

"All right, hold your meeting," he said reluctantly. "But Bolsheviks can't get anywhere with our crew."

Despite the absence of many of our comrades, who were on shore, a fairly large crowd assembled on the deck where religious services were held. The crew of the *Slava* listened with close attention to what we said, and when we had finished showered us with a mass of written questions. We replied in detail, carefully explaining how the Kronstadters viewed this problem and that.

Everything went well until, at last, I came to the matter of fraternization, which was then a burning question for the sailors and soldiers. Speaking out decisively against the offensive being prepared, I counterposed to this the practice of fraternization at the front and began to defend and justify this slogan. But my call for fraternization was not to someone's liking. "We've just come back from Tserel [near Riga]," shouted one of the sailors hysterically. "Every day the German aeroplanes rained down bombs on us, and you talk about fraternization! You should be in the trenches! See how you can fraternize there!"

I had to cool down somewhat the passion of the sailor, whose nerves had obviously been shattered by his experiences in action. But the sailors themselves immediately made him shut up and turning to me with a request to go on with my concluding speech, they added reassuringly: "Don't pay any attention, comrade, he is a provocateur among us."

In general the mood of this ship was quite favorable, but nevertheless it considerably lagged behind other ships where speeches had been greeted with much greater sympathy and enthusiasm. It was clear that during their isolated stationing off Tserel, the ship's crew had been well worked upon by the reactionary officers, led by Antonov himself. On the same battleship *Slava*, just before our delegation left it, an incident occurred. As we were saying goodbye to our sailor comrades and the officers who stood nearby, I came upon one young officer who refused to offer me his hand.

"Why didn't you give me your hand?" I asked.

"On account of your views," the officer answered defiantly.

"But, pardon me, I am a representative of a certain political party and I honestly and sincerely expressed the views which I profess. Tell me why I should deserve to be treated with such contempt that you refused to shake hands with me?"

"I didn't intend to insult you," muttered the young officer, embarrassed. "I acted as my feelings prompted me."

"But if your feelings have prompted you to hit me in the face," I replied, "then regardless of your intentions, that would have been an insult."

"If you consider yourself insulted, I apologize," the officer whispered, now quite confused.

I advised him to behave more carefully next time, and asked his name, which turned out to be Sub-Lieutenant Denyer. At once I went to see the ship's committee and told the member on duty that, while a guest on the battleship *Slava* I have been subjected to insult and considered that in my person the whole delegation, which shared my views, had been insulted. The committee member reacted very sympathetically to my statements, took note of what happened, and remarked about Sub-Lieutenant Denyer, "You have to realize what sort of a fellow he is. He has only been one week on the ship." I named as witnesses the sailor Baranov and a sub-lieutenant named Sminkevich. The ship's committee promised to let me know the outcome of this affair.

# III.

# THE JULY DAYS
# AND THE KORNILOV COUNTERREVOLUTION

*The great French revolutionary Louis Antoine de Saint-Just once remarked, "Those who make revolution halfway only dig their own graves." During the summer of 1917, workers, soldiers, and sailors in St. Petersburg did exactly what Saint-Just warned against. That is, with guns in hand, they marched to demand the Mensheviks (Tsereteli and Minister of Labor Matvey Skobelev) and SRs (Kerensky and Minister of Agriculture Victor Chernov) end the war, distribute land to the peasants, convene national elections, and grant workers' power in the factories. Confronted with the manifest refusal of these leaders to "take the power" away from the bourgeoisie, as one worker put it, the masses hesitated and fell back in a state of confusion and disappointment, thereby opening the door to reaction from the opposite end of the political spectrum. However, when reaction struck in the form of an attempted military coup by General Kornilov in August, Kornilov found the working class had already been inoculated against his conspiracy by their fighting experiences in 1905 and 1917. Further, the Bolshevik Party, now grown to some 150,000 members, helped the working class retreat in good order from its halfway revolution—they suffered dozens or hundreds of casualties, not thousands or tens of thousands, and the St. Petersburg working class lived to fight another day.*

# 12.

# The July Days

*Upon receiving news of the February Revolution, **Trotsky** left New York City with a group of exiles in hopes of getting around the German and Allied blockades. He was detained by the British navy and held captive for a month in Nova Scotia. Finally arriving in St. Petersburg on May 4, he temporarily joined the Mezhraiontsy group of independent revolutionary socialists as they negotiated with the Bolshevik Party for a merger. In 1905, Trotsky had been elected chairman of the St. Petersburg Soviet and now, being one of the most popular figures in the revolutionary movement, he was immediately elected to the All-Russian Executive Committee of the Soviet in June. By July, Trotsky had regained the stature he had earned in 1905 on the extreme left. Here he recounts the conflict that landed him back in prison, this time under the authority of Kerensky's government.[1]*

## July 2 to 5—Armed demonstrations

General Polovtsev published on the morning of July 4 an announcement that he was going to cleanse Petrograd of armed hordes. The inhabitants were strictly advised to lock their doors and not go into the streets except in case of absolute necessity. This threatening order fell flat. The commander of all the troops of the district was able to bring out against the demonstrators only petty detachments of Cossacks and Junkers. In the course of the day they caused some meaningless shootings and some bloody clashes. [ . . . ] The government was living by the authorization of the Executive Committee [of the Soviet]; the power of the Executive Committee derived in turn from the hopes of the masses that it might at last come to its senses and take the power.

The demonstration attained its highest point with the appearance on the Petrograd arena of the Kronstadt sailors. Delegates from the machine-gunners had been working the day before in the garrison of the naval fortress. A meeting had assembled in Yakorny Square, unexpectedly to the local organization, on the initiative of some anarchists from Petrograd. The orators had appealed to the sailors to come to the help of Petrograd. Roshal, a medical student, one of the young heroes of Kronstadt and a favorite on Yakorny Square, had tried to make a speech counseling moderation. Thousands of voices cut him off. Roshal, accustomed to a different welcome, had been compelled to leave the tribune. Not until night did it become known that in Petrograd the Bolsheviks were calling the masses into the streets. That settled the matter. The Left Social-Revolutionaries—and in Kronstadt there could be no Right ones—announced that they intended to take part in the demonstration. These people belonged to the same party with Kerensky, who at that very moment was at the front collecting troops to put down the demonstration. The mood at that night's session of the Kronstadt organization was such that even the timid commissar of the Provisional Government, Parchevsky, voted for the march on Petrograd. A plan was drawn up; transports were mobilized. For the necessities of this political siege, two and a half tons of arms and ammunition were given out from the stores. Crowded on tugs and passenger steamers, about 10,000 armed sailors, soldiers and workers came into the narrows of the Neva at twelve o'clock noon. Disembarking on both sides of the river, they formed a procession with bands playing and with rifles slung over their shoulders. Behind the detachments of sailors and soldiers came columns of workers from the Petrograd and Vassilievsky Island districts, interspersed with companies of the Red Guard flanked by armored cars and with innumerable standards and banners rising above them.

The Palace of Kshesinskaia was but two steps away. A little lank man, black as tar, Sverdlov—one of the basic organizers of the party elected to the Central Committee in the April conference—was standing on the balcony and in a businesslike manner, as always, shouting down instructions in his powerful bass voice: "Head of the procession, advance—close up ranks—rear ranks come closer." The demonstrators were greeted from the balcony by Lunacharsky, a man always easily infected by the moods of those around him, imposing in appearance and voice, eloquent in a declamatory way—none too reliable, but often irreplaceable. He was stormily applauded from below. But most of all the demonstrators wanted to hear Lenin himself. He had been summoned that morning, by the way, from his temporary Finland refuge. And the sailors so insisted on having their will that in spite of ill health Lenin could not beg off. An irresistible wave of ecstasy, a genuine Kronstadt wave, greeted the leader's appearance on the balcony. Impatiently—and as always with some embarrassment—awaiting the end of the greeting, Lenin began speaking before the voices died down. His speech, which the hostile press for weeks after growled over and tore to pieces in every possible manner, consisted of a few simple phrases: a greeting to the demonstrators; an expression of confidence that the slogan "All power to the soviets" would conquer in the end, an appeal for firmness and self-restraint. With renewed shouts the procession marched away to the music of the band.

Between this holiday introduction and the next stage of the proceedings, when blood began to flow, a curious episode intruded. The leaders of the Kronstadt Left Social-Revolutionaries noticed only after they arrived on Mars Field a colossal standard of the Central Committee of the Bolsheviks which had appeared at the head of the procession after the stop at the Palace of Kshesinskaia. Burning with party rivalry, they demanded its removal. The Bolsheviks refused. The Social-Revolutionaries then announced that they would withdraw entirely. However, none of the sailors or soldiers followed the leaders. The whole policy of the Left Social-Revolutionaries consisted of such capricious waverings, now comic and now tragic.

At the corner of the Nevsky and Liteiny, the rear guard of the demonstration was suddenly fired on, and several people were wounded. A crueler fire occurred on the corner of the Liteiny and Panteleimonov Street. The leader of the Kronstadt men, Raskolnikov, tells how "like a sharp pain to the demonstrators was their uncertainty where the enemy was, from what side he was shooting." The soldiers seized their rifles. Disorderly firing began in all directions. Several were killed and wounded. Only with great difficulty was order restored in the ranks. The procession again moved forward with music, but not a trace was left of its holiday spirit. "There seemed to be a hidden enemy everywhere; rifles no longer rested peacefully on the left shoulder, but were held ready for action." [ . . . ]

## Take power when they give it to you

The demonstrators again besieged the Tauride Palace and demanded their answer. At the moment the Kronstadt men arrived, some group or other brought Chernov out to them. Sensing the mood of the crowd, the word-loving minister pronounced upon this one occasion a very brief speech. Sliding over the crisis in the problem of power, he referred scornfully to the Cadets who had withdrawn from the government. "Good riddance!" he cried. Shouts interrupted him: "Then why didn't you say so before?" Miliukov even relates how "a husky worker, shaking his fist in the face of the minister, shouted furiously: 'Take the power, you son-of-a-bitch, when they give it to you.'" Even though nothing more than an anecdote, this expresses with crude accuracy the essence of the July situation. Chernov's answers have no interest; in any case, they did not win him the hearts of the Kronstadters. [ . . . ]

In just two or three minutes someone ran into the hall where the Executive Committee was sitting, and yelled that the sailors had arrested Chernov and were going to end him. With indescribable excitement the Executive Committee delegated several of its prominent members, exclusively internationalists and Bolsheviks, to rescue the minister. Chernov testified subsequently before a government commission that as he was descending from the tribune he noticed in the entrance behind the columns a hostile movement of several people. "They surrounded me and would not let me through to the door. . . . A suspicious-looking person in command of the sailors who were holding me back, kept pointing to an automobile standing near. . . . At that moment Trotsky, emerging from the Tauride Palace, came up and mounting on the front of the automobile in which I found myself [and] made a short speech." Proposing that Chernov be released, Trotsky asked all those opposed to raise their hands. "Not one hand was raised. The group which had conducted me to the automobile then stepped aside with a disgruntled look. Trotsky, as I remember, said: 'Citizen Chernov, nobody is hindering you from going back.'" [ . . . ]

## Could the Bolsheviks have seized the power in July?

The demonstration forbidden by the government and the Executive Committee had been a colossal one. On the second day not less than 500,000 people participated. Sukhanov, who cannot find words strong enough for the "blood and filth" of the July Days, nevertheless writes: "Political results aside, it was impossible not to look with admiration upon that amazing movement of the popular masses. Even while deeming it fatal, one could not but feel a rapture in its gigantic spontaneous scope." According to the reckonings of the Commission of Inquiry, 29 men were killed and 114 wounded—about an equal number on each side.

That the movement had begun from below, irrespective of the Bolsheviks— to a certain extent against their will—was at first recognized even by the Compromisers [the Menshevik/SR leaders]. But on the night of July 3, and yet more on the following day, official opinion began to change. The movement was declared an insurrection, the Bolsheviks its organizers. "Under the slogan, 'All power to the soviets,'" writes Stankevich, a man close to Kerensky, "there occurred an organized insurrection of the Bolsheviks against the majority of the soviets, consisting at that time of the defensist parties." This charge of organizing an insurrection was something more than a method of political struggle. During the month of June those people had well convinced themselves of the strong influence of the Bolsheviks on the masses, and they now simply refused to believe that a movement of workers and soldiers could have surged up over the heads of the Bolsheviks. Trotsky tried to explain the situation at a session of the Executive Committee: "They accuse us of creating the mood of the masses; that is wrong, we only tried to formulate it." In books published by their enemies after the October Revolution, particularly in Sukhanov, you will find it asserted that the Bolsheviks covered up their actual aim only in consequence of the defeat of the July insurrection, hiding behind the spontaneous movement of the masses. But could one possibly conceal, like a buried treasure, the plans of an armed insurrection which drew into its whirlpool hundreds of thousands of people? Were not the Bolsheviks compelled in October to summon the masses quite openly to insurrection, and to make preparations for it before the eyes of all? If no one discovered such a plan in July, it is only because there was none. [ . . . ]

The Bolsheviks made every effort to reduce the July movement to a demonstration. But did it not, nevertheless, by the very logic of things transcend these limits? This political question is harder to answer than the criminal indictment. Appraising the July Days immediately after they occurred, Lenin wrote: "An anti-government demonstration—that would be the most formally accurate description of the events. But the point is that this was no ordinary demonstration. It was something considerably more than a demonstration and less than a revolution." When the masses once get hold of some idea, they want to realize it. Although trusting the Bolshevik party, the workers, and still more the soldiers, had not yet acquired a conviction that they ought to come out only upon the summons of the party and under its leadership. The experiences of February and April had taught them rather the opposite. When Lenin said in May that the workers and peasants were a hundred times more revolutionary than the party, he undoubtedly generalized this February and April experience. But the masses had also generalized the experience in their own way. They were saying to themselves: "Even the Bolsheviks are dawdling and holding us back." The demonstrators were entirely ready in the July Days to liquidate the official government if that should seem necessary in the course of business. In case of resistance from the bourgeoisie they were ready to employ arms. To that extent there was an element of armed insurrection. If, in spite of this, it was not carried through even to the middle—to say nothing of the end—that is because the Compromisers confused the whole picture. [ . . . ]

The July demonstrators wanted to turn over the power to the soviets, but for this the soviets had to agree to take it. Even in the capital, however, where a majority of the workers and the active elements of the garrison were already for the Bolsheviks, a majority in the Soviet—owing to that law of inertia which applies to every representative system—still belonged to those petty-bourgeois parties who regarded an attempt against the power of the bourgeoisie as an attempt against themselves. The workers and soldiers felt clearly enough the contrast between their moods and the policy of the Soviet—that is, between their today and their yesterday. In coming out for a government of the soviets, they by no means gave their confidence to the compromisist majority in those soviets. But they did not know how to settle with this majority. To overthrow it by violence would have meant to dissolve the soviets instead of giving them the power. Before they could find the path to a change of the personal composition of the soviets, the workers and soldiers tried to subject the soviets to their will by the method of direct action. [ . . . ]

But if the Compromisers did not want to take the power, and the bourgeoisie did not have the strength to take it, maybe the Bolsheviks could have seized the helm in July? In the course of those two critical days the power in Petrograd completely dropped from the hands of the governmental institutions. The Executive Committee then felt for the first time its own complete impotence. In such circumstances it would have been easy enough for the Bolsheviks to seize the power. They could have seized the power, too, at certain individual points in the provinces. That being the case, was the Bolshevik party right in refraining from an insurrection? Might they not, fortifying themselves in the capital and in certain industrial districts, have subsequently extended their rule to the whole country? That is an important question. Nothing gave more help to the triumph of imperialism and reaction in Europe at the end of the war than those few months of Kerenskyism, exhausting revolutionary Russia and immeasurably damaging her moral authority in the eyes of the warring armies and of the toiling masses of Europe who had been hopefully awaiting some new word from the revolution. To shorten the birth pains of the proletarian revolution by four months would have been an immense gain. The Bolsheviks would have received the country in a less exhausted condition; the authority of the revolution in Europe would have been less undermined. This would not only have given the soviets an immense predominance in conducting the negotiations with Germany, but would have exerted a mighty influence on the fortunes of war and peace in Europe. The prospect was only too enticing!

But nevertheless, the leadership of the party was completely right in not taking the road of armed insurrection. It is not enough to seize the power—you have to hold it. When in October the Bolsheviks did decide that their hour had struck, the most difficult days came after the seizure of power. It requires the highest tension of the forces of the working class to sustain the innumerable attacks of an enemy. In July even the Petrograd workers did not yet possess that preparedness for infinite struggle. Although able to seize the power, they nevertheless offered it to the Executive Committee. The proletariat of the capital, although inclining toward the Bolsheviks in its overwhelming majority, had still not broken the February umbilical cord attaching it to the Compromisers. Many still cherished the illusion that everything could be obtained by words and demonstrations—that by frightening the Mensheviks and Social-Revolutionaries you could get them to carry out a common policy with the Bolsheviks. Even the advanced sections of the class had no clear idea by which roads it was possible to arrive at the power. [ . . . ]

## July as prototype

In April, June, and July, the principal actors were the same: the Liberals, the Compromisers and the Bolsheviks. At all these stages the masses were trying to crowd the bourgeoisie out of the government. But the difference in the political consequences of mass interference in the several cases was enormous. It was the bourgeoisie who suffered in consequence of the "April days." The annexation policy was condemned—in words at least; the Cadet party was humiliated; the portfolio of foreign affairs was taken from it. In June the movement came to nothing. A gesture was made against the Bolsheviks, but the blow was not struck. In July the Bolshevik party was accused of treason, shattered, deprived of food and drink. Whereas in April Miliukov had been forced out of the government, in July Lenin was forced underground. [ . . . ]

A prototype of the July Days is to be found in all the old revolutions—with various, but generally speaking unfavorable and frequently catastrophic, results. This stage is involved in the inner mechanics of a bourgeois revolution, inasmuch as that class which sacrifices most for the success of the revolution and hopes the most from it receives the least of all. The natural law of the process is perfectly clear. The possessing class which is brought to power by the revolution is inclined to think that with this the revolution has accomplished its mission, and is therefore most of all concerned to demonstrate its reliability to the forces of reaction. This "revolutionary" bourgeoisie provokes the indignation of the popular masses by those same measures with which it strives to win the good will of the classes it has overthrown. The disappointment of the masses follows very quickly; it follows even before their vanguard has cooled off after the revolutionary struggle. The people imagine that with a new blow they can carry through, or correct, that which they did not accomplish decisively enough before. Hence the impulse to a new revolution, a revolution without preparation, without program, without estimation of the reserves, without calculation of consequences. On the other hand those bourgeois layers which have arrived at the power are in a way only waiting for a stormy outbreak from below, in order to make the attempt decisively to settle accounts with the people. Such is the social and psychological basis of that supplementary semi-revolution, which has more than once in history become the starting point of a victorious counter-revolution. [ . . . ]

## Knowing how to hold back

Had the Bolshevik party, stubbornly clinging to a doctrinaire appraisal of the July movement as "untimely," turned its back on the masses, the semi-insurrection would inevitably have fallen under the scattered and uncoordinated leadership of anarchists, of adventurers, of accidental expressers of the indignation of the masses, and would have expired in bloody and bootless convulsions. On the other hand, if the party, after taking its place at the head of the machine-gunners and Putilov men, had renounced its own appraisal of the situation as a whole, and glided down the road to a decisive fight, the insurrection would indubitably have taken a bold scope. The workers and soldiers under the leadership of the Bolsheviks would have conquered the power—but only to prepare the subsequent shipwreck of the revolution. The question of power on a national scale would not have been decided, as it was in February, by a victory in Petrograd. The provinces would not have caught up to the capital. The front would not have understood or accepted the revolution. The railroads and the telegraphs would have served the Compromisers against the Bolsheviks. Kerensky and headquarters would have created a government for the front and the provinces. Petrograd would have been blockaded. Disintegration would have begun within its walls. The government would have been able to send considerable masses of soldiers against Petrograd. The insurrection would have ended, in those circumstances, with the tragedy of a Petrograd Commune.

At the July forking of historic roads, the interference of the Bolshevik Party eliminated both fatally dangerous variants—both that in the likeness of the June Days of 1848, and that of the Paris Commune of 1871 [when workers rose up without support outside the capital city]. Thanks to the Party's taking its place boldly at the head of the movement, it was able to stop the masses at the moment when the demonstration began to turn into an armed test of strength. The blow struck at the masses and the Party in July was very considerable, but it was not a decisive blow. The victims were counted by tens and not by tens of thousands. The working class issued from the trial, not headless and not bled to death. It fully preserved its fighting cadres, and these cadres had learned much.

# 13.

# The Kornilov Coup

*Despite the Bolsheviks' success in guiding an orderly retreat during and after the July Days, the right wing had its opportunity to strike. Although his interpretation is diametrically opposed to Trotsky's, **Kerensky** here confirms how he became entangled, wittingly or not, in the conspiracy that aimed to drown the revolution in blood.*[1]

## Late August—The conspirators take the offensive

I do not know to this day when and where the final decision was taken to make General Korniloff dictator. I believe the decision was made already previous to the appointment of Korniloff as commander of the Galician Front, i.e., between July 2 and 7. I am strengthened in this belief by the tone of the very first telegram addressed by Korniloff to the government in reply to his appointment as commander of the front. [. . .] General Korniloff wired:

> I, General Korniloff, whose entire life, from the very first day of my conscious existence, has been devoted only to serving my country, declare that the Motherland is perishing and, therefore, although not asked to express my opinion, I demand the immediate cessation of the offensive on all fronts. It is necessary to introduce immediately capital punishment in the territory of military operations.

I had already made the proper suggestion to General Brusiloff with regard to halting the offensive. The application of armed force in the struggle with deserters, looters and similar traitors had already been made obligatory on all commanders by my repeated orders. The demand for the restoration of capital

79

punishment at the front had been previously presented by army committees.

Thus, the significance of General Korniloff's telegram was not in the content but in its gesture—the gesture of a "strong man." [ . . . ]

In fact, I personally even liked General Korniloff's impulsive gesture. In the fourth month of the Revolution we of the Provisional Government could no longer be surprised by excesses of speech. Still less could our equilibrium be shattered by such utterances, for we had already had plenty of experience with the revolutionary "wild men" on the Left, who were properly tamed as soon as they were led into the harness of government and responsibility. I believe that General Korniloff and his close military friends would likewise be tamed and disciplined by the consciousness of responsibility.

On July 16, at an extraordinary military council summoned by me at General Headquarters, General Denikin, then commander of our Western Front, in the presence of General Alexeyeff, Brusiloff and other high commanders, delivered himself a veritable indictment against the Provisional Government. [ . . . ]

Terestchenko, the Minister of Foreign Affairs, and I, the Prime Minister and Minister of War and Navy, listened quite calmly to this cry of the scorched soul of an officer. At the conclusion of the grave philippic, amidst the confused and alarmed silence of all those present, I rose, shook hands with General Denikin and said: "I thank you, General, for your courageous and sincere words."

General Denikin's declaration constituted in reality a formulation of the military program upon which the propaganda of the supporters of the military conspiracy was based, which I then dubbed "the music of the future military reaction." This program was reiterated in even sharper form before the Moscow Conference [in mid-August] by General Kaledin of the Don Cossacks. This program was more than justified. Its substance was the demand for the restoration of normal military discipline and unity of command and the abolition of the system of commissars and army committees.

Shortly before the Moscow Conference Korniloff came to Petrograd. In a tête-à-tête in my office I sought to convince the general that there were no differences between the Provisional Government, on one side, and himself and his entourage on the other as far as questions bearing on the army were concerned. I tried to make Korniloff realize that any attempt at hasty and violent action would produce [an] adverse effect on the army. I repeated to him what in May I said at the front, namely, that if anyone should try to establish a personal dictatorship in Russia he would find himself the next day helplessly dangling in space, without railroads, without telegraphs and without an army. I pointed out to him the terrible fate awaiting the officers in event of failure of the coup d'état.

"Well, what of it?" said Kornilov as if thinking aloud. "Many will perish but the rest will finally take the army into their hands." [ . . . ]

## The drive against the Provisional Government

On August 17, the government returned to Petrograd, while Kornilov went back to General Headquarters. On August 19, the Germans launched a new attack on the Dvina, breaking through our lines and threatening Petrograd. On August 21, the Provisional Government made the following decisions:

1. To begin preparations for the government's removal to Moscow.

2. To transfer the troops of the Petrograd military district to the direct jurisdiction of the commander-in-chief.

3. To create a separate military area, consisting of Petrograd and its environs, under the jurisdiction of the Provisional Government.

4. To bring from the front a detachment of reliable troops, to be placed at the government's disposal.

In the order to his troops Krimoff declared that a Bolshevist revolution had broken out in Petrograd and that the government was unable to cope with it. On August 27, when according to the calculations of General Headquarters Krimoff's troops were to have arrived near Petrograd, there appeared before me in the Winter Palace a former member of the Provisional Government, Vladimir Lvoff, who placed before me a verbal ultimatum from General Korniloff. The ultimatum did not surprise me, but I still entertained doubt as to whether General Korniloff had actually lent his name to it. The entire tragic significance of what was being contemplated appeared clearly before me. Only by quick action was it possible to save the situation. I immediately took myself in hand and pretended that I did not believe in the authenticity of the ultimatum. Lvoff became greatly excited, assuring me on his word of honor that all he said was true. I then demanded that he put the ultimatum in writing. I told him this was necessary as otherwise the Provisional Government to whom I, as premier and war minister, was to carry Korniloff's ultimatum demanding the government's resignation would consider me mad. Lvoff wrote down the ultimatum point by point:

1. Proclamation of martial law in Petrograd.

2. Immediate resignation of the government.

3.  My departure the same night, together with Savinkoff, for General Headquarters, where we were to put ourselves at Korniloff's disposal.

I put the written ultimatum into my side pocket and agreed with Lvoff to meet him at seven o'clock in the evening at the long-distance telephone at the War Ministry, when we were to converse with General Korniloff at General Headquarters. En route to the War Ministry I still entertained some hope that the ultimatum and my whole conversation with Lvoff were a horrible dream. [ . . . ]

In an hour I submitted a report to the Provisional Government together with the incriminating ultimatum and received from the cabinet extraordinary powers for the liquidation of the Korniloff mutiny, which was about to begin with the arrival, expected at any moment, of Krimoff's troops in Petrograd.

I will not go into further details. As I foretold, the rebellious general found himself suddenly without troops and railways, and cut off at General Headquarters from the entire country. Without firing a single shot we were victorious. [ . . . ]

On August 30, the adventure was finished. On August 31, I issued an order to the Army and Navy presenting a picture of the anarchy and demoralization provoked anew by the Korniloff adventure.

Following the arrest of Korniloff and his immediate associates, the supporters of the Korniloff movement launched a widespread campaign through the press against the Provisional Government. Amply supplied with funds, they successfully spread the falsehood that there had been no conspiracy, that Korniloff was the victim of a "misunderstanding" between himself and the Provisional Government. It was even asserted that I had been in "agreement" with Korniloff through Savinkoff and "betrayed" him under pressure from the Soviet. This slanderous invention was immediately taken up by the Bolsheviki, who used it as dynamite with which, within a few days, they succeeded in destroying the confidence of the rank and file of the army in the Provisional Government. The Korniloff uprising destroyed the entire work of the restoration of discipline in the army, achieved after almost superhuman efforts.

Lenin, still in hiding, immediately grasped the significance of the service performed for him by the organizers of the Korniloff rebellion. "General Korniloff," wrote Lenin to the Central Executive Committee of the Bolshevist party from Finland, whither he had fled after the issuance of my July order for his arrest, "has opened for us quite unexpected perspectives. We must act at once."

# 14.

## Fight Kornilov, but Don't Support Kerensky

*Although often overlooked, the decision to work alongside Kerensky's forces to defeat Kornilov was remarkable. After all, Kerensky and the Provisional Government had imprisoned Trotsky, Raskolnikov, Kollontai, and dozens of leading Bolsheviks and driven Lenin and Zinoviev into hiding. In the fight between Kornilov and Kerensky, they might have been forgiven for adopting a "plague on both your houses" attitude. In the heat of the moment, **Lenin** explains how the Bolsheviks should react to the "unbelievably sharp turn of events."[1]*

### August 30—Letter to the Central Committee of the RSDLP

It is possible that these lines will come too late, for events are developing with a rapidity that sometimes makes one's head spin. I am writing this on Wednesday, August 30, and the recipients will read it no earlier than Friday, September 2. Still, on chance, I consider it my duty to write the following.

The Kornilov revolt is a most unexpected (unexpected at such a moment and in such a form) and downright unbelievably sharp turn in events.

Like every sharp turn, it calls for a revision and change of tactics. And as with every revision, we must be extra-cautious not to become unprincipled.

It is my conviction that those who become unprincipled are people who (like Volodarsky) slide into defensism or (like other Bolsheviks) into a bloc with the SRs, into supporting the Provisional Government. Their attitude is absolutely wrong and unprincipled. We shall become defensists only after the transfer of power to the proletariat, after a peace offer, after the secret treaties and ties with the banks have been broken—only afterwards. Neither the capture of Riga nor the capture of Petrograd will make us defensists. (I should very much like Volodarsky to read this.) Until then we stand for a proletarian revolution, we are against the war, and we are no defensists.

Even now we must not support Kerensky's government. This is unprincipled. We may be asked: aren't we going to fight against Kornilov? Of course we must! But this is not the same thing; there is a dividing line here, which is being stepped over by some Bolsheviks who fall into compromise and allow themselves to be carried away by the course of events.

We shall fight, we are fighting against Kornilov, just as Kerensky's troops do, but we do not support Kerensky. On the contrary, we expose his weakness. There is the difference. It is rather a subtle difference, but it is highly essential and must not be forgotten.

What, then, constitutes our change of tactics after the Kornilov revolt?

We are changing the form of our struggle against Kerensky. Without in the least relaxing our hostility towards him, without taking back a single word said against him, without renouncing the task of overthrowing him, we say that we must take into account the present situation. We shall not overthrow Kerensky right now. We shall approach the task of fighting against him in a different way, namely, we shall point out to the people (who are fighting against Kornilov) Kerensky's weakness and vacillation. That has been done in the past as well. Now, however, it has become the all-important thing and this constitutes the change.

The change, further, is that the all-important thing now has become the intensification of our campaign for some kind of "partial demands" to be presented to Kerensky: arrest Milyukov, arm the Petrograd workers, summon the Kronstadt, Vyborg and Helsingfors [radical] troops to Petrograd, dissolve the Duma, arrest Rodzyanko, legalize the transfer of the landed estates to the peasants, introduce workers' control over grain and factories, etc., etc. We must present these demands not only to Kerensky, and not so much to Kerensky, as to the workers, soldiers and peasants who have been carried away by the course of the struggle against Kornilov. We must keep up their enthusiasm, encourage them to deal with the generals and officers who have declared for Kornilov, urge them to demand the immediate transfer of land to the peasants, suggest to them that it is necessary to arrest Rodzyanko and Milyukov, dissolve the Duma, close down *Rech* and other bourgeois papers, and institute investigations against them. The "Left" SRs must be especially urged on in this direction.

It would be wrong to think that we have moved farther away from the task of the proletariat winning power. No. We have come very close to it, not directly, but from the side. At the moment we must campaign not so much directly against Kerensky as indirectly against him, namely, by demanding a more and more active, truly revolutionary war against Kornilov. The development of this war alone can lead us to power, but we must speak of this as little as possible in our propaganda (remembering very well that even tomorrow events may put power into our hands, and then we shall not relinquish it). It seems to me that this should be passed on in a letter (not in the papers) to the propagandists, to groups of agitators and propagandists, and to Party members in general. We must relentlessly fight against phrases about the defense of the country, about a united front of revolutionary democrats, about supporting the Provisional Government, etc., etc., since they are just empty phrases. We must say: now is the time for action; you SR and Menshevik gentlemen have long since worn those phrases threadbare. Now is the time for action; the war against Kornilov must be conducted in a revolutionary way, by drawing the masses in, by arousing them, by inflaming them (Kerensky is afraid of the masses, afraid of the people). In the war against the Germans, action is required right now; immediate and unconditional peace must be offered on precise terms. If this is done, either a speedy peace can be attained or the war can be turned into a revolutionary war; if not, all the Mensheviks and Socialist Revolutionaries remain lackeys of imperialism.

P.S. Having read six issues of *Rabochy* [the Bolshevik paper printed after *Pravda* was suppressed by Kerensky] after this was written, I must say that our views fully coincide. I heartily welcome the splendid editorials, press review and articles by V. M—n and Vol—y. As to Volodarsky's speech, I have read his letter to the editors, which likewise "eliminates" my reproaches. Once more, best wishes and greetings!

# 15.

# Use Kerensky as a Gun-Rest to Shoot at Kornilov

*In his account, Kerensky claims that his own "extraordinary powers for the liqui-*
*dation" of the Kornilov revolt prevented the coup; **Trotsky** tells a different story,*
*demonstrating how the Bolsheviks' decision to "use Kerensky as a gun-rest to shoot*
*at Kornilov" turned the tide.*[1]

## The Attempted Counterrevolution

The Executive Committee sent telephonegrams to Kronstadt and Vyborg asking for the dispatch of considerable detachments of troops to Petrograd. On the
morning of the 29th, the troops began to arrive. These were chiefly Bolshevik
units. In order that the summons of the Executive Committee should become
operative, it had to be confirmed by the Central Committee of the Bolsheviks.
A little earlier, at midday of the 28th, upon an order from Kerensky which
sounded very much like a humble request, sailors from the cruiser *Aurora* had
undertaken the defense of the Winter Palace. A part of the same crew were still
imprisoned in Kresty for participation in the July demonstration. During their
hours off duty the sailors came to the prison for a visit with the imprisoned Kronstadters, and with Trotsky, Raskolnikov and others. "Isn't it time to arrest the
government?" asked the visitors. "No, not yet," was the answer. "Use Kerensky
as a gun-rest to shoot Kornilov. Afterward we will settle with Kerensky." [ . . . ]

The entrance of Kornilov's troops into Petrograd would have meant first
of all the extermination of the arrested Bolsheviks. In his order to General
Bagration, who was to enter the capital with the vanguard, Krymov did not

forget this special command: "Place a guard in prisons and houses of detention, in no case let out the people now under restraint." This was a concerted program, inspired by Miliukov ever since the April days: "In no case let them out." There was not a single meeting in Petrograd in those days which did not pass resolutions demanding the release of the July prisoners. Delegation after delegation came to the Executive Committee, which in turn sent its leaders for negotiations to the Winter Palace. In vain! The stubbornness of Kerensky on this question is the more remarkable since during the first day and a half or two days he considered the position of the government hopeless, and was therefore condemning himself to the role of the old-time jail keeper—holding the Bolsheviks so that the generals could hang them.

It is no wonder that the masses led by the Bolsheviks in fighting against Kornilov did not place a moment of trust in Kerensky. For them it was not a case of defending the government, but of defending the revolution. So much the more resolute and devoted was their struggle. The resistance to the rebels grew out of the very road beds, out of the stones, out of the air. The railroad workers of the Luga station, where Krymov arrived, stubbornly refused to move the troop trains, alluding to a lack of locomotives. The Cossack echelons also found themselves immediately surrounded by armed soldiers from the Luga garrison, 20,000 strong. There was no military encounter, but there was something far more dangerous: contact, social exchange, inter-penetration. The Luga soviet had had time to print the government announcement retiring Kornilov, and this document was now widely distributed among the echelons. The officers tried to persuade the Cossacks not to believe the agitators, but this very necessity of persuasion was a bad sign.

On receiving Kornilov's order to advance, Krymov demanded under threat of bayonets that the locomotives be ready in half an hour. The threat seemed effective: the locomotives, although with some delays, were supplied; but even so, it was impossible to move, since the road out was damaged and so crowded with cars that it would take a good twenty-four hours to clear it. To get free of demoralizing propaganda, Krymov on the evening of the 28th, removed his troops several *versts* from Luga [a *verst* is about 3,500 feet]. But the agitators immediately turned up in the villages. These were soldiers, workers, railroad men—there was no refuge from them. They went everywhere. The Cossacks began even to hold meetings. Thus stormed with propaganda and cursing his impotence, Krymov waited in vain for [General] Bagration. The railroad workers were holding up the echelon of the Savage Division, which also in the coming hours was to undergo a most alarming moral attack. [ . . . ]

The railroad workers in those days did their duty. In a mysterious way echelons would find themselves moving on the wrong roads. Regiments would arrive in the wrong division, artillery would be sent up a blind alley, staffs would get out of communication with their units. All the big stations had their own soviets, their railroad workers' and their military committees. The telegraphers kept them informed of all events, all movements, all changes. The telegraphers also held up the orders of Kornilov. Information unfavorable to the Kornilovists was immediately multiplied, distributed, pasted up, passed from mouth to mouth. The machinists, the switchmen, the oilers became agitators. It was in this atmosphere that the Kornilov echelons advanced—or what was worse, stood still. The commanding staff, soon sensing the hopelessness of the situation, obviously did not hasten to move forward, and with their passivity promoted the work of the counter-conspirators of the transport system. Parts of the army of Krymov were in this way scattered about in the stations, sidings, and branch lines, of eight different railroads. If you follow on the map the fate of the Kornilov echelons, you get the impression that the conspirators were playing at blind man's buff on the railroad lines.

# 16.

# A Peaceful Road to All Power to the Soviets?

*Lenin wrote "On Compromises" to the Bolshevik Central Committee from hiding in the wake of the Kornilov coup. In it he demonstrates that the Bolsheviks' demand for "all power to the soviets" could encompass a proposal for the workers' parties in the soviets to overthrow the ruling class and its Provisional Government altogether and then work out their differences among themselves. Of course, **Lenin** fully expected new conflicts would arise within that new context between the Bolsheviks and their rivals, but this only goes to show that a united front has two goals: to win a concrete battle for the working class and, simultaneously, to clarify the differences between revolutionaries and reformists.[1]*

## September 1–3: Letter to the Central Committee of the RSDLP

The term *compromise* in politics implies the surrender of certain demands, the renunciation of part of one's demands, by agreement with another party. The usual idea the man in the street has about the Bolsheviks, an idea encouraged by a press which slanders them, is that the Bolsheviks will never agree to a compromise with anybody.

The idea is flattering to us as the party of the revolutionary proletariat, for it proves that even our enemies are compelled to admit our loyalty to the fundamental principles of socialism and revolution. Nevertheless, we must say that

91

this idea is wrong. Engels was right when, in his criticism of the Manifesto of the Blanquist Communists (1873), he ridiculed their declaration: "No compromises!" This, he said, was an empty phrase, for compromises are often unavoidably forced upon a fighting party by circumstances, and it is absurd to refuse once and for all to accept "payments on account." The task of a truly revolutionary party is not to declare that it is impossible to renounce all compromises, but to be able, through all compromises, when they are unavoidable, to remain true to its principles, to its class, to its revolutionary purpose, to its task of paving the way for revolution and educating the mass of the people for victory in the revolution.

To agree, for instance, to participate in the Third and Fourth Dumas was a compromise, a temporary renunciation of revolutionary demands. But this was a compromise absolutely forced upon us, for the balance of forces made it impossible for us for the time being to conduct a mass revolutionary struggle, and in order to prepare this struggle over a long period we had to be able to work even from inside such a "pigsty." History has proved that this approach to the question by the Bolsheviks as a party was perfectly correct.

Now the question is not of a forced, but of a voluntary compromise.

Our Party, like any other political party, is striving after political domination for itself. Our aim is the dictatorship of the revolutionary proletariat. Six months of revolution have proved very clearly, forcefully and convincingly that this demand is correct and inevitable in the interests of this particular revolution, for otherwise the people will never obtain a democratic peace, land for the peasants, or complete freedom (a fully democratic republic). This has been shown and proved by the course of events during the six months of our revolution, by the struggle of the classes and parties and by the development of the crises of April 20–21, June 9–10 and 18–19, July 3–5 and August 27–31.

The Russian revolution is experiencing so abrupt and original a turn that we, as a party, may offer a voluntary compromise—true, not to our direct and main class enemy, the bourgeoisie, but to our nearest adversaries, the "ruling" petty-bourgeois-democratic parties, the Socialist Revolutionaries and Mensheviks. We may offer a compromise to these parties only by way of exception, and only by virtue of the particular situation, which will obviously last only a very short time. And I think we should do so. The compromise on our part is our return to the pre-July demand of all power to the soviets and a government of SRs and Mensheviks responsible to the soviets.

Now, and only now, perhaps during only a few days or a week or two, such a government could be set up and consolidated in a perfectly peaceful way. In all probability it could secure the peaceful advance of the whole Russian revolution, and provide exceptionally good chances for great strides in the world movement towards peace and the victory of socialism.

In my opinion, the Bolsheviks, who are partisans of world revolution and revolutionary methods, may and should consent to this compromise only for the sake of the revolution's peaceful development—an opportunity that is extremely rare in history and extremely valuable, an opportunity that only occurs once in a while. The compromise would amount to the following: the Bolsheviks, without making any claim to participate in the government (which is impossible for the internationalists unless a dictatorship of the proletariat and the poor peasants has been realized), would refrain from demanding the immediate transfer of power to the proletariat and the poor peasants and from employing revolutionary methods of fighting for this demand. A condition that is self-evident and not new to the SRs and Mensheviks would be complete freedom of propaganda and the convocation of the Constituent Assembly without further delays or even at an earlier date.

The Mensheviks and SRs, being the government bloc, would then agree (assuming that the compromise had been reached) to form a government wholly and exclusively responsible to the soviets, the latter taking over all power locally as well. This would constitute the "new" condition. I think the Bolsheviks would advance no other conditions, trusting that the revolution would proceed peacefully and party strife in the soviets would be peacefully overcome thanks to really complete freedom of propaganda and to the immediate establishment of a new democracy in the composition of the soviets (new elections) and in their functioning. Perhaps this is already impossible? Perhaps. But if there is even one chance in a hundred, the attempt at realizing this opportunity is still worthwhile.

What would both "contracting" parties gain by this "compromise," i.e., the Bolsheviks, on the one hand, and the SR and Menshevik bloc, on the other? If neither side gains anything, then the compromise must be recognized as impossible, and nothing more is to be said. No matter how difficult this compromise may be at present (after July and August, two months equivalent to two decades in "peaceful," somnolent times), I think it stands a small chance of being realized. This chance has been created by the decision of the SRs and Mensheviks not to participate in a government together with the Cadets.

The Bolsheviks would gain the opportunity of quite freely advocating their views and of trying to win influence in the soviets under a really complete democracy. In words, "everybody" now concedes the Bolsheviks this freedom. In reality, this freedom is impossible under a bourgeois government or a government in which the bourgeoisie participate, or under any government, in fact, other than the soviets. Under a soviet government, such freedom would be possible (we do not say it would be a certainty, but still it would be possible). For the sake of such a possibility at such a difficult time, it would be worth compromising with the present majority in the soviets. We have nothing to fear from real democracy, for reality is on our side, and even the course of development of trends within the SR and Menshevik parties, which are hostile to us, proves us right.

The Mensheviks and SRs would gain in that they would at once obtain every opportunity to carry out their bloc's program with the support of the obviously overwhelming majority of the people and in that they would secure for themselves the "peaceful" use of their majority in the Soviets. [ . . . ]

The above lines were written on Friday, September 1, but due to unforeseen circumstances (under Kerensky, as history will tell, not all Bolsheviks were free to choose their domicile) they did not reach the editorial office that day. After reading Saturday's and today's (Sunday's) papers, I say to myself: perhaps it is already too late to offer a compromise. Perhaps the few days in which a peaceful development was still possible have passed too. Yes, to all appearances, they have already passed. In one way or another, Kerensky will abandon both the SR Party and the SRs themselves, and will consolidate his position with the aid of the bourgeoisie without the SRs, and thanks to their inaction... Yes, to all appearances, the days when by chance the path of peaceful development became possible have already passed. All that remains is to send these notes to the editor with the request to have them entitled: "Belated Thoughts." Perhaps even belated thoughts are sometimes not without interest.

# 17.

# Overview of the Situation in September 1917

*Morgan Philips Price covered the Eastern front as a reporter for the* Manchester Guardian *newspaper during World War I. He learned Russian at Cambridge University and, although not a socialist before the revolution, he became one of the Bolsheviks' most important English-language information outlets. He also became a convert to their cause, writing in* Dispatches from the Revolution, *"We are all compelled to provide one warm shirt and jacket for the revolutionary troops as a requisition without payment! We have got the dictatorship of the proletariat with a vengeance this time! But I rub my hands and chuckle with glee. May the day soon come when the proletariat of Western Europe does the same." Here he reviews the objective economic and social conditions that compelled a definitive political solution to the crisis, from either the left or the right, in the late summer of 1917.*[1]

Having briefly examined the economic and social conditions in Central Russia before the revolution, and having seen how these conditions made revolutionary changes inevitable, let us now see how these changes were effected in their different stages. We shall be better able then to compare the "law and order" of Tsarism and of the transitionary stage of the Kerensky government with the "anarchy and chaos" of the new regime. Now it was clear to any unprejudiced observer that even in the first days of the February Revolution the great peasant–proletarian–soldier mass, which had created the first Petrograd Soviet and was already imposing its will upon the timid Provisional Government, was bent on bringing about immense social change in the country. The complete breakdown, as the result of the war, of the corrupt and incompetent bureaucracy of Tsarism, which based its authority on old feudal privileges, opened for these masses a wide perspective.

The skilled factory laborers and the half-proletarian unskilled workers now had the chance by united action of freeing themselves from the ever-increasing exploitation under which they had lived and by which they were being threatened with famine. Something had to be done to raise their purchasing power so that they could cope with the ever-increasing cost of living, which far overstepped the meager increase in their wages. Something had to be done to shorten their hours, if only as the first step of insuring greater efficiency of labor and thereby an ultimate increase in production. Lastly, something had to be done to stop profiteering and to ensure that the products of the factory were properly and evenly distributed among the rural population, in exchange for which food could be obtained for the starving towns. This last meant that the factory-owners and swarms of middlemen and parasites, who were buying up and speculating in these necessaries of life, should be put under control. Instinctively the workmen in the first Petrograd Soviet and later in the thousands of provincial soviets all over the country felt the imperative need for action on these lines.

The peasant also saw in the collapse of Tsarism the possibility of at last freeing himself from his conditions of economic serfdom under the landlord. He saw that he could demand the recognition of the principle for which he had always contended, namely, that the land should not be the property of any individual, that it should belong to the whole community, who should allow its use to all citizens, and that property in land should be converted into property in the products of labor from the land. This meant the liquidation of the great estates, the passing of the latifundia [large agricultural estates] to the peasant communes, and the domain lands to some public authority.

Lastly, it was clear both to peasant, to urban worker and to half-proletarian that unless there was speedy peace between Russia and the peoples of the Central Powers, a terrible catastrophe would overtake the country, the shortage in food and raw materials would become a famine, speculation would increase to social parasitism, and the whole of Russia would become the prey to foreign banking capital, to be partitioned at pleasure between London, Berlin, Paris and New York.

It is not necessary here to describe the steps taken by the first All-Russian Soviet Executive with the unwilling assistance of Kerensky's bourgeois Provisional Government to bring about international peace by a "democratic" socialist conference. The failure of these attempts during the summer of 1917 only dashed the hopes of emancipation which the urban workers and the peasants had seen maturing for them earlier in the year. The policy of coalition between the "socialist" leaders and the representatives of the Russian propertied classes in the Provisional Government led to the complete shelving of all reforms and the ever-increasing degradation of the laborer and the peasant under the iron heel, not only of the "patriotic" Russian industrialists and landlords, but also of the increasingly powerful "financial capitalists" of the Allied countries, who like vultures were standing round a weak horse hoping it would die.

As soon therefore as the restraints imposed by the autocracy on political and economic association had been removed, the urban proletariat commenced to mobilize itself politically into Soviets, professionally into trade unions, and industrially into shop-stewards' committees. By the middle of the summer of 1917 the All-Russian Professional Alliance was formed with a membership of nearly two million. Large increases in wages for metal workers, cotton-mill hands, railwaymen and miners were demanded and obtained. But the effect of this on the conditions of the workers was nil. The factory-owners, free from all restraints, only raised wages in order to increase prices and thus forced the burden upon the workers again. Prices of food and necessaries continued to tower, forcing the government to inflate still further the currency. A bottom-less swamp was created into which the urban worker was sinking deeper and deeper every day. The Provisional Government's attempts to stop the "dance of the paper milliards" [inflation] and to control the war profiteers were a dis-mal failure. The industrial syndicates, which were formed under government control to concentrate the production of and supervise the distribution of the principal raw materials of industry, were in practice left to the tender mercies of the bank directors and factory-owners themselves. The latter easily succeeded in influencing the bourgeois members of the Provisional Government in the way they desired. Nor did the government's attempts to stop profiteering by introducing direct graduated taxation have any result. Capitalists only drew millions of paper [notes] out of the banks, did their own banking and gave incorrect returns.

More than once during the summer the Petrograd workmen tried to take the law into their own hands and through their shop-stewards' committees to control production in the interests of the workers and the consumers. But in every case the Menshevik members of the Provisional Government interfered with promises that they would "influence" the industrialists and bourgeois members of the Provisional Government in the desired direction. The Menshe-vik Minister of Labor, Skobelev, however, showed not only that he could not influence the capitalists, but that he was himself unconsciously their tool. For he hurried through a law forbidding the shop-stewards' committees to interfere with the work of the owners of the factories. But as if in defiance of even the most moderate reforms the owners began a campaign of sabotage. Several coal mine areas were closed down on the Don during the summer of 1917, while the Moscow cotton manufacturers threatened to stop the mills if they were not allowed a "free hand." Thus the industrial anarchy increased week by week and with the coming of the winter the urban worker and the half-proletarian saw nothing before him but cold and famine.

Nor was the peasant's lot any brighter. During the spring Victor Chernov, the Minister of Agriculture in the Provisional Government, had set up "land committees" in each province, which were temporarily to take on account all landlords' land and to work it in the interests of the community, pending the final decision of the Constituent Assembly. This pacified the peasants for a time. But as soon as it was known that the right to buy and sell land was restricted, the bankers and Cadet politicians commenced a furious attack on Chernov, who was compelled to resign, and his provisional land scheme collapsed with him. Then the landlords got bolder and commenced a hue and cry against the land committees. Their members were arrested by parties of officers, who had formed into secret White Guards, they were thrown into prison, some of them shot, and in many provinces the whole organization was broken up. The peasants replied by sacking many landlords' mansions with the aid of their soldier sons, who had returned from the front. A wave of agrarian pogroms swept over the governments of Tambov, Penza and Voronezh in September 1917. The landlords would not give way one tittle of their privileges in favor of the rural communes; the peasants on the contrary were determined to secure the recognition of their contention that the land belongs to the community that works it.

Two irreconcilables were thus clashing and, as a result, complete anarchy was reigning in the central provinces of Russia on the eve of the Bolshevik revolution. The Kerensky government, brought into existence by the popular uprising in February on the understanding that it would remove the economic and social privileges of the Russian landlord and capitalist class and of foreign banking syndicates, had not only failed to accomplish anything but had intensified the very evil which was rampant under Tsarism and had thus made the outlook of the masses more hopeless than ever.

# IV.

## DEBATING INSURRECTION

*After the defeat of the Kornilov coup, support for the Bolsheviks (and the Left Socialist Revolutionaries) grew rapidly. In early September, an enormous wave of sympathy propelled the Bolsheviks to majority status in soviets across Russia, including the biggest cities: St. Petersburg, Moscow, Ivanovo-Voznesensk, Kronstadt, and Krasnoyarsk, among others. On September 4, Trotsky and other Bolshevik leaders were released from prison and, within weeks, Trotsky was elected chairman of the St. Petersburg Soviet. As the Bolsheviks' call for "All power to the soviets" more or less openly promised to depose the Provisional Government, a series of sharp debates broke out within the party regarding relations with other parties, the nature of the capitalist state, and the tactics of insurrection as a component of working-class revolution.*

# 18.

## The Provisional Government and the Soviet

*Arthur Ransome* *went to Russia to cover World War I for the* Daily News, *a left-leaning English publication. Best known as a naturalist and a children's-book author, Ransome had no strong political commitments and considered himself an objective, if sympathetic, reporter. In this account, he explains the social gap opening up between the policies and personnel of the Provisional Government, on the one hand, and the soviets on the other.*[1]

There were thus formed two bodies, each of which claimed to represent the revolutionary nation. The first of these was the Provisional Government, which was appointed by an Executive Committee of the Duma, and so did indirectly represent that body, which, never fully representative of the people, had lost in the course of the war any claim to stand for anything except the bourgeois and privileged classes. The second of these was the Soviet of Workmen's and Soldiers' Deputies. Each thousand workmen had the right to send one member to the Soviet, and each company of soldiers. From the very first there could be no sort of doubt in the mind of an unprejudiced observer as to which of these two bodies best represented the Russian people. I do not think I shall ever again be so happy in my life as I was during those first days when I saw working men and peasant soldiers sending representatives of their class and not of mine. I remembered Shelley's

> *Shake your chains to earth like dew*
> *Which in sleep had fallen on you—*
> *Ye are many—they are few. [ . . . ]*

Immediately there became visible a definite fissure, soon a wide gulf, between the ideals of these two bodies, the Government and the representatives of the people. The people, the working classes, the peasants, who suffered most from the war, demanded that steps should be taken to secure peace. They did not want to fight to get territory for the sake of some phantasmagoric gain which did not affect them, which they did not understand. They were starving already, and saw worse starvation ahead. The Government, on the other hand, was, if anything, except for the presence in it of Kerensky, the labor member, more definitely imperialistic than the autocracy whose place it had taken.

The gulf between the working classes and the Government became suddenly deeper when it was realized that the future of the revolution depended on the possession of the army. If the army were not to be swept into the revolution, if it were allowed to remain apart from politics, it would be a passive weapon in the hands of the Government, which would thus be able to suppress the Soviets, and so the true expression of the people's will, whenever it should think fit. If the Government had been able to retain possession of the army, then Miliukov might have had his way and the bourgeoisie would have secured the profits of the revolt of the masses.

This, however, was not to be, and immediately the contradiction between a revolution and war of the imperialistic kind became evident. The army, which at that time meant practically the whole of the younger peasantry, took the share in politics it had a right to take. From that moment the future of the Soviets was assured, and the bourgeois Government was doomed to be a government only by the good will of the Soviets, who, within a few days of the beginning of the revolution, were the only real power in the country. [ . . . ]

Then began the long struggle of the summer. The Soviets, in which the moderates, who, mistrusting their own abilities, desired to keep the Government as a sort of executive organ, were in a majority, exerted all their influence on the Government in the direction of peace. The Government made its representations to the Allies, but, at any rate at first, gambled in the future, and pretended that things were not so bad, and that Russia could still take an active part in the war. There was a decisive moment [in April] when Miliukov wrote a note to the Allies calculated to lull them to believe that the changes in Russia meant nothing and that Russia stood by her old claims. The soldiers and people poured into the streets in protest, and that lie had to be publicly, withdrawn.

Already there was serious opposition to the Moderate party in the Soviets from the Bolsheviki, who urged that coalition with the bourgeoisie was merely postponing peace and bringing starvation and disaster nearer. The Moderates proposed a Stockholm conference, at which the socialist groups of all countries should meet and try to come to a common understanding. This was opposed by the Allied Governments and by the Bolsheviki, on the ground that the German Majority Socialists would be the agents of the German Government. One deadlock followed another. Each successive deadlock strengthened the party of the Bolsheviki, who held that the Provisional Government was an incubus and that all authority should belong to the Soviets.

The Bolshevik leaders, Lenin and Trotsky, had come from exile in western countries not merely to take their share in a Russian revolution, but to use Russia in kindling the world revolution. They called for peace, but peace, for them, was not an end in itself. They could say, with Christ, that they brought not peace but a sword. For they hoped that in stirring the working classes of the world to demand peace from their governments, they would be putting into their hands the sword that was necessary for the Social Revolution, in which cause they had both, like many of their friends, spent the best years of their lives.

In their own country, at any rate, they have proved that they were right in their calculation. The struggle for peace, the failure to obtain it, shook the Government into the disastrous adventure of the Galician advance, shook it again with the Galician retreat, weakened it with every telegram from Allied countries that emphasized the continuance of the war. Each shock to the Government was also a shock for the Moderate party in the Soviets. The struggle in Russia became, as the Bolsheviki wished it should become, a struggle between the classes, a struggle in which the issue became ever clearer between the working and the privileged classes. The Government went to Moscow for moral support, and came back without it. The Kornilov mutiny, a definite attempt against the Soviets by a handful of the privileged classes, merely strengthened the organizations it was intended to overthrow. Within the Soviets the Moderate party, which had already come by force of events to be a sort of annex of the bourgeoisie, grew weaker and weaker. Just as the Government went to Moscow to seek support in a conference, so the Moderate party, feeling support slipping from under it, knowing that the next meeting of the All-Russian Assembly of Soviets would find it in a minority, treacherously sought new foothold in an artificial democratic assembly. Not even the tactics of the Moderate party shook the actual fabric of the Soviets, and when, in October, first Petrograd, then Moscow, showed a huge Bolshevik majority, the Bolshevik leaders were so confident that they had the country behind them that they made every single arrangement for the ejection of the Government openly over the telephone, and, notwithstanding, neither the Government nor the old Moderates (now in a minority) could muster authority to prevent them.

The point that I wish to make is this: that, from the first moment of the revolution to the present day, the real authority of the Soviets has been unshaken. The October revolution did not give authority to the Soviets. That had always been theirs; by their very nature. It was merely a public open illustration of the change of opinion brought about in the Soviets themselves by the change of opinion in the working men and soldiers who elected them. The October revolution cleared away the waste growths that hid the true government of Russia from the world, and, as the smoke of the short struggle died away, it was seen that that Government had merely to formulate an authority it already possessed.

# 19.

# Marxism and Insurrection

*Having spent nearly seven months advocating "all power to the soviets," the Bolsheviks were confronted with a problem: What if the Provisional Government refused to give up formal state power? After all, Kerensky had jailed Bolshevik leaders when he had the chance after the July Days, and Kornilov's coup had demonstrated that the officer corps had no intention of giving up without a fight. Thus, **Lenin** argued that if soviet power were to be accomplished, the Provisional Government would have to be forcibly removed from the scene. Other Bolshevik leaders, principally Kamenev and Zinoviev, agreed "in principle" but were afraid that the Bolsheviks would be isolated if they didn't have the support of at least parts of the Mensheviks and SR parties.[1]*

## September 13–14—A Letter to the Central Committee of the RSDLP

One of the most vicious and probably most widespread distortions of Marxism resorted to by the dominant "socialist" parties is the opportunist lie that preparation for insurrection, and generally the treatment of insurrection as an art, is "Blanquism." Bernstein, the leader of opportunism, has already earned himself unfortunate fame by accusing Marxism of Blanquism, and when our present-day opportunists cry Blanquism they do not improve on or "enrich" the meager "ideas" of Bernstein one little bit. Marxists are accused of Blanquism for treating insurrection as an art! Can there be a more flagrant perversion of the truth, when not a single Marxist will deny that it was Marx who expressed himself on this score in the most definite, precise and categorical manner, referring to insurrection specifically as an art, saying that it must be treated as an art, that you must win the first success and then proceed from success to success, never ceasing the offensive against the enemy, taking advantage of his confusion, etc., etc.?

To be successful, insurrection must rely not upon conspiracy and not upon a party, but upon the advanced class. That is the first point. Insurrection must rely upon a revolutionary upsurge of the people. That is the second point. Insurrection must rely upon that turning-point in the history of the growing revolution when the activity of the advanced ranks of the people is at its height, and when the vacillations in the ranks of the enemy and in the ranks of the weak, half-hearted and irresolute friends of the revolution are strongest. That is the third point. And these three conditions for raising the question of insurrection distinguish Marxism from Blanquism.

Once these conditions exist, however, to refuse to treat insurrection as an art is a betrayal of Marxism and a betrayal of the revolution. To show that it is precisely the present moment that the Party must recognize as the one in which the entire course of events has objectively placed insurrection on the order of the day and that insurrection must be treated as an art, it will perhaps be best to use the method of comparison, and to draw a parallel between July 3–4 and the September days. On July 3–4 it could have been argued, without violating the truth, that the correct thing to do was to take power, for our enemies would in any case have accused us of insurrection and ruthlessly treated us as rebels. However, to have decided on this account in favor of taking power at that time would have been wrong, because the objective conditions for the victory of the insurrection did not exist.

(1) We still lacked the support of the class which is the vanguard of the revolution. We still did not have a majority among the workers and soldiers of Petrograd and Moscow. Now we have a majority in both Soviets. It was created solely by the history of July and August, by the experience of the "ruthless treatment" meted out to the Bolsheviks, and by the experience of the Kornilov revolt.

(2) There was no country-wide revolutionary upsurge at that time. There is now, after the Kornilov revolt; the situation in the provinces and assumption of power by the Soviets in many localities prove this.

(3) At that time there was no vacillation on any serious political scale among our enemies and among the irresolute petty bourgeoisie. Now the vacillation is enormous. Our main enemy, Allied and world impe-

rialism (for world imperialism is headed by the "Allies"), has begun to waver between a war to a victorious finish and a separate peace directed against Russia. Our petty-bourgeois democrats, having clearly lost their majority among the people, have begun to vacillate enormously, and have rejected a bloc, i.e., a coalition, with the Cadets.

(4) Therefore, an insurrection on July 3–4 would have been a mistake; we could not have retained power either physically or politically. We could not have retained it physically even though Petrograd was at times in our hands, because at that time our workers and soldiers would not have fought and died for Petrograd. There was not at the time that "savageness," or fierce hatred both of the Kerenskys and of the Tseretelis and Chernovs. Our people had still not been tempered by the experience of the persecution of the Bolsheviks in which the Socialist Revolutionaries and Mensheviks participated.

We could not have retained power politically on July 3–4 because, before the Kornilov revolt, the army and the provinces could and would have marched against Petrograd.

Now the picture is entirely different. We have the following of the majority of a class, the vanguard of the revolution, the vanguard of the people, which is capable of carrying the masses with it. [ . . . ]

All the objective conditions exist for a successful insurrection. We have the exceptional advantage of a situation in which only our victory in the insurrection can put an end to that most painful thing on earth, vacillation, which has worn the people out; in which only our victory in the insurrection will give the peasants land immediately; a situation in which only our victory in the insurrection can foil the game of a separate peace directed against the revolution—foil it by publicly proposing a fuller, more just and earlier peace, a peace that will benefit the revolution.

Finally, our Party alone can, by a victorious insurrection, save Petrograd; for if our proposal for peace is rejected, if we do not secure even an armistice, then we shall become "defensists," we shall place ourselves at the head of the war parties, we shall be the war party *par excellence*, and we shall conduct the war in a truly revolutionary manner. We shall take away all the bread and boots from the capitalists. We shall leave them only crusts and dress them in *bast* [birch bark] shoes. We shall send all the bread and footwear to the front. And then we shall save Petrograd.

The resources, both material and spiritual, for a truly revolutionary war in Russia are still immense; the chances are a hundred to one that the Germans will grant us at least an armistice. And to secure an armistice now would in itself mean to win the whole world. [ . . . ]

There is no middle course. Delay is impossible. The revolution is dying. By putting the question in this way, by concentrating our entire group in the factories and barracks, we shall be able to determine the right moment to start the insurrection.

In order to treat insurrection in a Marxist way, i.e., as an art, we must at the same time, without losing a single moment, organize a headquarters of the insurgent detachments, distribute our forces, move the reliable regiments to the most important points, surround the Alexandriusky Theatre, occupy the Peter and Paul Fortress, arrest the General Staff and the government, and move against the officer cadets and the Savage Division with those detachments which would rather die than allow the enemy to approach the strategic points of the city. We must mobilize the armed workers and call them to fight the last desperate fight, occupy the telegraph and the telephone exchange at once, move our insurrection headquarters to the central telephone exchange and connect it by telephone with all the factories, all the regiments, all the points of armed fighting, etc.

Of course, this is all by way of example, only to illustrate the fact that at the present moment it is impossible to remain loyal to Marxism, to remain loyal to the revolution, unless insurrection is treated as an art.

# 20.

# The Bolsheviks Vote on Insurrection

*By early October, the Bolshevik Central Committee had decided to prepare an insurrection to overthrow the Provisional Government. But conflict raged about just what this meant in practice. For the first time since July, Lenin came out of hiding to personally join in the debate. He faced resistance from Zinoviev and Kamenev, who did their best to block any concrete action they feared would risk isolating the Bolsheviks as had happened in July. Compounding these political debates, the Bolshevik leadership sought to establish a common assessment, as recorded in these* **Central Committee minutes** *about the state of their forces and those of their enemies.*[1]

## Session of the Central Committee of the Bolshevik Party—October 10

Present: Lenin, Zinoviev, Kamenev, Trotsky, Stalin, Sverdlov, Uritsky, Dzerzhinsky, Kollontai, Bubnov, Sokolnikov, Lomov [Oppokov]. Chairman Sverdlov.

Comrade Lenin speaks on the current situation. He maintains that since the beginning of September a certain indifference to the question of insurrection has been noticeable. Yet if we are seriously promoting the slogan of a seizure of power by the Soviets, this cannot be allowed. That is why attention should have been given to the technical side of the matter long ago. Now, apparently, considerable time has been lost.

Nonetheless, the question is urgent and the decisive moment is near. The international situation is such that we must take the initiative. What is being done to surrender as far as the Narva and to surrender Peter[sburg] makes it even more imperative for us to take decisive action. The political position is also working impressively in this direction. On July 3–5, positive action on our part would have failed because the majority was not behind us. Since then we have gone up in leaps and bounds. Absenteeism and indifference among the masses can be explained by the fact that the masses are fed up with words and resolutions.

The majority is now behind us. Politically, the situation is completely ripe for a transfer of power. The agrarian movement is going in the same direction, for it is clear that it would need heroic forces to quell this movement. The slogan for all land to be transferred has become the general slogan of the peasants. So the political circumstances are ripe. We have to talk about the technical side. That is the crux of the matter. Yet we, in the wake of the defensists, are inclined to regard the systemic preparation of an insurrection as something akin to a political sin. It is senseless to wait for the Constituent Assembly, which will clearly not be on our side, for this means complicating our task. The Regional Congress and the proposal from Minsk must be used as the starting point for decisive action.

Comrade Lomov [Oppokov] takes the floor with information about the position of the Moscow Regional Bureau and the Moscow Committee, and also about the situation in Moscow.

Comrade Uritsky maintains that we are not only weak technically but also in all the other aspects of our work, too. We have passed a mass of resolutions but taken no positive action. The Petrograd Soviet is disorganized, there are few meetings etc. What forces can we rely on? The workers in Petrograd have 40,000 rifles but that will not settle the matter; that is nothing. After the July Days, the garrison cannot inspire great hope. But in any case, if an insurrection is the aim, then something effective must be done in this direction. We have to decide on certain actions.

Comrade Sverdlov tells what he knows about the state of affairs in Russia as a whole.

A resolution is approved in the following form:

> The CC recognizes that the international position of the Russian revolution (the insurrection in the German navy, e.g.) is an extreme sign of the way the world socialist revolution has grown throughout Europe; then the imperialists' threat of a peace aimed at stifling the revolution in Russia, as well as the military position (the decision undoubtedly made by the Russian bourgeoisie and Kerensky and Co. to surrender Peter[sburg] to the Germans) and the fact that the proletarian party has acquired a ma-

jority in the Soviets—all this taken together with the peasant revolt and the swing in popular confidence towards our Party (the Moscow elections, e.g.) and, finally, the obvious preparations being made for a second Kornilov revolt (troops being withdrawn from Peter, Cossacks moved towards Peter, Minsk encircled by Cossacks, etc.)—all this puts an armed rising on the order of the day.

Recognizing therefore that an armed rising is inevitable and that its time has come, the CC suggests that all Party organizations be guided by this and approach the discussion and solution of all practical issues from this point of view (the Congress of Northern Region Soviets, the withdrawal of troops from Peter, the action of our people in Moscow and Minsk, etc.).

Ten expressed themselves in favor, two against [Zinoviev and Kamenev].

* * *

## An enlarged meeting of Bolshevik leaders debates insurrection—October 16

Present: Members of the CC, the Executive Commission of the Petrograd Committee, the Military Organization, the Petrograd Soviet, trade unions, factory committees, the Petrograd Area Committee and the railwaymen.
Comrade Sv[erdlov] in the chair. [ . . . ]

### I. Report on the last CC meeting.
Comrade Lenin reads out the resolution the CC adopted at its last session. He announces that the resolution was passed with two votes against. If the dissenting comrades want to say something, a debate can be held but in the meantime he gives the reasons for this resolution.

If the Menshevik and SR Parties had broken with conciliation, it might have been possible to offer them a compromise. The proposal had been made but it was clear that the Parties in question rejected this compromise. By that time, on the other hand, it had already become clear that the masses were supporting us. That was before the Kornilov revolt. He cites the election figures in Peter and in Moscow as evidence. The Kornilov revolt itself pushed the masses even more decisively towards us. The balance of forces at the Democratic Conference. The position is clear: either a Kornilov dictatorship or a dictatorship of the proletariat and the poorest strata of the peasants. One cannot be guided by the mood of the masses, for it is changeable and not to be calculated; we must go by an objective analysis and assessment of the revolution. The masses have put their faith in the Bolsheviks and demand deeds, not words, from them, a determined policy in both the struggle against the war and the struggle with disruption. On the basis of a political analysis of the revolution, it becomes quite clear that even anarchic outbursts confirm this now.

He goes on to analyze the situation in Europe and shows that revolution is even more difficult there than here; if things have gone as far as a revolt in the navy in a country like Germany, then this shows that things have already gone a long way there, too. Certain objective facts about the international situation indicate that in acting now we will have the whole European proletariat on our side; he shows that the bourgeoisie wants to surrender Peter. We can only escape that when we have taken control of Petrograd. From all this, the conclusion is clear, the armed insurrection talked of in the CC resolution is on the agenda.

As far as practical conclusions to be drawn from the resolution are concerned, it would be better to deal with them after hearing the reports from representatives from the centers. A political analysis of the class struggle both in Russia and in Europe points to the need for a very determined and active policy, which can only be an armed insurrection.

## II. Reports from representatives.

Comrade Sverdlov of the CC reports on behalf of the CC secretariat on the state of affairs in the localities. The Party has grown on a gigantic scale; it can be estimated that it now encompasses no fewer than 400,000 (he furnishes evidence). Our influence has grown in the same way, especially in the Soviets (evidence) and similarly in the army and navy. He goes on to give the facts about the mobilization of counterrevolutionary forces (Donetsk district, Minsk, Northern Front).

Comrade Boky of the Petrograd Committee. He gives information district by district:

> Vasil'evskii Island—mood not militant, military preparations being made.
> Vyborg District the same but they are preparing for an insurrection; a
>  Military Council has been formed; if there were action, the masses
>  would be in support. They consider that the initiative ought to come
>  from above.

1st City District: The mood is difficult to assess. There is a Red Guard.

2nd [City District]: A better mood.

Moscow District: A reckless mood, will come out if the Soviet calls but not the Party.

Narva District: Not eager for action but no falling off in the Party's authority. The anarchists are getting stronger at the Putilov [factory].

Neva District: The mood has swung sharply in our favor. Everyone will follow the Soviet.

Okhten District: Things are bad.

Petersburg District: An expectant mood.

Rozhdestvensk District: Doubt here, too, on whether they will rise, anarchists have strengthened their influence.

Porokhov District: The mood has improved in our favor.

Schluesselburg: Mood in our favor.

Comrade Krylenko of the Military Bureau announces that they differ sharply in their assessment of the mood. Personal observations of the mood in the regiments indicate that they are ours to a man, but information from comrades working in the districts differs; they say that they would have to be positively stung by something for a rising, that is: the withdrawal of troops. The Bureau believes that morale is falling. Most of the Bureau thinks there is no need to do anything in practice to intensify things, but the minority thinks that it is possible to take the initiative oneself.

Comrade Step[anov] of the Area Organization. In Sestroretsk, Kolpino, the workers are arming, the mood is militant and they are preparing for a rising. In Kolpino, an anarchist mood is developing. The atmosphere in Narva is grave because of the dismissals. Three thousand have already been dismissed. Where the garrisons are concerned, the mood is depressed but Bolshevik influence is very strong (two machine-gun regiments). Work in the regiment in N[ovyi] Petergof has fallen off a bit and the regiment is disorganized. Krasnoe Selo—176th [Regiment] is completely Bolshevik, the 172nd [Regiment] nearly, but apart from that the cavalry is there. Luga—a garrison of 30,000; the Soviet is defensist. A Bolshevik mood and there are elections ahead. In Gdov—the regiment is Bolshevik.

Comrade Boky adds that according to the information he has, matters are not so good in Krasnoe Selo. In Kronstadt, morale has fallen and the local garrison there is no use for anything in a militant sense.

Comrade Volodarsky from the Petrograd Soviet. The general impression is that no one is ready to rush out on the streets but everyone will come if the Soviet calls.

Comrade Ravich confirms this and adds that some have indicated that also at the Party's call.

Comrade Shmidt of the trade unions. The total number organized is more than 500,000. Our Party's influence predominates but it is weak in unions more of the handicraft type (especially among the office workers and the printers) but even there it is beginning to grow, particularly since there is dissatisfaction with pay regulations. The mood is one where active demonstrations cannot be expected, especially because of the fear of dismissals. To a certain extent, this is a restraining factor. Because of certain economic conditions, colossal unemployment can be anticipated in the near future; this, too, makes the mood expectant. Everyone recognizes that there is no way out of the situation apart from a struggle for power. They demand all power to the Soviets.

Comrade Shliapnikov adds that Bolshevik influence predominates in the metalworkers' union but a Bolshevik rising is not popular; rumors of this even produce panic. The mood among metalworkers in Russia as a whole is also predominantly Bolshevik; they pass Bolshevik resolutions but they are not conscious that they are capable of organizing production for themselves. The union faces the struggle to raise wages. The issue of control will be linked with this fight.

Comrade Skrypnik from the factory committees. He states that a craving for practical results has been noted everywhere; resolutions are no longer enough. It is felt that the leaders do not fully reflect the mood of the masses; the former are more conservative; a growth of anarcho-syndicalist influence is noted, particularly in the Narva and Moscow Districts.

Comrade Sverdlov gives additional information that as a result of the CC resolution, steps have been taken in Moscow to clarify the position about a possible insurrection.

Comrade Moskvin from the railwaymen. The railwaymen are starving and embittered, organization is weak, especially among the telegraph employees.

Comrade Shmidt adds that the strike has led to a crisis among the railwaymen. Dissatisfaction with the committee is especially marked at the Moscow junction. In general, the Peter[sburg] and Moscow junctions are closer to the Bolsheviks.

Comrade Boky. The post and telegraph employees. There is no separate organization. The telegraph apparatus is mostly under the control of the Cadets. The postmen report that they will be able to take control of the post offices at the decisive moment.

Comrade Shmidt. The postal workers' union is more radical than the railwaymen. The lower employees are essentially Bolshevik but not the higher ones; while they keep control of the union, there has to be a struggle with them. [ . . . ]

*[A debate ensues over the balance of forces and whether to take action on the CC's resolution from the previous day.]*

Comrade Le[nin]. If all resolutions were defeated in this manner, one could not wish for anything better. Now Zinoviev is saying down with the "power to the Soviets" slogan and bring pressure on the government. To say that an insurrection is ripe means there is no need to talk of conspiracy. If an insurrection is inevitable politically, it must be treated as an art. And politically, its time has come. There is only bread for one day, and that is why we cannot wait for the Constituent Assembly. He moves that the resolution be confirmed, that preparations get positively under way and that it should be for the CC and the Soviet to decide when.

Comrade Zinoviev. This revolution has been compared with the February Revolution. There is no comparison because then the old regime had nothing on its side and now it is a war against the whole bourgeois world. We did not launch the slogan "power to the Soviets" in the abstract. If the Congress puts pressure on the Constituent Assembly, this cannot be compared with Menshevik policy. If the insurrection is tabled as a long-term prospect, there can be no objection, but if it is an order for tomorrow or the day after, then this is adventurism. We must not start an insurrection before our comrades have held the Congress and there has been consultation. [ . . . ]

*[More debate follows.]*

[Kamenev objects.] To fix a date for the rising is adventurism. We ought to explain to the masses that we will not summon them to a rising in the next three days but that we consider an insurrection inevitable. He moves a vote on the resolution, and makes a proposal that the central organ should publish a statement that there will be no appeal for a rising before the [Second All-Russian Congress of Soviets].

Comrade Skrypnik proposes an appeal to the masses to get ready for an insurrection.

Comrade Lenin objects to Zinoviev that this revolution should not be seen in contrast to the February evolution. On the substance, he proposes the resolution:

The meeting unreservedly welcomes and entirely supports the CC resolution, calls on all organizations and all workers and soldiers to make comprehensive and intensive preparations for an armed insurrection and to support the center created for this by the Central Committee and expresses its full confidence that the CC and the Soviet will be timely in indicating the favorable moment and the appropriate methods of attack.

Zinoviev. He replies to Lenin on the subject of the February Revolution. These two months will not be the worst in the pages of our Party's history. On the substance, he moves his own resolution:

> While going ahead with the work of reconnaissance and preparation, to consider that any demonstrations in advance of a conference with the Bolshevik section of the Congress of Soviets are inadmissible.

Comrade Lenin's resolution voted on in principle. In favor 20, against 2, abstained 3.

# 21.

# Preparing October

*Albert Rhys Williams paints a picture of how growing social breakdown could only be reversed by a social force taking power. After the Bolshevik leadership agreed on plans for the uprising, they explained their intentions to the St. Petersburg working class and soldiery in a series of mass meetings—without quite tipping their hand in terms of how they planned to act, lest Kerensky get the jump on them.*[1]

Another winter is bearing down upon hungry, heartsick Russia. For last October leaves are falling from the trees, the last bit of confidence in the government is falling with them. Everywhere recklessness and orgies of speculation. Food trains are looted. Floods of paper money pour from the presses. The newspapers list columns of holdups, murderers, and suicides. Nightlife and gambling halls run full blast with enormous stakes won and lost. Reaction is open and arrogant. Kornilov, instead of being tried for high treason, is lauded as the Great Patriot by the bourgeoisie. But with them patriotism is tawdry talk and a sham. They pray for the Germans to come and cut off Petrograd, the Head of the Revolution. Rodzianko, ex-president of the Duma, brazenly writes: "Let the Germans take the city. Though they destroy the fleet they will throttle the Soviets." The big insurance companies announce one third off rates after the German occupation. "Winter always was Russia's best friend," say the bourgeoisie. "It may rid us of this cursed Revolution."

Winter, sweeping down out of the North, hailed by the privileged, brings terror to the suffering masses. As the mercury drops toward zero, the prices of food and fuel go soaring up. Bread ration grows shorter. The queues of shivering women standing all night in the icy streets grown longer. Lockouts and strikes add to the millions of workless. The rancor in the hearts of the masses flares out in bitter speeches like this from my Viborg workingman: "Patience, patience, they are always counseling us. But what have they done to make us patient? Has Kerensky given us more to eat than the Tsar? More words and promises—yes! But not more food. All night long we wait in the lines for shoes and bread and meat, while, like fools, we write *Liberty* on our banners. The only liberty we have is the same old liberty to slave and starve."

Russia is plunging headlong towards the abyss. Over the spectacle of misery and ruin designs a handful of talkers called the Provisional Government. It is almost a corpse, treated to hyperdermic injections of threats and promises from the Allies [. . .] to all the demands of the people it has just one reply, "Wait." First it was, "Wait until the end of the year." Now, "Wait till the Constituent Assembly." But the people will wait no longer. Their last shred of faith in the government has gone. They have faith in themselves; faith that they can alone save Russia from going over the precipice to ruin and night; faith alone in the institutions of their own making. They now look to the new authority created out of their own midst. They looked to the Soviets.

Summer and fall have seen a steady growth of the soviets. They have drawn to themselves the vital forces in each community. They have been schools for the training of the people, giving them confidence. The network of local soviets is wrought into a wide, firmly built organization, a new structure which has risen within the shell of the old. As the old apparatus was going to pieces, the new one was taking over its functions. The soviets in many ways were already acting as the government. It was necessary only to proclaim them the government. Then the soviets would be in name what they were already in reality.

From the depths now lifted up a mighty cry: "All power to the Soviets." The demand of the capital in July became a demand of the country, like wildfire that swept thru the land. Sailors on the Baltic Fleet flung it out to their comrades on the Black and White and Yellow Seas, and from them it came echoing back. Farm and factory, barracks and battlefront joint in the cry, swelling louder, more insistent every hour.

Petrograd came thundering into the chorus on Sunday, October 22, in sixty meetings. Trotsky having read the "Reply of the Baltic Fleet" to my greetings asked me to speak at the People's House. Here great waves of human beings—against the doors, swirled inside and sluice along the core doors. They poured into the halls, filling them full, splashing hundreds up on the girders where they hung like garlands of foam. Out of the eddying throngs, a mighty voice rose and fell and broke like surf, thundering on the shore—hundreds of thousands of throats roaring "Down with the Provisional Government." "All Power to the Soviets." Hundreds of thousands of hands were raised [. . .] to fight and die for the Soviets. [ . . . ]

These insurgent masses go home to organize committees, draw up lists, form Red Cross units, collect rifles. Hands lifted in a vote for Revolution are now holding guns. To get ready for the forces of the Counter-Revolution now mobilizing against them. In Smolny sits the Military Revolutionary Committee from which these messengers take orders. There is another committee, the Committee of a Hundred Thousand; that is, the masses themselves. There are no side streets, no barracks, no buildings where this committee does not penetrate. It reaches into the councils of the Black Hundreds, the Kerensky government, the intelligentsia. They see everything, hear everything, report everything to headquarters. Thus, forewarned, they can checkmate every move of the enemy. Every attempt to strangle or sidetrack the Revolution they paralyze at once.

# V.

# THE OCTOBER REVOLUTION

*The October Revolution of 1917 began in earnest on October 24, the day before the Second All-Russian Congress of the Soviets was due to meet. After Kerensky ordered police to raid Bolshevik newspaper offices and attempted to call in troops loyal to him, the Military Revolutionary Committee of the St. Petersburg Soviet began operations to disarm counterrevolutionary troops, secure strategic points in the city, and seize the Winter Palace, where the Provisional Government and its ministers sat. By late in the day on October 25, the Congress convened and a battle royale ensued between the Bolsheviks (their left-wing allies) and the SR and Menshevik moderate socialists over the formation of a Soviet government. At two in the morning on October 26, the Winter Palace fell. Later that same day, the Soviet reconvened and began the construction of the world's first socialist government, passing decrees calling for immediate peace, land distribution, and workers' control in the factories.*

# 22.

# Smolny and the Winter Palace

*American journalist **Louise Bryant** enjoyed incredible access to most of the leading figures in the drama, risking life and limb to get the story of the fall of the Winter Palace. Her book,* Six Months in Revolutionary Russia, *appeared in the United States before John Reed's more famous account and was one of the first records of the October Revolution to reach an American audience.*[1]

## Smolny

Smolny Institute, headquarters of the Bolsheviki, is on the edge of Petrograd. Years ago it was considered "way out in the country," but the city grew out to meet it, engulfed it and finally claimed it as its own. Smolny is an enormous place; the great main building stretches in a straight line for hundreds of feet with an ell jutting out at each end and forming a sort of elongated court. Close up to the north ell snuggles the lovely little Smolny Convent with its dull blue dome with the silver stars. Once young ladies of noble birth from all over Russia came here to receive a "proper" education.

I came to know Smolny well while I was in Russia. I saw it change from a lonely, deserted barracks into a busy humming hive, heart and soul of the last revolution. I watched the leaders once accused, hunted and imprisoned raised by the mass of the people of all Russia to the highest places in the nation. They were borne along on the whirling wind of radicalism that swept and is still sweeping Russia and they themselves did not know how long or how well they would be able to ride that whirlwind. [ . . . ]

I ate many of my meals in the great mess hall on the ground floor with the soldiers. There were long, rough wooden tables and wooden benches and a great air of friendliness pervaded everywhere. You were always welcome at Smolny if you were poor and you were hungry. We ate with wooden spoons, the kind the Russian soldiers carry in their big boots, and all we had to eat was cabbage soup and black bread. We were always thankful for it and always afraid that perhaps tomorrow there would not be even that. [. . .] We stood in long lines at the noon hour chattering like children. "So you are an American, *tavarishe* [comrade], well, how does it go now in America?" they would say to me.

Upstairs in a little room tea was served night and day. Trotsky used to come there and Kollontay and Spiradonova and Kaminoff and Volodarysky and all the rest except Lenine. I never saw Lenine at either of these places. He held aloof and only appeared at the largest meetings and no one got to know him very well. But the others I mentioned would discuss events with us. In fact, they were very generous about giving out news.

In all the former classrooms typewriters ticked incessantly. Smolny worked twenty-four hours a day. For weeks Trotsky never left the building. He ate and slept and worked in his office on the third floor and strings of people came in every hour of the day to see him. All the leaders were frightfully overworked, they looked haggard and pale from loss of sleep. In the great white hall, once the ballroom, with its graceful columns and silver candelabra, delegates from the Soviets all over Russia met in all-night sessions. Men came straight from the first line trenches, straight from the fields and the factories. Every race in Russia met there as brothers. Men poured out their souls at these meetings and they said beautiful and terrible things. I will give you an example of the speeches of the soldiers. A tired, emaciated little soldier mounts the rostrum. He is covered with mud from head to foot and with old blood stains. He blinks in the alarming light. It is the first speech he has ever made in his life and he begins it in a shrill hysterical shout:

> *Tavarishi*! I come from the place where men are digging their graves and calling them trenches! We are forgotten out there in the snow and the cold. We are forgotten while you sit here and discuss politics! I tell you the army can't fight much longer! Something's got to be done! Something's got to be done! The officers won't work with the soldiers' committees and the soldiers are starving and the Allies won't have a conference. I tell you something's got to be done or the soldiers are going home!

Then the peasants would get up and plead for their land. The Land Committees, they claimed, were being arrested by the Provisional Government; they had a religious feeling about land. They said they would fight and die for the land, but they would not wait any longer. If it was not given to them now they would go out and take it. And the factory workers told of the sabotage of the bourgeoisie, how they were ruining the delicate machinery so that the workmen could not run the factories; they were shutting down the mills so they would starve. It was not true, they cried, that the workers were getting fabulous sums. They couldn't live on what they got! Over and over and over like the beat of the surf came the cry of all starving Russia: "Peace, land and bread!" [ . . . ]

Antonoff, the War Minister, had an office in Smolny, as well as Krylenko and Dubenko, so it was the nerve center for the army and navy, as well as the political center. In the corridors were stacks of literature which the people gobbled up eagerly. Pamphlets, books and official newspapers of the Bolshevik party like *Rabotchi Poot* and [the Soviet newspaper] *Isvestia* by the thousands were disposed of daily. Soldiers, dead-weary, slept in the halls and on chairs and benches in unused rooms. Others stood alert and on guard before all sorts of committee rooms, and if you didn't have a pass…you didn't get in. The passes were changed frequently to keep out spies. In many windows were machine guns pointing blind eyes into the cold winter air. Rifles were stacked along the walls, and on the stone steps before the main entrance were several cannon. In the court were armored cars ready for action. Smolny was always well guarded by volunteers.

No matter how late the meetings lasted, and they usually broke up about four o'clock in the morning, the streetcar employees kept the cars waiting. When the heaviest snowstorms blocked up the traffic, soldiers and sailors and working women came out on the streets and kept the tracks clear to Smolny. Often it was the only line running in the city. [ . . . ]

## The fall of the Winter Palace

October 24th was crowded with events. After the ludicrous disbanding of the Council of the Russian Republic at two o'clock in the afternoon by the Cronstadt sailors, with two other Americans, John Reed and Albert Rhys Williams, I started for the Winter Palace to find out what was happening to Kerensky. Junker guards were everywhere. They let us pass after solemnly examining our American passports. Once past the guards we were at liberty to roam all over the palace and so we went directly to Kerensky's office. In the ante-room we found one of his smart-looking aides who greeted us in an agitated manner. Babushka, he told us, had gone two days before and Kerensky had also fled after an embarrassing experience which might have caused his capture. At the last moment he found that he did not have enough gasoline for his automobile, and couriers had to be sent into the Bolshevik lines. [ . . . ]

Everybody in the palace was tremendously excited; they were expecting an attack at any minute and no one knew just what to do. There was very little ammunition and it was only a matter of hours before they would have to give up. The Winter Palace was cut off from all outside help and the ministers of the Provisional Government were inside. [. . .] When we left Kerensky's office we walked straight to the front of the palace. Here were hundreds of Junkers all armed and ready. Straw beds were on the floor and a few were sleeping, huddled up on their blankets. They were all young and friendly and said they had no objection to our being in the battle; in fact, the idea rather amused them.

For three hours we were there. I shall never forget those poor, uncomfortable, unhappy boys. They had been reared and trained in officers' schools, and now they found themselves without a court, without a Tsar, without all the traditions they believed in. The Miliukov government was bad enough, the Provisional Government was worse and now this terrible proletarian dictatorship. [. . .] It was too much; they couldn't stand it. A little group of us sat down on a window ledge. One of them said he wanted to go to France "where people lived decently." Another enquired the best method to get into the American army. One of them was not over eighteen. He told me that in case they were not able to hold the palace, he was "keeping one bullet for himself." All the others declared that they were doing the same. Someone suggested that we exchange keepsakes. We brought out our little stores. I recall a silver Caucasian dagger, a short sword presented by the Tsar and a ring with this inscription: "God, King and Lady." When conversation lagged they took us away to show us the Gold Room of which they were very proud. They said that it was one of the finest rooms in all Europe. All the talk was sprinkled with French phrases just to prove they were really cultured. Russia had moved several centuries beyond these precious young men. [ . . . ]

[The next day, October 25] at Smolny a hot battle of words was being waged between the Mensheviki and Socialist Revolutionists on one side and the Left Socialist Revolutionists, Bolsheviki and Menshevik Internationalists on the other. The former were claiming that all important matters must be put off until after the Constituent Assembly. But the majority of the gathering would not listen to them. Finally, an inspired speaker declared that the cruiser *Aurora* was at that very moment shelling the Winter Palace, and if the whole uprising was not stopped at once, the delegates from the Menshevik and Socialist Revolutionist parties, together with certain members of the City Duma, would march unarmed through the firing lines and die with the Provisional Government. This came as a complete surprise to many of the delegates who were to be sacrificed, but nevertheless a number of them impulsively followed the speaker; others sat uneasily in their seats looking as if they felt this was carrying party principles altogether too far. The affair, dramatic as it was, did not have much effect on the general assembly; five minutes after the delegates left the hall they proceeded with their regular business. The soldiers seemed to think it was a particularly good joke and kept slapping each other on the back and guffawing. Of course we followed the bolting delegates.

All the street cars had stopped and it was two miles to the Winter Palace. A huge motor truck was just leaving Smolny. We hailed it and climbed on board. We found we had for companions several sailors and soldiers and a man from the Wild Division, wearing his picturesque, long black cape. They warned us gaily that we'd probably all get killed, and they told me to take off a yellow hatband, as there might be sniping. Their mission was to distribute leaflets all over town, and especially along the Nevsky Prospect. The leaflets were piled high over the floor of the truck together with guns and ammunition. As we rattled along through the wide, dim-lit streets, they scattered the leaflets to eager crowds. People scrambled over the cobbles fighting for copies. We could only make out the headlines in the half-light: "Citizens! The Provisional Government is deposed. State power has passed into the organ of the Petrograd Soviet of Worker' and Soldiers' Deputies."

Before I left Smolny I had secured a pass from the new famous Military Revolutionary Committee. My pass read:

No. 1. Military Revolutionary Committee of the Petrograd Council of Workers' and Soldiers' Deputies gives Tavarishe Louise Bryant free passage through the city.

—Signed by the Chairman and Secretary of the Military Revolutionary Committee, and stamped by the Military Division.

Where the Ekaterina Canal crosses the Nevsky, guards informed the driver that we could go no further. So we jumped down and found ourselves witnesses to as fantastic a political performance as ever took place in history. Huddled together in the middle of the Nevsky were the delegates of the Socialist Revolutionist and Menshevik parties [who had walked out of the Soviet Congress soon after it had opened earlier in the day]. Unto themselves they had since gathered various wives and friends and those members of the City

Duma who were not Bolsheviki, Left Socialist Revolutionists or Menshevik Internationalists—so that their number was something over 200. It was then two o'clock in the morning. [ . . . ]

For a time, I confess, we were all pretty much impressed by these would-be martyrs; any body of unarmed people protesting against armed force is bound to be impressive. In a little while, however, we couldn't help wondering why they didn't go ahead and die as long as they had made up their minds to it; and especially since the Winter Palace and the Provisional Government might be captured at any moment. When we began to talk to the martyrs we were surprised to find that they were very particular about the manner in which they were to die—and not only that but they were trying to persuade the sailor guards that they had been given permission to pass by the Military Revolutionary Committee. If our respect for their bravery weakened, our interest in the uniqueness of their political tricks grew a good deal; it was clear that the last thing the delegates wanted to do was to die, although they kept shouting that they did at the top of their voices. "Let us pass! Let us sacrifice ourselves!" they cried like bad children.

Only twenty husky sailors barred the way. And to all arguments they continued stubborn and unmoved. "Go home and take poison," they advised the clamoring statesmen, "but don't expect to die here. We have orders not to allow it."

"What will you do if we suddenly push forward?" asked one of the delegates.

"We may give you a good spanking," answered the sailors, "but we will not kill one of you—not by a damn sight!"

This seemed to settle the business. Prokopovitch, Minister of Supplies, walked to the head of the company and announced in a trembling voice: "Comrades: Let us return, let us refuse to be killed by switchmen!" Just exactly what he meant by that was too much for my simple American brain, but the martyrs seemed to understand perfectly, for off they marched in the direction from which they had come and took up headquarters in the City Duma. When we showed our passes, it was like magic, the sailors smiled and let us go forward without a word. At the Red Arch, soldiers informed us that the Winter Palace had just surrendered. We ran across the Square after the Bolshevik troops, a few bullets whistled by, but it was impossible to tell from which direction they came. Every window was lit up as if for a fête and we could see people moving about inside. Only a small entrance was open and we poured through the narrow door.

Inside the Junkers were being disarmed and given their liberty. They had to file past the door through which we had come. When those we had been with in the afternoon recognized us they waved friendly greetings. They looked relieved that it was all over, they had forgotten about the "one bullet" they were keeping for themselves. [. . .] The ministers of the Provisional Government were betrayed by the employees in the palace, and they were quickly hauled out of all sorts of secret back rooms and passages. They were sent to Peter and Paul Fortress. We sat on a long bench by the door and watched them going out. Tereschenko impressed me more than the others. He looked so ridiculous and out of place; he was so well groomed and so outraged. [ . . . ]

About five o'clock the same morning [now October 26], we left the Winter Palace and called at the City Duma. Here we found the indignant and no longer self-sacrificing politicians furiously forming what they ingeniously chose to call the "Committee for Saving the Country and the Revolution." Soon after it fell into their hands, the Soviet government turned the Winter Palace into a People's Museum.

# 23.

# Women Fighters in the October Revolution

*Alexandra Kollontai was a member of the Bolshevik Central Committee and was named the People's Commissar of Welfare by the Second All-Russian Congress of Soviets. During the July Days she was, along with Trotsky and others, arrested by the Kerensky government. Here she recounts the leading role women played in the insurrection.*[1]

The women who took part in the Great October Revolution—who were they? Isolated individuals? No, there were hosts of them; tens, hundreds of thousands of nameless heroines who, marching side by side with the workers and peasants behind the red flag and the slogan of the Soviets, passed over the ruins of tsarist theocracy into a new future. [ . . . ]

If one looks back into the past, one can see them, these masses of nameless heroines whom October found living in starving cities, in impoverished villages plundered by war. [ . . . ] A scarf on their head (very rarely, as yet, a red kerchief), a worn skirt, a patched winter jacket. [ . . . ] Young and old, women workers and soldiers' wives, peasant women and housewives from among the city poor. More rarely, much more rarely in those days, office workers and women in the professions, educated and cultured women. But there were also women from the intelligentsia among those who carried the red flag to the October victory—teachers, office employees, young students at high schools and universities, women doctors. They marched cheerfully, selflessly, purposefully. They went wherever they were sent. To the front? They put on a soldier's cap and became fighters in the Red Army. If they put on red armbands, then

131

they were hurrying off to the first-aid stations to help the Red Front against Kerensky at Gatchina. They worked in army communications. They worked cheerfully, filled with the belief that something momentous was happening, and that we are all small cogs in the one class of revolution.

In the villages, the peasant women (their husbands had been sent off to the front) took the land from the landowners and chased the aristocracy out of the nests they had roosted in for centuries. [ . . . ]

However, out of this sea of women's heads in scarves and worn caps there inevitably emerge the figures of those to whom the historian will devote particular attention when, many years from now, he writes about the Great October Revolution and its leader, Lenin. The first figure to emerge is that of Lenin's faithful companion, Nadezhda Konstantinovna Krupskaya, wearing her plain grey dress and always striving to remain in the background. She would slip unnoticed into a meeting and place herself behind a pillar, but she saw and heard everything, observing all that happened so that she could then give a full account to Vladimir Ilyich, add her own apt comments and light upon a sensible, suitable and useful idea. In those days Nadezhda Konstantinovna did not speak at the numerous stormy meetings at which the people argued over the great question: would the Soviets win power or not? But she worked tirelessly as Vladimir Ilyich's right hand, occasionally making a brief but telling comment at party meetings. In moments of greatest difficulty and danger, when many stronger comrades lost heart and succumbed to doubt, Nadezhda Konstantinovna remained always the same, totally convinced of the rightness of the cause and of its certain victory. She radiated unshakable faith, and this staunchness of spirit, concealed behind a rare modesty, always had a cheering effect upon all who came into contact with the companion of the great leader of the October Revolution.

Another figure emerges—that of yet another faithful companion of Vladimir Ilyich, a comrade-in-arms during the difficult years of underground work, secretary of the Party Central Committee, Yelena Dmitriyevna Stassova. A clear, high brow, a rare precision in and an exceptional capacity for work, a rare ability to "spot" the right person for the job. Her tall, statuesque figure could be seen first at the Soviet at the Tavrichesky palace, then at the house of Kshesinskaya, and finally at Smolny. In her hands she holds a notebook, while around her press comrades from the front, workers, Red Guards, women workers, members of the party and of the Soviets, seeking a quick, clear answer or order.

Stassova carried responsibility for many important matters, but if a comrade faced need or distress in those stormy days, she would always respond, providing a brief, seemingly curt answer, and herself doing anything she could.

She was overwhelmed with work, and always at her post. Always at her post, yet never pushing forward to the front row, to prominence. She did not like to be the center of attention. Her concern was not for herself, but for the cause. For the noble and cherished cause of communism, for which Yelena Stassova suffered exile and imprisonment in tsarist jails, leaving her with broken health . . . In the name of the cause she was as hard as steel. But to the sufferings of her comrades she displayed a sensitivity and responsiveness that are found only in a woman with a warm and noble heart.

Klavdia Nikolayeva was a working woman of very humble origins. She had joined the Bolsheviks as early as 1908, in the years of reaction, and had endured exile and imprisonment. [ . . . ] In 1917 she returned to Leningrad and became the heart of the first magazine for working women, *Kommunistka*. She was still young, full of fire and impatience. But she held the banner firmly, and boldly declared that women workers, soldiers' wives and peasant women must be drawn into the party. "To work, women! To the defense of the Soviets and communism!" She spoke at meetings, still nervous and unsure of herself, yet attracting others to follow. She was one of those who bore on her shoulders all the difficulties involved in preparing the way for the broad, mass involvement of women in the revolution, one of those who fought on two fronts—for the Soviets and communism, and at the same time for the emancipation of women. The names of Klavdia Nikolayeva and Konkordia Samoilova, who died at her revolutionary post in 1921 (from cholera), are indissolubly linked with the first and most difficult steps taken by the working women's movement, particularly in Leningrad. Konkordia Samoilova was a party worker of unparalleled selflessness, a fine, businesslike speaker who knew how to win the hearts of working women. Those who worked alongside her will long remember Konkordia Samoilova. She was simple in manner, simple in dress, demanding in the execution of decisions, strict both with herself and others.

Particularly striking is the gentle and charming figure of Inessa Armand, who was charged with very important party work in preparation for the October Revolution, and who thereafter contributed many creative ideas to the work conducted among women. With all her femininity and gentleness of manner, Inessa Armand was unshakable in her convictions and able to defend what she believed to be right, even when faced with redoubtable opponents. After the revolution, Inessa Armand devoted herself to organizing the broad movement of working women, and the delegate conference is her creation.

Enormous work was done by Varvara Nikolayevna Yakovleva during the difficult and decisive days of the October Revolution in Moscow. On the battleground of the barricades she showed a resolution worthy of a leader of party headquarters. [ . . . ] Many comrades said then that her resolution and unshakable courage gave heart to the wavering and inspired those who had lost heart. "Forward!"—to victory.

As one recalls the women who took part in the Great October Revolution, more and more names and faces rise up as if by magic from the memory. Could we fail to honor today the memory of Vera Slutskaya, who worked selflessly in preparation for the revolution and who was shot down by Cossacks on the first Red Front near Petrograd? Could we forget Yevgenia Bosh, with her fiery temperament, always eager for battle? She also died at her revolutionary post. Could we omit to mention here two names closely connected with the life and activity of V.I. Lenin—his two sisters and comrades-in-arms, Anna Ilyinichna Yelizarova and Maria Ilyinichna Ulyanova? And comrade Varya, from the railway workshops in Moscow, always lively, always in a hurry? And Fyodorova, the textile worker in Leningrad, with her pleasant, smiling face and her fearlessness when it came to fighting at the barricades?

It is impossible to list them all, and how many remain nameless? The heroines of the October Revolution were a whole army, and although their names may be forgotten, their selflessness lives on in the very victory of that revolution, in all the gains and achievements now enjoyed by working women in the Soviet Union. It is a clear and indisputable fact that, without the participation of women, the October Revolution could not have brought the red flag to victory. Glory to the working women who marched under that red banner during the October Revolution. Glory to the October Revolution that liberated women!

# 24.

# The Soviets Take Power

*John Reed was one of the best-known radical journalists in the United States prior to World War I. He supported the Industrial Workers of the World, rode with Pancho Villa during the Mexican Revolution, and helped found the Communist Labor Party in 1919 upon returning from Russia. His book* Ten Days that Shook the World *introduced tens of thousands to the October Revolution and included an introduction from Lenin himself. "Unreservedly do I recommend it to the workers of the world," wrote Lenin. "Here is a book which I should like to see published in millions of copies and translated into all languages. It gives a truthful and most vivid exposition of the events so significant to the comprehension of what really is the Proletarian Revolution and the Dictatorship of the Proletariat." These selections focus on the debate between the Bolsheviks, Left SRs, Mensheviks, and others at the opening of the Second All-Russian Congress of Soviets.*[1]

## October 24—The fall of the Provisional Government

The massive facade of Smolny blazed with lights as we drove up, and from every street converged upon it streams of hurrying shapes dim in the gloom. Automobiles and motorcycles came and went; an enormous elephant-colored armored automobile, with two red flags flying from the turret, lumbered out with screaming siren. It was cold, and at the outer gate the Red Guards had built themselves a bonfire. At the inner gate, too, there was a blaze, by the light of which the sentries slowly spelled out our passes and looked us up and down. The canvas covers had been taken off the four rapid-fire guns on each side of the doorway, and the ammunition belts hung snakelike from their breeches. A dun herd of armored cars stood under the trees in the courtyard, engines going. The long, bare, dimly-illuminated halls roared with the thunder of feet, calling, shouting. [ . . . ] There was an atmosphere of recklessness. A crowd came pouring down the staircase, workers in black blouses and round black fur hats, many of them with guns slung over their shoulders, soldiers in rough dirt-colored coats and grey fur *shapki* pinched flat, a leader or so—Lunacharsky, Kameniev—hurrying along in the center of a group all talking at once, with harassed anxious faces, and bulging portfolios under their arms. The extraordinary meeting of the Petrograd Soviet was over. I stopped Kameniev—a quick moving little man, with a wide, vivacious face set close to his shoulders. Without preface he read in rapid French a copy of the resolution just passed:

> The Petrograd Soviet of Workers' and Soldiers' Deputies, saluting the victorious Revolution of the Petrograd proletariat and garrison, particularly emphasizes the unity, organization, discipline, and complete cooperation shown by the masses in this rising; rarely has less blood been spilled, and rarely has an insurrection succeeded so well [ . . . ]

"You consider it won then?"

He lifted his shoulders. "There is much to do. Horribly much. It is just beginning."

On the landing I met Riazanov, vice-president of the Trade Unions, looking black and biting his grey beard. "It's insane! Insane!" he shouted. "The European working class won't move! All Russia—" He waved his hand distractedly and ran off. Riazanov and Kameniev had both opposed the insurrection, and felt the lash of Lenin's terrible tongue.

It had been a momentous session. In the name of the Military Revolutionary Committee Trotzky had declared that the Provisional Government no longer existed. "The characteristic of bourgeois governments," he said, "is to deceive the people. We, the Soviets of Workers', Soldiers' and Peasants' Deputies, are going to try an experiment unique in history; we are going to found a power which will have no other aim but to satisfy the needs of the soldiers, workers, and peasants."

Lenin had appeared, welcomed with a mighty ovation, prophesying worldwide social revolution. And Zinoviev, crying, "This day we have paid our debt to the international proletariat, and struck a terrible blow at the war, a terrible body-blow at all the imperialists and particularly at Wilhelm the Executioner."

Then Trotzky, that telegrams had been sent to the front announcing the victorious insurrection, but no reply had come. Troops were said to be marching against Petrograd—a delegation must be sent to tell them the truth.

Cries, "You are anticipating the will of the All-Russian Congress of Soviets!"

Trotzky, coldly, "The will of the All-Russian Congress of Soviets has been anticipated by the rising of the Petrograd workers and soldiers!"

## October 25—Opening of the Second All-Russian Congress of Soviets

So we came into the great meeting hall, pushing through the clamorous mob at the door. In the rows of seats, under the white chandeliers, packed immovably in the aisles and on the sides, perched on every windowsill, and even the edge of the platform, the representatives of the workers and soldiers of all Russia waited in anxious silence or wild exultation the ringing of the chairman's bell. There was no heat in the hall but the stifling heat of unwashed human bodies. A foul blue cloud of cigarette smoke rose from the mass and hung in the thick air. Occasionally someone in authority mounted the tribune and asked the comrades not to smoke; then everybody, smokers and all, took up the cry "Don't smoke, comrades!" and went on smoking. Petrovsky, anarchist delegate from the Obukhov factory, made a seat for me beside him. Unshaven and filthy, he was reeling from three nights' sleepless work on the Military Revolutionary Committee.

On the platform sat the leaders of the old Tsay-ee-kah [acronym for the All-Russian Central Executive Committee of the Soviets]—for the last time dominating the turbulent Soviets, which they had ruled from the first days, and which were now risen against them. It was the end of the first period of the Russian revolution, which these men had attempted to guide in careful ways. The three greatest of them were not there: Kerensky, flying to the front through country towns [ . . . ]; Tcheidze, the old eagle, who had contemptuously retired to his own Georgian mountains, there to sicken with consumption; and the high-souled Tsereteli, also mortally stricken, who, nevertheless, would return and pour out his beautiful eloquence for a lost cause. Gotz sat there, Dan, Lieber, Bogdanov, Broido, Fillipovsky—white-faced, hollow-eyed and indignant. Below them the second session of the All-Russian Soviets boiled and swirled, and over their heads the Military Revolutionary Committee functioned white-hot, holding in its hands the threads of insurrection and striking with a long arm. It was 10:40 P.M.

Dan, a mild-faced, baldish figure in a shapeless military surgeon's uniform, was ringing the bell. Silence fell sharply, intense, broken by the scuffling and disputing of the people at the door. "We have the power in our hands," he began sadly, stopped for a moment, and then went on in a low voice.

> Comrades! The Congress of Soviets is meeting in such unusual circumstances and in such an extraordinary moment that you will understand why the Tsay-ee-kah considers it unnecessary to address you with a political speech. This will become much clearer to you if you will recollect that I am a member of the Tsay-ee-kah, and that at this very moment our party comrades are in the Winter Palace under bombardment, sacrificing themselves to execute the duty put on them by the Tsay-ee-kah.

(Confused uproar.) "I declare the first session of the Second Congress of Soviets of Workers' and Soldiers' Deputies open!"

The election of the presidium took place amid stir and moving about. Avanessov announced that by agreement of the Bolsheviki, Left Socialist Revolutionaries and Mensheviki Internationalists, it was decided to base the presidium upon proportionality. Several Mensheviki leaped to their feet protesting. A bearded soldier shouted at them, "Remember what you did to us Bolsheviki when we were the minority!" Result: fourteen Bolsheviki, seven Socialist Revolutionaries, three Mensheviki and one Internationalist (Gorky's group). Hendelmann, for the right and center Socialist Revolutionaries, said that they refused to take part in the presidium; the same from Kintchuk, for the Mensheviki; and from the Mensheviki Internationalists, that until the verification of certain circumstances, they too could not enter the presidium. Scattering applause and hoots. One voice, "Renegades, you call yourselves socialists!" A representative of the Ukrainian delegates demanded, and received, a place. Then the old Tsay-ee-kah stepped down, and in their places appeared Trotzky, Kameniev, Lunacharsky, Madame Kollontai, Nogin. The hall rose, thundering. How far they had soared, these Bolsheviki, from a despised and hunted sect less than four months ago, to this supreme place, the helm of great Russia in full tide of insurrection!

The order of the day, said Kameniev, was first, Organization of Power; second, War and Peace; and third, the Constituent Assembly. Lozovsky, rising, announced that upon agreement of the bureau of all factions, it was proposed to hear and discuss the report of the Petrograd Soviet, then to give the floor to members of the Tsay-ee-kah and the different parties, and finally to pass to the order of the day.

But suddenly a new sound made itself heard, deeper than the tumult of the crowd, persistent, disquieting—the dull shock of guns. People looked anxiously toward the clouded windows, and a sort of fever came over them. Martov, demanding the floor, croaked hoarsely,

> The civil war is beginning, comrades! The first question must be a peaceful settlement of the crisis. On principle and from a political standpoint we must urgently discuss a means of averting civil war. Our brothers are being shot down in the streets! At this moment, when before the opening of the Congress of Soviets the question of Power is being settled by means of a military plot organized by one of the revolutionary parties—"

For a moment he could not make himself heard above the noise,

> All of the revolutionary parties must face the fact! The first *vopros* (question) before the Congress is the question of Power, and this question is already being settled by force of arms in the streets! We must create a power which will be recognized by the whole democracy. If the Congress wishes to be the voice of the revolutionary democracy it must not sit with folded hands before the developing civil war, the result of which may be a dangerous outburst of counter-revolution. The possibility of a peaceful outcome lies in the formation of a united democratic authority. We must elect a delegation to negotiate with the other Socialist parties and organization.

Always the methodical muffled boom of cannon through the windows, and the delegates, screaming at each other. So, with the crash of artillery, in the dark, with hatred, and fear, and reckless daring, new Russia was being born.

The Left Socialist Revolutionaries and the United Social Democrats supported Martov's proposition. It was accepted. A soldier announced that the All-Russian Peasants' Soviets had refused to send delegates to the Congress; he proposed that a committee be sent with a formal invitation. "Some delegates are present," he said. "I move that they be given votes." Accepted.

Kharash, wearing the epaulets of a captain, passionately demanded the floor. "The political hypocrites who control this Congress," he shouted, "told us we were to settle the question of Power—and it is being settled behind our backs, before the Congress opens! Blows are being struck against the Winter Palace, and it is by such blows that the nails are being driven into the coffin of the political party which has risked such an adventure!" Uproar.

Followed him Gharra: "While we are here discussing propositions of peace, there is a battle on in the streets. The Socialist Revolutionaries and the Mensheviki refuse to be involved in what is happening, and call upon all public forces to resist the attempt to capture the power."

Kutchin, delegate of the 12th Army and representative of the Troudoviki: "I was sent here only for information, and I am returning at once to the Front, where all the Army Committees consider that the taking of power by the Soviets, only three weeks before the Constituent Assembly, is a stab in the back of the Army and a crime against the people!"

Shouts of "Lie! You lie!" When he could be heard again, "Let's make an end of this adventure in Petrograd! I call upon all delegates to leave this hall in order to save the country and the Revolution!" As he went down the aisle in the midst of a deafening noise, people surged in upon him, threatening. Then Khintchuk, an officer with a long brown goatee, speaking suavely and persuasively: "I speak for the delegates from the Front. The Army is imperfectly represented in this Congress, and furthermore, the Army does not consider the Congress of Soviets necessary at this time, only three weeks before the opening of the Constituent." Shouts and stamping, always growing more violent. "The Army does not consider that the Congress of Soviets has the necessary authority." Soldiers began to stand up all over the hall.

"Who are you speaking for? What do you represent?" they cried.

"The Central Executive Committee of the Soviet of the Fifth Army, the Second F— regiment, the First N— Regiment, the Third S— Rifles."

"When were you elected? You represent the officers, not the soldiers! What do the soldiers say about it?" Jeers and hoots.

"We, the Front group, disclaim all responsibility for what has happened and is happening, and we consider it necessary to mobilize all self-conscious revolutionary forces for the salvation of the Revolution! The Front group will leave the Congress. The place to fight is out on the streets!"

Immense bawling outcry. "You speak for the Staff—not for the Army!"

"I appeal to all reasonable soldiers to leave this Congress!"

"Kornilovitz! Counter-revolutionist! Provocateur!" were hurled at him.

On behalf of the Mensheviki, Khintchuk then announced that the only possibility of a peaceful solution was to begin negotiations with the Provisional Government for the formation of a new Cabinet, which would find support in all strata of society. He could not proceed for several minutes. Raising his voice to a shout he read the Menshevik declaration:

> Because the Bolsheviki have made a military conspiracy with the aid of the Petrograd Soviet, without consulting the other factions and parties, we find it impossible to remain in the Congress, and therefore withdraw, inviting the other groups to follow us and to meet for discussion of the situation!

"Deserter!" At intervals in the almost continuous disturbance Hendelmann, for the Socialist Revolutionaries, could be heard protesting against the bombardment of the Winter Palace. "We are opposed to this kind of anarchy."

Scarcely had he stepped down than a young, lean-faced soldier, with flashing eyes, leaped to the platform, and dramatically lifted his hand: "Comrades!" he cried and there was a hush.

My *familia* (name) is Peterson—I speak for the Second Lettish Rifles. You have heard the statements of two representatives of the Army committees; these statements would have some value if their authors had been representatives of the Army.

Wild applause.

But they do not represent the soldiers!

Shaking his fist.

The Twelfth Army has been insisting for a long time upon the re-election of the Great Soviet and the Army Committee, but just as your own Tsay-ee-kah, our Committee refused to call a meeting of the representatives of the masses until the end of September, so that the reactionaries could elect their own false delegates to this Congress. I tell you now, the Lettish soldiers have many times said, "No more resolutions! No more talk! We want deeds—the Power must be in our hands!" Let these impostor delegates leave the Congress! The Army is not with them!

The hall rocked with cheering. In the first moments of the session, stunned by the rapidity of events, startled by the sound of cannon, the delegates had hesitated. For an hour hammer-blow after hammer-blow had fallen from that tribune, welding them together but beating them down. Did they stand then alone? Was Russia rising against them? Was it true that the Army was marching on Petrograd? Then this clear-eyed young soldier had spoken, and in a flash they knew it for the truth. This was the voice of the soldiers—the stirring millions of uniformed workers and peasants were men like them, and their thoughts and feelings were the same. [ . . . ]

Then came Abramovitch, for the Bund, the organ of the Jewish Social Democrats—his eyes snapping behind thick glasses, trembling with rage. "What is taking place now in Petrograd is a monstrous calamity! The Bund group joins with the declaration of the Mensheviki and Socialist Revolutionaries and will leave the Congress!" He raised his voice and hand.

Our duty to the Russian proletariat doesn't permit us to remain here and be responsible for these crimes. Because the firing on the Winter Palace doesn't cease, the Municipal Duma together with the Mensheviki and Socialist Revolutionaries, and the Executive Committee of the Peasants' Soviet, has decided to perish with the Provisional Government, and we are going with them! Unarmed we will expose our breasts to the machine guns of the Terrorist. We invite all delegates to this Congress.

The rest was lost in a storm of hoots, menaces and curses which rose to a hellish pitch as fifty delegates got up and pushed their way out.

Kameniev jangled the bell, shouting, "Keep your seats and we'll go on with our business!" And Trotzky, standing up with a pale, cruel face, letting out his rich voice in cool contempt, "All these so-called Socialist compromisers, these frightened Mensheviki, Socialist Revolutionaries, Bund—let them go! They are just so much refuse which will be swept into the garbage-heap of history!"

Riazanov, for the Bolsheviki, stated that at the request of the City Duma the Military Revolutionary Committee had sent a delegation to offer negotiations to the Winter Palace. "In this way we have done everything possible to avoid blood-shed."

We hurried from the place, stopping for a moment at the room where the Military Revolutionary Committee worked at furious speed, engulfing and spitting out panting couriers, dispatching Commissars armed with power of life and death to all the corners of the city, amid the buzz of the telephonographs. The door opened, a blast of stale air and cigarette smoke rushed out, we caught a glimpse of dishevelled men bending over a map under the glare of a shaded electric-light. Comrade Josephov-Dukhvinski, a smiling youth with a mop of pale yellow hair, made out passes for us.

## October 26—Plunging ahead: The Soviets take power

Riazanov was coming up the front steps, explaining in a sort of humorous panic that he, Commissar of Commerce, knew nothing whatever of business. In the upstairs cafe sat a man all by himself in the corner, in a goat-skin cape and clothes which had been—I was going to say "slept in," but of course he hadn't slept—and a three days' growth of beard. He was anxiously figuring on a dirty envelope, and biting his pencil meanwhile. This was Menzhinsky, Commissar of Finance, whose qualifications were that he had once been clerk in a French bank. And these four half-running down the hall from the office of the Military Revolutionary Committee, and scribbling on bits of paper as they run—these were Commissars dispatched to the four corners of Russia to carry the news, argue, or fight—with whatever arguments or weapons came to hand.

The Congress was to meet at one o'clock [in the afternoon], and long since the great meeting-hall had filled, but by seven P.M. there was yet no sign of the presidium. The Bolshevik and Left Social-Revolutionary factions were in session in their own rooms. All the livelong afternoon Lenin and Trotzky had fought against compromise. A considerable part of the Bolsheviki were in favor of giving way so far as to create a joint all-Socialist government. "We can't hold on!" they cried. "Too much is against us. We haven't got the men. We will be isolated, and the whole thing will fall." So Kameniev, Riazanov and others. But Lenin, with Trotzky beside him, stood firm as a rock. "Let the compromisers accept our program and they can come in! We won't give way an inch. If there are comrades here who haven't the courage and the will to dare what we dare, let them leave with the rest of the cowards and conciliators! Backed by the workers and soldiers we shall go on."

At five minutes past seven [in the evening] came word from the Left Socialist Revolutionaries to say that they would remain in the Military Revolutionary Committee.

"See!" said Lenin. "They are following!" [ . . . ]

It was just 8:40 p.m. when a thundering wave of cheers announced the entrance of the presidium, with Lenin—great Lenin—among them. A short, stocky figure, with a big head set down in his shoulders, bald and bulging. Little eyes, a snubbish nose, wide, generous mouth, and heavy chin; clean-shaven now, but already beginning to bristle with the well-known beard of his past and future. Dressed in shabby clothes, his trousers much too long for him. Unimpressive, to be the idol of a mob, loved and revered as perhaps few leaders in history have been. A strange popular leader—a leader purely by virtue of intellect; colorless, humorless, uncompromising and detached, without picturesque idiosyncrasies—but with the power of explaining profound ideas in simple terms, of analyzing a concrete situation. And combined with shrewdness, the greatest intellectual audacity.

Kameniev was reading the report of the actions of the Military Revolutionary Committee; abolition of capital punishment in the Army, restoration of the free right of propaganda, release of officers and soldiers arrested for political crimes, orders to arrest Kerensky and confiscation of food supplies in private store-houses. Tremendous applause.

Again the representative of the Bund. The uncompromising attitude of the Bolsheviki would mean the crushing of the Revolution; therefore, the Bund delegates must refuse any longer to sit in the Congress. Cries from the audience, "We thought you walked out last night! How many times are you going to walk out?"

Then the representative of the Mensheviki Internationalists. Shouts, "What! You here still?" The speaker explained that only part of the Mensheviki

Internationalists left the Congress; the rest were going to stay. "We consider it dangerous and perhaps even mortal for the Revolution to transfer the power to the Soviets," interruptions, "but we feel it our duty to remain in the Congress and vote against the transfer [of power] here!"

Other speakers followed, apparently without any order. A delegate of the coal-miners of the Don Basin called upon the Congress to take measures against Kaledin, who might cut off coal and food from the capital. Several soldiers just arrived from the Front brought the enthusiastic greetings of their regiments. Now Lenin, gripping the edge of the reading stand, letting his little winking eyes travel over the crowd as he stood there waiting, apparently oblivious to the long-rolling ovation, which lasted several minutes. When it finished, he said simply, "We shall now proceed to construct the Socialist order!" Again that overwhelming human roar.

> The first thing is the adoption of practical measures to realize peace. . . . We shall offer peace to the peoples of all the belligerent countries upon the basis of the Soviet terms—no annexations, no indemnities, and the right of self-determination of peoples. At the same time, according to our promise, we shall publish and repudiate the secret treaties. . . . The question of War and Peace is so clear that I think that I may, without preamble, read the project of a Proclamation to the Peoples of All the Belligerent Countries.

By crowd vote it was quickly decided that only representatives of political factions should be allowed to speak on the motion and that speakers should be limited to fifteen minutes.

First Karelin for the Left Socialist Revolutionaries. "Our faction had no opportunity to propose amendments to the text of the proclamation; it is a private document of the Bolsheviki. But we will vote for it because we agree with its spirit."

For the Social Democrats Internationalists Kramarov, long, stoop-shouldered and near-sighted—destined to achieve some notoriety as the Clown of the Opposition. Only a Government composed of all the Socialist parties, he said, could possess the authority to take such important action. If a Socialist coalition were formed, his faction would support the entire program; if not, only part of it. As for the proclamation, the Internationalists were in thorough accord with its main points.

Then one after another, amid rising enthusiasm; Ukrainian Social Democracy, support; Lithuanian Social Democracy, support; Populist Socialists, support; Polish Social Democracy, support; Polish Socialists support—but would prefer a Socialist coalition; Lettish Social Democracy, support. Something was kindled in these men. One spoke of the "coming World Revolution, of which we are the advance-guard," another of "the new age of brotherhood, when all the peoples will become one great family." An individual member claimed the floor. "There is contradiction here," he said. "First you offer peace without annexations and indemnities, and then you say you will consider all peace offers. To consider means to accept."

Lenin was on his feet.

We want a just peace, but we are not afraid of a revolutionary war. Probably the imperialist Governments will not answer our appeal—but we shall not issue an ultimatum to which it will be easy to say no. If the German proletariat realizes that we are ready to consider all offers of peace, that will perhaps be the last drop which overflows the bowl—revolution will break out in Germany.

We consent to examine all conditions of peace, but that doesn't mean that we shall accept them. For some of our terms we shall fight to the end—but possibly for others will find it impossible to continue the war. Above all, we want to finish the war.

It was exactly 10:35 P.M. when Kameniev asked all in favor of the proclamation to hold up their cards. One delegate dared to raise his hand against, but the sudden sharp outburst around him brought it swiftly down. Unanimous.

Suddenly, by common impulse, we found ourselves on our feet, mumbling together into the smooth lifting unison of the Internationale. A grizzled old soldier was sobbing like a child. Alexandra Kollontai rapidly winked the tears back. The immense sound rolled through the hall, burst windows and doors and seared into the quiet sky. "The war is ended! The war is ended!" said a young workman near me, his face shining. And when it was over, as we stood there in a kind of awkward hush, someone in the back of the room shouted, "Comrades! Let us remember those who have died for liberty!" So we began to sing the Funeral March, that slow, melancholy and yet triumphant chant, so Russian and so moving. The Internationale is an alien air, after all. The Funeral March seemed the very soul of those dark masses whose delegates sat in this hall, building from their obscure visions a new Russia—and perhaps more.

*You fell in the fatal fight*
*For the liberty of the people, for the honor of the people . . .*
*You gave up your lives and everything dear to you,*
*You suffered in horrible prisons,*
*You went to exile in chains.*

*Without a word you carried your chains because you could not ignore your*
*suffering brothers,*
*Because you believed that justice is stronger than the sword.*
*The time will come when your surrendered life will count*
*That time is near; when tyranny falls the people will rise, great and free!*
*Farewell, brothers, you chose a noble path,*

*You are followed by the new and fresh army ready to die and to suffer.*
*Farewell, brothers, you chose a noble path,*
*At your grave we swear to fight, to work for freedom and the people's happiness.*

For this did they lie there, the martyrs of March, in their cold Brotherhood Grave on Mars Field; for this thousands and tens of thousands had died
in the prisons, in exile, in Siberian mines. It had not come as they expected
it would come, nor as the intelligentsia desired it; but it had come—rough,
strong, impatient of formulas, contemptuous of sentimentalism; real.

# 25.

# The Intelligentsia Desert

*While political arguments raged in the Soviet Congress, **Albert Rhys Williams** noticed a strange sociological phenomenon. The Russian intelligentsia had long terrorized the Tsar with assassination plots and attempts to foment peasant and working-class rebellion, but now, at the apex of the revolution, a disproportionate number of them shrank back. Of course, many workers opposed the Bolsheviks, and the Bolsheviks contained many intellectuals in their ranks, but as a social layer the intellectuals recoiled. Williams offers his explanation.[1]*

Now comes one of the startling paradoxes of history, and one of its colossal tragedies—the refusal of the intelligentsia. Among the delegates were scores of these intellectuals. They have made the "dark people" the object of their devotion. "Going to the people" was a religion. For them they have suffered poverty, prison and exile. They had stirred the quiescent masses with revolutionary ideas, inciting them to revolt. The character and the nobility of the masses had been ceaselessly extolled. In short, the intelligentsia had made a god of the people. Now the people were rising with the wrath and thunder of a god, imperious and arbitrary. They were acting like a god.

But the intelligentsia reject a god who will not listen to them and over whom they have lost control. Straightaway the intelligentsia became atheists. They disavow all faith in their former god, the people. They deny their right to rebellion.

Like Frankenstein before this monster of their own creation, the intelligentsia quail, trembling with fear, trembling with rage. It is a bastard thing, a devil, a terrible calamity, plunging Russia into chaos, "a criminal rebellion against authority." They hurl themselves against it, storming, cursing, beseeching, raving. As delegates [to the soviet] they refused to recognize this Revolution. They refuse to allow this Congress to declare the soviets the government of Russia.

So futile! So impotent! They may as well refuse to recognize a tidal wave, or an erupting Volcano as to refuse to recognize this Revolution. This Revolution is elemental, inexorable, it is everywhere, in the barracks, in the trenches, in the factories, in the streets. It is here in this Congress, officially, in hundreds of workmen, soldiers and peasant delegates. It is here unofficially in the masses crowding every inch of space, climbing up on pillars and windowsills, making the assembly hall white with fog from their close-packed steaming bodies, electric with the intensity of their feelings.

The people are here to see that their revolutionary will is done; that the Congress declares the soviets the government of Russia. On this point they are inflexible. Every attempt to becloud the issue, every effort to paralyze or evade their will evokes blasts of angry protest. The parties on the right have long resolutions to offer. The crowd is impatient. "No more resolutions! No more words! We want deeds! [We] want the soviets!"

The intelligentsia, as usual, wish to compromise the issue by [forming] a coalition of all parties. "Only one coalition is possible," is the retort, "the coalition of workers, soldiers and peasants."

Martov calls out for "a peaceful solution of the impending civil war." "Victory! Victory!—The only possible solution," is the answering cry.

The officer Kutchin tries to terrify them with the idea that the Soviets are isolated, and that the whole army is against him. "Liar! Staff!" yell the soldiers. "You speak for the staff—not the men in the trenches. We soldiers demand 'All power to the soviets.'"

Their will is steel. No entreaties or threats avail to break or bend it. Nothing can deflect them from their goal. Finally stung to fury, Abromovich cries out, "We cannot remain here and be responsible for these crimes. We invite all delegates to leave this Congress." With a dramatic gesture he steps from the platform and stalks towards the door. About eighty delegates rise from their seats and push their way after him.

"Let them go," cries Trotsky, "Let them go! They are just so much refuse that will be swept into the garbage-heap of history."

In a storm of hoots, jeers and taunts of "Renegades! Traitors!" from the proletarians, the intelligentsia pass out of the hall and out of the Revolution. A supreme tragedy! The intelligentsia rejecting the revolution they had helped to create, deserting the masses in the crisis of their struggle. Supreme folly, too. Behind the soviets are rolling up solid battalions of support.

# 26.

# The Mensheviks Walk Out and Split

*Nikolai Sukhanov, having joined Julius Martov's left-wing Menshevik Interna-*
*tionalist faction, reveals the inability of the wavering (but pro-soviet) factions to*
*offer an alternative to the Bolsheviks or join them. Instead, although the Menshevik*
*Internationalists supported many of the Bolsheviks' aims, they walked out of the Con-*
*gress, an action Sukhanov would later consider his greatest "crime." Astonishingly,*
*these left-wing Mensheviks acted almost exactly as Lenin had predicted they would*
*in his April pamphlet, "Political Parties in Russia and the Tasks of the Proletariat."*[1]

It was around 8 o'clock [in the evening] and I returned to Smolny. There
seemed to be even more chaos and disorder. As I went and I met old Martynov,
of our fraction. "Well?"

"The fraction's in session. Of course we shall leave the Congress. [. . .]"

"What? Leave the Congress? Our fraction?"

I was thunderstruck. Nothing like this had ever entered my head. It was
thought possible that the right Mensheviks would apply a specifically Bolshevik tactic and subject the Congress to a boycott. For *our* fraction such a possibility seemed to me absolutely excluded.

First of all, no one contested the legality of the Congress. Second, it represented the most authentic worker-peasant democracy; and it must be said that
not a small part of it consisted of the participants in the first Congress in June
[ . . . ] of that great mass of delegates who had once followed the Mensheviks,
and had been enticed away by Lenin, while most of the Right SRs were becoming Left SRs, if not Bolsheviks. Third, the question was: *where* would the Right

149

Mensheviks and the SRs leave the Congress for? Where were they to go to from the soviets? The soviet, after all, was the revolution itself. Without the soviet it never existed, nor could it. It was in the soviet, the combat instrument of the revolution, that the revolutionary masses were always organized and rallied. So where could one go from the soviet? It meant a formal break with the masses and with the revolution.

And why? Because the Congress had proclaimed a Soviet regime in which the minute Menshevik-SR minority would not be given a place! I myself considered this fatal for the revolution, but why link this with abandoning the supreme representative organ of the workers, soldiers, and peasants? The "Coalition," after all, was no less odious to the Bolsheviks than a "Soviet regime" was to the old Soviet bloc; the Bolsheviks, not long ago, under the dictatorship of the Star Chamber, themselves constituted the same impotent minority as the Mensheviks and SRs now, but they did not and could not draw the conclusion that they had to leave the Soviet.

The old bloc could not swallow its defeat in the Bolshevik dictatorship. With the bourgeoisie and with Kornilovites—yes; but with the workers and peasants they have thrown into the arms of Lenin with their own hands—impossible. [ . . . ]

*[Martov proposed negotiations in the middle of the Winter Palace assault; the Right SRs and Mensheviks had already walked out of Congress. In fact, the Congress passed Martov's resolution without much opposition because no one was opposed to looking into a peaceful solution "in principle." Sukhanov continues.]*

In some detail Martov analyzed the motives for his resolution. Then he proposed that the Congress pass a decree on the necessity for a peaceful settlement of the crisis by forming a general democratic government and electing a delegation to negotiate with all socialist parties. [ . . . ]

Martov's reply came from Trotsky, who was standing at his side in the crowd that packed the platform. Now that the Rightists had left, Trotsky's position was as strong as Martov's was weak.

"A rising of the masses of the people," Trotsky rapped out, "needs no justification."

> What has happened is an insurrection, and not a conspiracy. We hardened the revolutionary energy of the Petersburg workers and soldiers. We openly forged the will of the masses for an insurrection, and not a conspiracy. The masses of the people followed our banner and our insurrection was victorious. And now we are told: renounce your victory, make concessions, compromise. With whom? I ask: with whom ought we compromise? With those

wretched groups who have left us or who are making this proposal? But after all we've had a full view of them. No one in Russia is with them any longer. [. . .] No, here no compromise is possible. To those would have left and those who tell us to do this we must say: you are miserable bankrupts, your role is played out: go where you want to be: into the dust bin of history!

"Then we'll leave," Martov shouted from the platform, amid stormy applause for Trotsky.

No, excuse me, Comrade Martov! Trotsky's speech, of course, was a clear and unambiguous reply. But rage at an opponent, and Martov's emotional state, still did not bind the fraction to a decisive and fatal act. Martov, enraged and upset, began pushing his way off the platform. And I called an emergency conference of our fraction, scattered throughout the hall. [ . . . ]

During this time our fraction, extremely tense and nervous, was discussing the situation. Having settled ourselves in any sort of order just inside the door, about thirty of us, some standing up, others sitting on some kind of garden benches, were quarreling bitterly. I was vigorously attacking, very excited, and not mincing my words. Martov, having yielded to theatricality at the plenary session, defended himself more calmly and patiently. He seemed to feel that he had no firm ground beneath him, but at the same time to be aware that the whole conjunction of circumstances irrevocably compelled him to break with the Congress and go out after Dan—even though only halfway. [ . . . ]

I gave a good account of myself and did as much as I could. Throughout the revolution I have never defended my position with such conviction and ardor. Not only logic, political science, and elementary revolutionary truth seem to be on my side, but also a technical consideration: after all, the question put by Martov had not yet been debated in the Congress, and we still only had Trotsky as the Congress's reply. Leaving the Congress now would not only be criminal in general, but also dishonest and frivolous in particular.

Alas! It was clear that Martov was a victim of Menshevik indecisiveness. He was indeed! For the rupture with the bourgeois Compromisers and adherence to Smolny entailed the most decisive struggle and a definite camp. No place was left for neutrality. [ . . . ] to remain in Smolny with nobody but the Bolsheviks—no, that was beyond our strength. The fraction divided. About fourteen votes against twelve—Martov had won. I felt that I had suffered a disaster worse than any before in the revolution. I returned to the great hall completely numb. [ . . . ]

So the thing was done. We had left, not knowing where or why, after breaking with the Soviet, getting ourselves mixed up with counterrevolutionary elements, discrediting and debasing ourselves in the eyes of the masses, and ruining the entire future of our organization and our principles. And that was the least of it: in leaving we completely untied the Bolsheviks' hands, making them masters of the entire situation and yielding to them the whole arena of the revolution.

A struggle at the Congress for united democratic front *might* have had some success. For the Bolsheviks as such, for Lenin and Trotsky, it was more odious than the possible Committees of Public Safety or another Kornilov march on Petersburg. The exit of the "pure-in-heart" freed the Bolsheviks from this danger. By quitting the Congress and leaving the Bolsheviks with only the Left SR youngsters and the feeble little *Novaya Zhizn* group, we gave the Bolsheviks with our own hands a monopoly of the soviet, of the masses, and of the revolution. By our own irrational decision we ensured the victory of Lenin's whole "line."

I personally committed not a few blunders and errors in the revolution. But I consider my greatest and most indelible crime the fact that I failed to break with the Martov group immediately after our fraction voted to leave, and didn't stay on at the Congress. To this day I have not ceased regretting this October 25 crime of mine.

# 27.

# The October Days

*One of the key organizers of the Bolshevik underground and Lenin's partner,*
**Nadezdha Krupskaya**, *recalls Lenin's negotiations with Left SR leader Maria Spiridonova, aimed at cementing a pro-Soviet alliance and support for soviet power from poor and middle-class peasants.*[1]

The Second Congress of the Soviets was to be opened that evening [October 25]. It was to proclaim the power of the soviets and give official recognition to the victory of the revolution. Agitation was carried on among the delegates when they began to arrive. The government of the workers was to lean upon the peasantry, rally it behind them. The party that was supposed to express the views of the peasantry was the Socialist Revolutionaries. The rich peasantry, the kulaks, had their ideologists in the person of the Right Socialist Revolutionaries. The ideologists of the peasant masses, the Left Socialist Revolutionaries, were typical representatives of the petty bourgeoisie, which wavered between the bourgeoisie and the proletariat. The leaders of the Petrograd Committee of the Socialist Revolutionaries were Natanson, Spiridonova and Kamkov. Ilyich had met Natanson during his first emigration. At that time, in 1904, Natanson had stood fairly close to the Marxists, except that he had believed the Social Democrats to be underestimating the role of the peasantry. Spiridonova was a popular figure at that time. During the first revolution, in 1906, she, then a girl of seventeen, had assassinated Luzhenovsky, the suppressor of the peasant movement in the Tambov Gubernia. After being brutally tortured, she was condemned to penal servitude in Siberia, where she remained until the February Revolution.

The Left Socialist Revolutionaries of Petrograd were strongly influenced by the Bolshevik temper of the masses. They were more favorably inclined towards the Bolsheviks than any of the others. They saw that the Bolsheviks were out in all earnest to confiscate all the lands of the landowners and hand them over to the peasants. The Left Socialist Revolutionaries believed in introducing a system of equalized land tenure; the Bolsheviks realized that a complete reconstruction of agriculture on socialist lines was necessary. However, Ilyich considered that the most important thing at the moment was to confiscate the landowners' lands. As to what turn further reconstruction would take, experience itself would show. And he gave his thoughts to the drafting of a decree on the land.

The reminiscences of M.V. Fofanova contain a very interesting item. "I remember," she writes, "Vladimir Ilyich asking me to get him all the back numbers of *Izvestia*, the organ of the All-Russian Soviet of Peasants' Deputies, which I did, of course. I do not remember exactly how many numbers there were, but they made a solid batch of material for study. Vladimir Ilyich spent two days over it, working even at night. In the morning, he says to me,"

> "Well, I think I've studied these SRs inside out. All that remains is for me to read the mandate of their peasant electors." Two hours later he called me in and said cheerfully, slapping one of the newspapers (I saw it to be the August 19 issue of the peasant *Izvestia*): "Here's a ready-made agreement with the Left SRs. It's no joke—this mandate has been signed by 242 local deputies. We shall use it as the basis for our law concerning the land and see if the Left SRs dare to reject it." He showed me the paper with blue pencil markings all over it and added: "The thing is to find a means by which we could afterwards reshape their socialization idea after our own pattern."

Marguerite was an agronomist by profession and she came up against these problems in her work. It was, therefore, a subject on which Ilyich willingly spoke to her. Would the Left Socialist Revolutionaries quit the congress or not?

The Second All-Russian Congress of Soviets opened at 10:45 P.M. on October 25. That evening the congress was to be constituted, was to elect a presidium and define its powers. Of the 670 delegates, only 300 were Bolsheviks; 193 were Socialist Revolutionaries [divided between Left and Right SRs] and 68 Mensheviks. The Right Socialist Revolutionaries, Mensheviks and Bundists foamed at the mouth and thundered denunciations at the Bolsheviks. They read out a declaration of protest against the "military plot and seizure of power engineered by the Bolsheviks behind the backs of the other parties and factions represented on the Soviet" and walked out. Some of the Menshevik Internationalists quit too. The Left Socialist Revolutionaries, who formed the overwhelming majority of the SR delegates (169 out of 193), remained. Altogether fifty delegates quit the congress. [ . . . ]

When there was no doubt left that victory had been won [after the Winter Palace fell] and that the Left Socialist Revolutionaries would not quit the congress, Vladimir Ilyich, who had hardly slept the previous night and had taken an active part all the time in directing the uprising, left Smolny and went to sleep at the Bonch-Bruyeviches', who lived in Peski, not far from Smolny. He was given a room to himself, but he could not fall asleep for a long time. He got up quietly so as not to wake anybody and began to write the Decree on Land, which he had already thought out in every detail. Addressing the congress on the evening of October 26, in support of the Decree on Land, Ilyich said:

> Voices are being raised here that the decree itself and the mandate were drawn up by the Socialist Revolutionaries. What of it? Does it matter who drew them up? As a democratic government, we cannot ignore the decision of the rank and file of the people, even though we may disagree with it. In the fire of experience, applying the decree in practice, and carrying it out locally, the peasants will themselves realize where the truth lies. [ . . . ] Life is the best teacher and it will show who is right. Let the peasants solve this problem from one end and we shall solve it from the other.

We have all of Ilyich in those words—an Ilyich free from petty conceit (it does not matter who said it, so long as it says the right thing), taking into consideration the opinion of the rank and file, appreciating the power of revolutionary creative work, clearly understanding that the masses are best convinced by practice and experience, and that the hard facts of life would show them that the Bolsheviks' point of view had been correct. [ . . . ]

The decrees on Peace and Land were passed at the evening session on October 26. On these points agreement was reached with the SRs. On the question of forming a government, however, the position was worse. The Left SRs had not quitted the congress because they had realized that such an action would have cost them their influence among the peasant masses, but the withdrawal on October 25 of the Right SRs and the Mensheviks, and their outcries against the adventurism of the Bolsheviks, the seizure of power, etc., etc., had deeply affected them. After the Right SRs and the others had left the congress, Kamkov, one of the leaders of the Left SRs, declared that they stood for a united democratic government, and that the Left SRs would do everything they could to have such a government set up. The Left SRs said they wanted to act as mediators between the Bolsheviks and the parties who had left the congress.

The Bolsheviks did not refuse to negotiate, but Ilyich understood perfectly well that nothing would come of such talks. The Bolsheviks had not seized the power and made the revolution in order to hitch a swan, a pike and a crab to the Soviet cart, to form a government that would be incapable of pulling together and getting things done. Cooperation with the Left SRs, in Ilyich's opinion, was possible.

A talk on this question with representatives of the Left SRs was held a couple of hours before the congress opened on October 26. I remember the surroundings in which that conference was held. It was a room in Smolny with small settees upholstered in dark red. On one settee sat Spiridonova, and next to her stood Ilyich, arguing with her in a sort of gentle earnest manner. No agreement was reached with the Left SRs. They did not want to join the government. Ilyich proposed the appointment of Bolsheviks alone to the posts of socialist ministers. [ . . . ]

Eino Rahja relates that when the list of first People's Commissars was being discussed at a meeting of the Bolshevik group, he had been sitting in a corner listening. One of the nominees had protested that he had no experience in that kind of work. Vladimir Ilyich had burst out laughing and said: "Do you think any of us has had such experience?" None had any experience, of course.

# 28.

# A New Power

*Trotsky describes the process of constructing an entirely new form of government from the ashes of the old capitalist state as well as the intense ongoing negotiations with other left-wing parties over power sharing. And alongside the intricacies of their new responsibilities, he relays the psychological impact of political power on the workers and peasants who fought, and won, the revolution.[1]*

The capital awoke under a new power. [ . . . ]

The reactionary French journalist, Claude Anet, wrote on this day: "The victors are singing a song of victory. And quite rightly too. Among all these blabbers they alone acted. [ . . . ] Today they are reaping the harvest. Bravo! Fine work." The Mensheviks estimated the situation quite otherwise. "Twenty-four hours have passed since the 'victory' of the Bolsheviks," wrote Dan's paper, "and the historic fates have already begun to take their cruel revenge. [ . . . ] Around them is an emptiness created by themselves. [ . . . ] They are isolated from all. [ . . . ] The entire clerical and technical machinery refuses to serve them. [ . . . ] They are sliding at the very moment of their triumph into the abyss."

During that day, the Central Committee of the Bolsheviks was at work in Smolny. It was deciding the problem of the new government of Russia. No minutes were kept—or they have not been preserved. Nobody was bothering about future historians, although a lot of trouble was being prepared for them right there. The evening session of the Congress was to create a cabinet of ministers. *M-i-n-i-s-t-e-r-s*? What a sadly compromised word! It stinks of the high bureaucratic career, the crowning of some parliamentary ambition. It was decided to call the government the Soviet of People's Commissars: that at least had a fresher sound. Since the negotiations for a coalition of the "entire democracy" had come to nothing, the question of the party and personal staff of the government was simplified. The Left Social-Revolutionaries minced and objected. Having just broken with the party of Kerensky, they themselves hardly knew what they wanted to do. The Central Committee adopted the motion of Lenin as the only thinkable one: to form a government of Bolsheviks only. [ ... ]

Lenin, whom the Congress has not yet seen, is given the floor for a report on peace. His appearance in the tribune evokes a tumultuous greeting. The trench delegates gaze with all their eyes at this mysterious being whom they had been taught to hate and whom they have learned without seeing him to love. "Now Lenin, gripping the edges of the reading-stand, let little winking eyes travel over the crowd as he stood there waiting, apparently oblivious to the long-rolling ovation, which lasted several minutes. When it finished, he said simply, 'We shall now proceed to construct the socialist order.'"

The minutes of the Congress are not preserved. The parliamentary stenographers, invited in to record the debates, had abandoned Smolny, along with the Mensheviks and Social-Revolutionaries. That was one of the first episodes in the campaign of sabotage. The secretarial notes have been lost without a trace in the abyss of events. There remain only the hasty and tendentious newspaper reports, written to the tune of the artillery or the grinding of teeth in the political struggle. Lenin's speeches have suffered especially. Owing to his swift delivery and the complicated construction of his sentences, they are not easily recorded even in more favorable conditions. That initial statement which John Reed puts in the mouth of Lenin does not appear in any of the newspaper accounts. But it is wholly in the spirit of the orator. Reed could not have made it up. Just in that way Lenin must surely have begun his speech at the Congress of Soviets—simply, without unction, with inflexible confidence: "We shall now proceed to construct the socialist order." [ ... ]

Sukhanov, an attentive although also prejudiced observer, noticed more than once at that first session the listlessness of the Congress. Undoubtedly the delegates—like all the people, indeed—were tired of meetings, congresses, speeches, resolutions, tired of the whole business of marking time. They had no confidence that this Congress would be able and know how to carry the thing through to the end. Will not the gigantic size of the task and the insuperable opposition compel them to back down this time too? An influx of confidence had come with the news of the capture of the Winter Palace, and afterward with the coming over of the bicycle men to the insurrection. But both these facts still had to do with the mechanics of insurrection. Only now was its historic meaning becoming clear in action. The victorious insurrection had built under this congress of workers and soldiers an indestructible foundation of power. The delegates were voting this time not for a resolution, not for a proclamation, but for a governmental act of immeasurable significance.

Listen, nations! The revolution offers you peace. It will be accused of violating treaties. But of this it is proud. To break up the leagues of bloody predation is the greatest historic service. The Bolsheviks have dared to do it. They alone have dared. Pride surges up of its own accord. Eyes shine. All are on their feet. No one is smoking now. It seems as though no one breathes. The præsidium, the delegates, the guests, the sentries, join in a hymn of insurrection and brotherhood. "Suddenly, by common impulse"—the story will soon be told by John Reed, observer and participant, chronicler and poet of the insurrection—"we found ourselves on our feet, mumbling together into the smooth lifting unison of the Internationale. A grizzled old soldier was sobbing like a child. Alexandra Kollontai rapidly winked the tears back. The immense sound rolled through the hall, burst windows and doors and seared into the quiet sky." Did it go altogether into the sky? Did it not go also to the autumn trenches, that hatch-work upon unhappy, crucified Europe, to her devastated cities and villages, to her mothers and wives in mourning?

"Arise ye prisoners of starvation! Arise ye wretched of the earth!" The words of the song were freed of all qualifications. They fused with the decree of the government, and hence resounded with the force of a direct act. Everyone felt greater and more important in that hour. The heart of the revolution enlarged to the width of the whole world. "We will achieve emancipation. The spirit of independence, of initiative, of daring, those joyous feelings of which the oppressed in ordinary conditions are deprived—the revolution had brought them now [ . . . ] with our own hand!" The omnipotent hand of those millions who had overthrown the monarchy and the bourgeoisie would now strangle the war. The Red Guard from the Vyborg district, the grey soldier with his scar, the old revolutionist who had served his years at hard labor, the young black-bearded sailor from the *Aurora*—all vowed to carry through to the end this "last and deciding fight." "We will build our own new world!" We will build! In that word eagerly spoken from the heart was included already the future years of the civil war and the coming five-year periods of labor and privation.

"Who was nothing shall be all!" And if the actualities of the past have often been turned into song, why shall not a song be turned into the actuality of the future? Those trench coats no longer seemed the costumes of galley-slaves. The *papakhi* [wool hats] with their holes and torn cotton took on a new aspect above those gleaming eyes. "The race of man shall rise again!" Is it possible to believe that it will not rise from the misery and humiliation, the blood and filth of this war? [ . . . ]

What the Congress experienced during those minutes was experienced on the next day, although less compactly, by the whole country. "It must be said," writes Stankevich, in his memoirs, "that the bold gesture of the Bolsheviks, their ability to step over the barbed-wire entanglements which had for four years divided us from the neighboring peoples, created of itself an enormous impression."

Baron Budberg expresses himself more crudely but no less succinctly in his diary:

> The new government of Comrade Lenin went off with a decree for immedi-ate peace. [ . . . ] This was now an act of genius for bringing the soldier masses to his side. I saw this in the mood of several regiments which I made the rounds of today; the telegram of Lenin on an immediate three months' armi-stice and then peace, created a colossal impression everywhere, and evoked stormy joy. We have now lost the last chance of saving the front.

Lenin is again in the tribune—this time with the little sheets of a Decree on Land. He begins with an indictment of the overthrown government and the compromisist parties, who by dragging out the land question have brought the country to a peasant revolt. "Their talk about pogroms and anarchy in the country rings false with cowardly deceit. Where and when have pogroms and anarchy been caused by 'reasonable measures?' The draft of the decree has not been multigraphed for distribution. The speaker has the sole rough draft in his hands, and it is written so badly," Sukhanov remembers, "that Lenin stumbles in the reading, gets mixed up, and finally stops entirely. Somebody from the crowd jammed around the tribune comes to his help. Lenin eagerly yields his place and the undecipherable paper." These rough spots did not, however, in the eyes of that plebeian parliament diminish by an iota the grandeur of which was taking place. [ . . . ]

A last problem remains: the creation of a government. Kamenev reads a proposal drawn up by the Central Committee of the Bolsheviks. The man-agement of the various branches of the state life is allotted to commissions who are to carry into action the program announced by the Congress of So-viets "in close union with the mass organization of working men and women, sailors, soldiers, peasants and clerical employees." The governmental power is concentrated in the hands of a collegium composed of the presidents of these commissions, to be called the Soviet of People's Commissars. Control over the activities of the government is vested in the Congress of Soviets and its Central Executive Committee. [ . . . ] All fifteen candidates, four workers and eleven intellectuals, have behind them years of imprisonment, exile and emigrant life. Five of them have been imprisoned even under the régime of the democratic republic. The future prime minister had only the day before emerged from the democratic underground. [ . . . ]

A representative of the Left Social-Revolutionaries, Karelin, spoke. [ . . . ] It is impossible to carry out the program adopted without those parties which have withdrawn from the Congress. To be sure "the Bolsheviks are not to blame for their withdrawal." But the program of the Congress ought to unite the entire democracy.

> We do not want to take the road of isolating the Bolsheviks, for we understand that with the fate of the Bolsheviks is bound up the fate of the whole revolution. Their ruin will be the ruin of the revolution. If they, the Left Social-Revolutionaries, have nevertheless declined the invitation to enter the government, their purpose is a good one: to keep their hands free for mediation between the Bolsheviks and the parties which have abandoned the Congress. In such mediations . . . the Left Social-Revolutionaries see their principal task at the present moment.

The Left Social-Revolutionaries will support the work of the new government in solving urgent problems. At the same time they vote against the proposed government. In a word the young party has got mixed up as badly as it knows how. [ . . . ]

The Council of People's Commissars was ratified by an overwhelming majority. Avilov's resolution [along the lines of Karelin's quote above], according to the excessively generous estimate of Sukhanov, got 150 votes, chiefly Left Social-Revolutionaries. The Congress then unanimously confirmed the membership of the new Central Executive Committee: out of 101 members—62 Bolsheviks, 29 Left Social-Revolutionaries. The Central Executive Committee was to complete itself in the future with representatives of the peasant soviets and the re-elected army organizations. The factions who had abandoned the Congress were granted the right to send their delegates to the Central Executive Committee on the basis of proportional representation.

The agenda of the Congress was completed! The Soviet government was created. It had its program. The work could begin. And there was no lack of it. At 5:15 in the morning [on October 27] Kamenev closed the Constituent Congress of the Soviet regime. To the stations! Home! To the front! To the factories and barracks! To the mines and the far-off villages. In the decrees of the Soviet, the delegates will carry the leaven of the proletarian revolution to all corners of the country.

On that morning the central organ of the Bolshevik Party, again under the old name *Pravda*, wrote:

> They wanted us to take the power alone, so that we alone should have to contend with the terrible difficulties confronting the country. [ . . . ] So be it! We take the power alone, relying upon the voice of the country and counting upon the friendly help of the European proletariat. But having taken the power, we will deal with the enemies of revolution and its saboteurs with an iron hand. They dreamed of a dictatorship of Kornilov. [ . . . ] We will give them the dictatorship of the proletariat.

# VI.

# WORKERS' POWER

*Although the Bolsheviks had hoped to enjoy a more or less extended period of transition, in which workers and peasants could wrest control by degree from their former masters, this was not to be. Rather than submit to the democratic will expressed by the Soviets, the ruling class, the old tsarist/capitalist state bureaucracy, and the officers did everything in their power to sabotage the new workers state in hopes of its early collapse. October did not mark the end of the revolution; far from it. It entered a phase of civil war; only now it was the capitalists, landlords, and officers who were scattered and divided, while the workers created their own state instrument to suppress the counterrevolution, initiate peace negotiations, guarantee workers' control in the factories, and safeguard the peasants' control over the land.*

# 29.

# Kerensky Is Coming!

*After he escaped capture at the Winter Palace, Kerensky fled to the outskirts of St. Petersburg, to a suburb called Gatchina. While the October uprising was relatively bloodless in St. Petersburg itself, reactionary forces, now with Kerensky at their head, immediately attempted to retake power. Here, **John Reed** races to the front lines to provide this account of what happened next, along the way showing how creativity, spontaneity, and not a small amount of improvisation held the revolution together in its earliest days.*[1]

"Kerensky is coming!"

In Smolny Institute, where the Bolsheviks rode the rocking insurrection, there was half-panic, half-desperation among all the leaders except Lenin, Trotsky, and one or two others; among the soldiers hesitation; among the workmen and the Cronstadt sailors a fierce exultant defiance. Kerensky, hurling proclamations and threats as he came, rolled up from the southwest with a horde of Cossacks, to win back the capital.

It was October 29. The Bolsheviks had been in control three days, with the world against them. Under their iron hands the city seethed and boiled. At the Duma, around which were grouped all the anti-Bolshevik elements—the moderate and conservative socialists as well the "bourgeois" parties—a great crowd was gathered, composed of business and professional men, socialist "intellectuals," and the officials of the Government; there were present no common soldiers, no workingmen, no peasants.

At this particular moment the Committee for Salvation of Country and

165

Revolution was forming a new government, and debating hotly whether or not the representatives of the Bolshevik party should be admitted. Around it swarmed army officers, journalists, and the foreign diplomats.

Kerensky was only twelve miles away—eight miles—four miles, with an army of five thousand—ten thousand—twenty thousand men. He had captured [the town of] Gatchina, the Gatchina Soviet had fled, half the garrison had surrendered and the other half had fallen back in disorder on Petrograd. He was at the gates of Tsarskoe Selo. He would triumphantly enter the city in two days [or] twelve hours.

Up at Smolny, the Military Revolutionary Committee roared like a flywheel day and night, throwing off spark-like showers of orders. Here the dim corridors echoed to the tramp of hurrying factory-workers with crossed bandoleers, and rifles, grim, silent men, hollow-eyed from loss of sleep, and with aimless wandering bands of soldiers. On piles of heaped-up newspapers and proclamations in the committee rooms hundreds snored in utter exhaustion. Couriers came and went, running or in commandeered automobiles; and commissars, common soldiers, workmen, armed with the power of life and death, invested with the authority of the risen proletariat, dashed out to the four corners of the city, the front, and all vast Russia, to command, plead, argue, fight.

In the great white ballroom the Petrograd Soviet met, a bristle of bayonets, and in the next chamber the Central Executive Committee of the All-Russian Soviets, the new parliament of proletarian Russia. Consider these Bolsheviks. Alone they had set up a Government in which the Minister of Finance was appointed because he had once been a clerk in a French bank—there was no other man to put there; in which the Minister of Commerce and Industry was a historian, without the slightest conception of commerce. The army and navy were under the command of a common sailor, Dubenko, a cadet, Krilenko, and a civilian, Antonov.

All the Government employees had declared a strike against them. The Post and Telegraph Employees' Union refused to transmit their telegrams or deliver their mail. The Railway Workers' Union would not transport them. Their very telephone wires were cut.

They could not communicate with the provinces, with the front, or with Europe. They did not know what was going on anywhere. Outside of a few trained and educated men they were supported only by the masses of the Petrograd workmen and women and soldiers. Was Russia like Petrograd? Were the workmen everywhere ready for insurrection? Would the Army at the front rise? Would the peasants support them? Lenin believed that Russia was ripe.

The All-Russian Soviets had met on October 26 and endorsed the Revolution by an overwhelming majority—and now the delegates were speeding back to their homes, to the corners of Russia, carrying word of what had happened in Petrograd. Volodarski told me that even if the All-Russian Soviets had been prevented from meeting, still there would have been an insurrection. "We are realists," he said. As a matter of fact, success depended on the correctness of the hypothesis that the Russian proletariat was ready for revolt.

In the courtyard of Smolny Institute stood an automobile, upon the running-board of which soldiers were trying to fasten two bicycles. The chauffeur protested violently. True, he was a Bolshevik, and the automobile had been [duly requisitioned], it was to carry the Ministers of War and of the Navy to the front, and the bicycles were for the use of the couriers; but the automobile was nicely enameled, and the chauffeur's professional pride revolted at the damage which would be done to the enamel. So the bicycles were abandoned.

Leaning against the side of the machine was a slight man with a thin beard and heavy glasses over eyes fixed and red-rimmed from three days and nights without rest, his shirt collar filthy, his conversation painful and chaotic from terrible fatigue. A great bearded sailor, with the clear eyes of youth, prowled restlessly about, absently toying with an enormous blue-steel revolver, which never left his hand. These were Antonov and Dubenko.

Could we go with them to the front? We could not. The automobile would only hold five—the two Ministers, two couriers and the chauffeur. My Russian comrade, however, whom I will call Koslov, calmly got in and sat down, nor could any argument dislodge him; so finally Antonov and Dubenko gave up.

I see no reason to disbelieve Koslov's story of the trip. As they went down the Souvorovsky Prospect, someone mentioned that they might be out for three or four days, in a country indifferently provisioned. Antonov stopped the car and asked Koslov to get out and buy provisions—about fifty rubles' worth. Money? The Minister of War looked through his pockets—he hadn't a kopek. The Minister of the Navy was broke. So was the chauffeur. So were the couriers. Koslov bought the provisions.

When they reached the Nevsky the automobile blew out a tire, and all got out. "Commandeer an automobile!" suggested Dubenko, waving the revolver. Antonov stood in the middle of the street and signaled to a passing machine to halt.

"I want that automobile!" he said to the lone soldier who was driving.

"You won't get it," responded the soldier.

"Do you know who I am?" asked Antonov, producing a paper upon which was written a commission appointing him Commander-in-Chief of all the armies of the Russian Republic. "In this paper it says that all my orders must be obeyed without question."

"I don't care if you are the devil himself," retorted the soldier. "This automobile belongs to the committee of the First Machine Gun Regiment, and we're carrying ammunition in it, and you can't have it." Whereupon he drove on.

The difficulty, however, was soon solved by the appearance of an old battered machine flying the Italian flag (in time of trouble private machines were registered in the name of some foreign consulate, so as to be safe from requisition), from the interior of which was dislodged a fat citizen in an expensive fur coat, and the party continued on its way.

Arrived at Colpinno, a factory town about twenty miles out on the Nicolai Railway, Antonov asked for the commandant of the Red Guard. He was led to the edge of town where about 500 factory workmen had dug trenches and were waiting for the Cossacks.

"Everything all right here, comrade?" asked Antonov.

"Everything is perfect, comrade," answered the commander, "except that we have no ammunition."

"In Smolny there are two billion rounds," Antonov told him. "I will give you an order." He felt in his pockets. "Has anybody a piece of paper?"

Dubenko had none. The chauffeur had none—neither had the couriers or the commander. Koslov offered his notebook, from which a page was torn.

"Have you got a pencil?" asked Antonov, rummaging through his clothes. Dubenko had no pencil—neither, needless to say, had anyone—except Koslov.

Meanwhile late in the afternoon I took a train for Tsarskoe Selo. In the station nobody knew just where Kerensky was, or where the front lay. Trains went no further, however, than Tsarskoe Selo. The train was full of commuters and country people going home. They had the evening papers in their hands, and the talk was all of the Bolshevik rising. Outside of that, however, you would never have realized that civil war was splitting mighty Russia in two, and that the train was headed into the zone of battle.

Out of the window we could see, in the swift-deepening darkness, masses of soldiers going irregularly along the muddy road toward the city, flinging their arms out in argument. That was all. Back along the flat horizon the glow of the city's lights faded down the night. A streetcar crawled distantly along a far-flung suburban street. Tsarskoe Selo station was calm, though knots of soldiers stood here and there talking in low tones and looking uneasily down the empty track that led to Gatchina. I asked some of them what side they were on. "Well," said a spokesman, "we don't know exactly the rights of the matter. There is no doubt that Kerensky is a provocateur, but we do not consider it right for Russian men to be shooting Russian men."

The commandant of the station proved to be a big, jovial, bearded common soldier, wearing the armband of a regimental committee. Our credentials from Smolny Institute commanded immediate respect. He was plainly for the Soviets, but bewildered.

"There was a commissar from the Soviets here this morning, but he went away when the Cossacks came."

"The Cossacks are here, then?"

He nodded, gloomily. "There has been a battle. The Cossacks came this morning. They captured two or three hundred of our troops, and killed about twelve."

"Where are the Cossacks?"

"Well, they didn't come down here. I don't know just where they are. Off that way." He waved his arm vaguely west.

We had dinner—an excellent dinner, by the way, much better and cheaper than could be got in Petrograd—in the station restaurant, and sallied out into the town. Just outside the door were two soldiers, evidently on guard, with the rifles and bayonets fixed. They were surrounded by crowded businessmen, Government officials, and students, who were attacking them with a passionate argument and epithet. The soldiers were uncomfortable and hurt, like children who are being unjustly scolded. A tall young man with a supercilious expression, dressed in a uniform of the student, was leading the attack.

"You realize, I presume," he said insolently, "that by taking up arms against your brothers you are making yourself the tools of murderers and traitors?"

"Now brother," answer the soldier earnestly, "you don't understand. There are two classes don't you see, the proletariat and the bourgeoisie. We—"

"Oh, I know that silly talk!" broke in the student rudely. "A bunch of ignorant peasants like you hear somebody bawling a few catch words. You don't understand what they mean. You just echo them like a lot of parrots." The crowd laughed. "Now I've been a Socialist for twenty years. I'm a Marxian student. And I tell you that this isn't Socialism that you are fighting for. It's just plain pro-German anarchy!"

"Oh yes, I know," answered the soldier, with sweat dripping from his brow. "You are an educated man, that is easy to see, and I only a simple man. But it seems to me—"

"I suppose," interrupted the other contemptuously, "that you believe Lenin is a real friend of the proletariat?"

"Yes, I do," answered the soldier, suffering.

"Well my friend, do you know that Lenin was sent through Germany in a closed car? Do you know that Lenin took money from the Germans?"

"Well, I don't know much about that," answered the soldier stubbornly, "but it seems to me that what he says is what I want, and all the simple men like me. Now there are two classes, the bourgeoisie and the proletariat—"

"You are a fool! Why, my friend, I spent two years in Shlisselburg [Prison] for revolutionary activity, when you were still shooting down revolutionists and singing 'God Save the Tsar.' My name is Vasili Georgevitch Panim. Didn't you ever hear of me?"

"I'm sorry to say I never did," answered the soldier with humility. "But then, I am not an educated man. You are probably a great hero."

"I am," said the student with conviction. "And I am opposed to the Bolsheviks, who are destroying our Russia, our free revolution. Now how do you account for that?"

The soldier scratched his head. "I can't account for it at all," he said, grimacing with the pain of his intellectual processes. "To me it seems perfectly simple—but then, I'm not well-educated. It seems like there are only two classes, the proletariat and the bourgeoisie—"

"There you go again with your silly formula!" cried the student.

"—only two classes," went on the soldier, doggedly. "And whoever isn't on one side is on the other." [ . . . ]

The next morning the Cossacks entered Tsarskoe Selo, Kerensky himself riding a white horse. From the top of a little hill beyond the town he could see the golden spires and many-colored cupolas, the sprawling grey immensity of the capital spread out along the dreary plain, and beyond, the steely Gulf of Finland. Every hour General Krasnov was issuing proclamations, "In the name of the Supreme Commandant, at the head of the loyal troops under Petrograd," calling upon the Petrograd garrison to return to their duty, and "all those who have been led astray by false counsels or the vain promises of the usurpers"—under pain of dire punishment when the city fell. Ten miles away! The Bolshevik troops falling back in the direst confusion; a revolution ready to break in the capital; the Bolsheviks isolated.

[As it turned out,] there was no battle in Tsarskoe after all. But Kerensky made one fatal mistake. Ascertaining that there were "neutral" regiments in the vicinity, he adopted a high-handed method of dealing with them. To the barracks of the Second Tsarskoe Selo Rifles he sent a message to surrender their arms and gave them ten minutes to think it over in. Now this savored too much of the old regime to the soldiers, who, after all, had been governing themselves by committing for half a year. They were not Bolsheviks, they did not want to fight Kerensky; but they would not submit to peremptory authority. At the end of the ten minutes Kerensky's artillery dropped a shell or two on their barracks; seven were killed, more wounded; and from that moment the Second Tsarskoe Selo Rifles ceased to be neutral.

In Petrograd, Smolny was a huge uproar. A delegation from the Semionov Regiment, sent out to stop the Cossacks, was trying to explain to the Military Revolutionary Committee how it was that most of them had been surrounded and captured. The regiments of the garrison, it was reported, had been corrupted by commissars of the City Duma, who had been around trying to persuade the soldiers to remain "neutral," so that the Cossacks and *junkers* might be turned loose in the city; Krilenko started out in a fast automobile to make the rounds of the barracks and win them back. We had witnessed, in the vast half-gloom of the Mikhailovsky Manege, the battle of speakers over the Armored Car Division, the far-famed *Brunnoviki;* where, in the bitter cold, two thousand great child-like men stood, listening with painful intensity to the arguments of the different speakers for five long hours, and finally went Bolshevik with the ponderous roar of an avalanche

A message arrived from Pulkova, this side of the Tsarskoe Selo, where the Bolsheviks were digging trenches, asking for "two truck-loads of orators." This is the Russian way of making civil war. It was the *propaganda* of the revolutionary troops which destroyed the forces of Kornilov. Russians will always listen. In this case the old proclamations and pamphlets used against Kornilov were resurrected and shipped to the front. Eighteen agitators were collected by the Military Revolutionary Committee, and hurtled off down the street in motor trucks, to corrupt the enemy.

On Saturday at three o'clock, the Military Revolutionary Committee loosed the full revolutionary force of the proletariat; a telephonogram was sent out to the factories to shut down and turn out the Red Guard. All around the grey horizon the whistles blew, and the hundreds of thousands of workers poured out in tides, bristling. Petrograd hummed like a beaten hive. Along the broad roads white with the first light fall of snow, the city belched its slums. As far as the eye could reach the roads were crowded with rifles—and crossed cartridge belts over their working clothes—women, some with guns, some with spades, picks, some carrying rolls of bandages, red crosses pinned on their arms, children [too]. Such an immense, spontaneous outpouring of a city was never seen! They rolled along torrent-like, companies of soldiers borne with them, guns, auto-trucks, wagons—the revolutionary proletariat defending with its naked breast the capital of the Socialist republic.

That night Kerensky and his Cossacks attacked all along a wide front, and untrained masses of people made a stand. What had happened to all that disorganization, panic? What change had come over those halves of garrisons which had retreated in disorder? Who had brought order out of chaos, and coordinated between the thousands of wavering regulars and hundreds of thousands of untrained workers? Nobody—nothing—but the concerted desire that the new revolution should win, that forever the powers of "coalition" and the Cossacks should be smashed. Things were done that night at Krasnoe Selo, at Pulkova, which will never be forgotten in the history of revolutions. The Red Guards rushed in masses, rushed the cannon, rushed the Cossacks and pulled them from their horses. Hundreds of workers were killed, and the plain was full of riderless Cossack steeds when morning came, and truce.

Zalkind, later Trotsky's adjunct in the Commissariat of Foreign Affairs, was riding in an automobile with Vera Sloutskaya, a veteran woman revolutionist, after both sides had agreed to stop firing. The train on which Kerensky rode carried a cannon, and I suppose the gunner couldn't resist the temptation to take a shot at the lone machine with the red flag floating over it. The shell went through the automobile, carrying away a door. Zalkind, who was in the midst of a discussion with Sloutskaya, turned around in the middle of a sentence to find himself addressing a corpse—Sloutskaya's chin and breast had been torn off. [ . . . ]

Kerensky was at Gatchina. The Cossacks were discontented. They had been beaten and then, too, it seemed that all Russia was up against them, whereas they had been told that Petrograd, rich Petrograd, would hold out welcoming arms. In this frame of mind "two truckloads of orators" descended upon their outposts. And toward nightfall arrived the redoubtable Dubenko, alone.

What Dubenko said no one knows, but the fact is that General Krasnov and his staff and several thousand Cossack troopers surrendered, and advised Kerensky to do the same. General Krasnov advised Kerensky to go to Petrograd with an escort, proudly, as head of the Provisional Government, and deal face to face with the Bolsheviks in Smolny. If Kerensky had followed this advice, he might still have been a power in Russia. But instead, he promised to do so, and then disguised himself in a sailor's uniform and ran away. And that was the end of Kerensky.

I went back to Petrograd riding on the front seat of an auto truck, driven by a workman, and filled with Red Guards. We had no kerosene, so our lights were not burning. The road was crowded with the proletarian army going home, and new reserves pouring out to take their places. Immense trucks like ours, columns of artillery, wagons, loomed up in the night, without lights, as we were. We hurtled furiously on, wrenched right and left to avoid collisions that seemed inevitable, scraping wheels, followed by the epithets of pedestrians. Across the horizon spread the glittering lights of the capital, immeasurably more splendid by night than by day, like a low dike of jewels heaped on the barren plain.

The old workman who drove held the wheel in one hand, while with the other he swept the far-gleaming capital in an exultant gesture.

"Mine!" he cried, his face all alight. "All mine now! My Petrograd!"

# 30.

# The Fall of the Constituent Assembly

*The Left Socialist Revolutionaries (or Social-Revolutionaries, as they were also known), led by Maria Spiridonova, provided provisional support for the October Revolution; however, it was not until weeks afterwards that the Left SRs constituted themselves as a formal party independent from the anti-Soviet Right SRs, led by Victor Chernov, the former agriculture minister in the now-deposed Provisional Government. By mid-November, attempts by the Left SRs and Bolsheviks like Kamenev and Zinoviev to create a broader pro-Soviet coalition had failed, thanks to opposition from Right Mensheviks and SRs, as well as Lenin and Trotsky's unwillingness to make significant concessions in terms of the Soviet's program. Nevertheless, the Left SRs agreed to join the Council of People's Commissars, taking seven positions to the Bolsheviks' fifteen, including **Isaac Nachman Steinberg**, who served as the People's Commissar for Justice.*

*One of the main debates in the Bolshevik/Left SR coalition was whether to convene the Constituent Assembly, which the Bolsheviks had long championed prior to October. Today it is often presented as an example of the Bolsheviks' antidemocratic practice. Here, Steinberg shows why the Right SR majority in the Constituent Assembly was illegitimate and why responsibility for the collapse of the Constituent Assembly lay predominantly with the Right SRs, even if he apportioned part of the blame to Lenin and Trotsky as well.[1]*

And in the meantime a new crisis loomed. The Constituent Assembly was still due to convene. To all political parties, without exception, the forthcoming Assembly seemed like an iceberg, its dangerous bulk hidden beneath the political

175

waves. All moderate socialists hoped that the Constituent Assembly, with the prestige of its majestic name, would overrun the entire Soviet system. The Bolsheviks foresaw a violent collision between these two pretenders to power in revolutionary Russia. Given the chance, they would have prevented this unpredictable Assembly from ever appearing before the people.

The Left Social-Revolutionaries disagreed vehemently. They demanded that the people witness the Assembly—which they had waited so long for—in action and then decide on its role within the new historic situation created after October. That is why on December 18, 1917, four Left Social-Revolutionary Peoples Commissars—Karelin, Kalegayev, Trutovsky, Steinberg—introduced a written motion that the next session of the Council of People's Commissars discuss the convening of the Constituent Assembly. [ . . . ]

The Left Social-Revolutionaries had few illusions about the approaching crisis. They knew that a large section of the deputies would belong to the Social-Revolutionary Party, which represented the most numerous class in the people, that is, the peasants. But had the voters during the elections for the Constituent Assembly known the difference between the right and left wings of the party? The list of candidates for the Social-Revolutionary Party had been made up some time before the October upheaval, when the left wing had had no separate existence. This upheaval had divided the two wings into opposing camps. Would the two come to an agreement in the Constituent Assembly?

The protracted, painful negotiations between socialist parties concerning the establishment of a unified government had been broken off at the end of November. The moderates had refused to yield on any of their dogmatic conditions because of their intransigence toward the Soviet revolt. And they would all return in the Constituent Assembly: the same personalities, demands, and emotions. Was any agreement possible?

There was no agreement. When, on January 5, deputies from all over Russia assembled in the Tauride Palace, they were sharply divided. It was a patent fact that the Constituent Assembly was no longer the only sovereign institution as had been intended during the long months of the year 1917; alongside it, and really above it, was the Soviet power. And the most fundamental aspect of the explosive situation was that while the Constituent Assembly was still only a political idea and a promise, the Soviet Government had already emerged as a fighting and active force, changing and reforming the country. The government was already conducting negotiations for peace; it had already published the decree on land socialization; it had already admitted the workers to the production process.

And so the magnificent hall of the Tauride Palace held the two camps: the "democratic" Social-Revolutionaries and the soviets, the Bolsheviks and the Left Social-Revolutionaries. (It is important to emphasize that neither the Mensheviks nor the Kadets played any role in that drama.) Once more the split was immediately apparent in the two names proposed for presidency of the Assembly: the right wing proposed Victor Chernov; the left, Maria Spiridinova. Chernov won the contest by 244 votes to 153 and, in his "speech from the throne," he gave no indication of a desire to find a common ground with the already existing political reality.

Of all possible attitudes toward the soviets, Chernov (and the Right Social-Revolutionary Party that stood behind him) chose the most dangerous, if not the most foolish, tactic: he simply *ignored* the soviets, as if they did not exist at all. His major speech, which naturally encompassed all cardinal issues of the revolution, was delivered with the incredible pretense that the Constituent Assembly had convened in a social vacuum. He announced that negotiations for peace would be started with the Allied powers; that the socialization of land would be carried through; that the federative rights of all nationalities would be proclaimed. Now with a single word he mentioned that all these vital tasks had already been realized in the country and followed with intense interest in the whole world.

What did all this mean? By implication it was a challenge to the Soviets and the masses that stood by them. For the Constituent Assembly, the only chance of survival lay in some compromise with the revolutionary forces that had already struck roots. It would have been easy to find some legal, constitutional, and political form for such understanding—had but will been there on both sides. But this one way of averting civil war within the camp of the working people was ignored by the majority. Did it then hope that the Soviets would simply capitulate?

There were no agreements. No common language was found even though both camps had, at the start of this memorable session, sung the Internationale in unison. A tragic pall hung over the agitated Council Chamber. Rarely had so many socialist leaders, martyrs, and fighters of Russia assembled in one place. Hundreds of their names were engraved as living legends in the memory of the people. And yet there was no hope of fraternity. The left wing—first the Bolsheviks and much later also the Left Social-Revolutionaries—read statements saying that, under the circumstances, they could not remain in the Assembly and were withdrawing from it. Thus the structure of this institution was crippled.

Chernov continued the session as if nothing happened and in great haste let the Assembly—without debates—adopt a series of laws based on the program of his major speech. But everybody felt, how unreal, ghostlike were these laws in the heated atmosphere of the moment. It was about four o'clock in the morning of January 6, 1918, when Chernov declared the session officially closed and announced that the Assembly would meet again the next day.

The deputies left the Tauride Palace unmolested and quickly vanished in the city. No attempt was made by the Soviet authorities to disperse them by violence.

The leaders of the Constituent Assembly did not make any determined effort to assemble for a second session. [ . . .] Neither did the masses of Petrograd rise in defense of the Constituent Assembly that January 6, 1918, as many in the country had expected. And that proved more tellingly than any argument that there was no longer room for the pre-October Constituent Assembly in this new phase of Russian history.

# 31.

# Radek at Brest-Litovsk

*The Bolsheviks dispatched Trotsky, his close friend and confidant Adolf Joffe, and Karl Radek, an Austrian citizen of Jewish ancestry active in Polish and German revolutionary politics, to the Polish city of Brest-Litovsk to negotiate peace with Germany. Rather than carry on as diplomats, the Bolshevik team distributed antiwar leaflets to the assembled German soldiers, denounced their adversaries as imperialists, and called on working people in Germany and Austria to rise up and overthrow their rulers, just as the Bolsheviks had done.*

*The talks failed and, on February 18, 1918, the Germans attacked on a broad front, quickly seizing Belarus, the Ukraine, and the Baltic states. Lenin convinced the majority of the Bolshevik leadership to sue for peace, concluding the Brest-Litovsk Treaty on March 3 and relinquishing much of Russia's food supply, industrial base, fuel supplies, and communications with Western Europe. But a little more than seven months later, sailors, soldiers, and workers overthrew the German Kaiser, declaring a democratic republic and bringing the war to a swift end. William Hard reports the testimony of American colonel **Ray Robins** of the Red Cross about Radek's role at Brest-Litovsk.[1]*

Radek was the most powerful propagandist, as well as the most powerful journalist, among the Bolsheviks. Like many other men prominent at Smolny, he had been badly treated by the Teutonic autocracy, which Allied diplomats accused him of loving and serving.

He was an Austrian and his front teeth had been knocked out by the German-Austrian police in a revolutionary street-battle. Afterward, in Switzerland, in

179

1915, when Radek was writing socialist revolutionary propaganda for distribution among the German soldiers on the Western front, the German government demanded that the Swiss government expel him from Swiss soil. Radek, at Brest-Litovsk, two years later, met the Austrian and German governments face to face. His specialty was to make them feel insecure about their own peoples and about their own futures.

Count Czernin alluded to him one day as a "Russian." "My nationality, Count," said Radek, "is not Russian. It is the same as yours—Austrian. It's not nationality that puts us on the other side of the table from you."

To Brest-Litovsk Radek carefully carried a certain book. It was a book well known in Germany and suppressed there. It was an argument for the military proposition (not unnoted by Napoleon) that in war the final factor is numbers. Therefore, in the end, against the Germans the Allies must win. The German generals at Brest-Litovsk were fully acquainted with this book. Radek kept it prominently on the table before their eyes. "In the end," he once said, "the Allies will put a Brest-Litovsk Treaty on *you*."

Radek also introduced at Brest-Litovsk a practice which frankly revealed the social notions and the social purposes of the Russian delegates. The Germans treated the Russian delegates as professional diplomats, as excellencies, as persons now in the high world of the ruling classes. They treated them so, and they wanted them to behave so. Radek expressed the Soviet contempt for all of it and the Soviet farewell to all of it by shaking hands with the German privates who stood about as attendants and by addressing them cordially and prophetically, in the presence of their officers, as "comrades."

Back in Petrograd Radek's opinion of the Teutonic governments appeared profusely in his daily writings. It was expressed in a hundred such phrases as "Austro-German vultures."

But Radek wrote equally viciously about the "Anglo-French vultures." To him, as to Trotzky, the Allies and the Germans were two equal maws of imperialism, the one opening for Mesopotamia and the scattered ends of the earth, and the other opening for a compact and consolidated prey in mid-Europe from Antwerp to Odessa. Against all European "capitalistic" governments Radek wrote without compromise. He also wrote without rest and with an eloquence unceasingly and savagely brilliant. He had a slight body, all wire, all electric wire. He had a mind heavily stored with historical facts and economic facts and socialist explosives. He scattered them everywhere. Day after day, in *Pravda* and in *Izvestia* and in pamphlets and in leaflets and in journals of the army and in journals of the navy, he blazed out on Russian opinion with a popular power far beyond that of any other journalist or propagandist in the Bolshevik world.

# 32.

# The Far Eastern Soviet in Siberia

*As the civil war intensified, the Allied governments sent troops to strangle the Revolution—including a well-armed Czech Legion stationed in the Russian Far East that had fought under the auspices of the Russian Army before the October Revolution. The Bolsheviks and their international supporters struggled to get news through the blockade. Here, the editors of the US* Liberator—*the successor to* The Masses, *which had been censored and suppressed by the Democratic administration of President Woodrow Wilson in 1917 for opposing American entry into the war—provide a verbatim report of a conversation with* **Gertrude M. Tobinson,** *wife of Krasnochokov, president of the Far Eastern Soviet in Siberia. This selection exposes the US military's role in the counterrevolution while offering insights into the early days of the revolution.*[1]

Q. Mrs. Tobinson, what was your husband's business in Chicago?

A. He was the superintendent of the Workers' Institute. It is an institution controlled by the working men—a sort of proletarian university.

Q. Was your husband born in Russia?

A. Yes, he was born in Kiev. He came to this country in 1902 and studied at the Chicago University, and worked at painting. Then he studied law and passed the bar examinations in 1911. He had an office and practiced law for five or six years. It was in July 1917 that we left for Russia.

Q. Did you go back at the expense of the Russian Government with the rest?

A. Our party consisted of about a hundred Russian people. Yes, we went at their expense.

Q. That was at the expense of the Kerensky Government?

A. Yes. And when we came to Vladivostok, the second day after we came, my husband was made the secretary of the Central Union. There were many who knew him from Chicago of course. We stayed four weeks in Vladivostok and then he was urged to go to Nikolsk, a small city about six hours' ride from Vladivostok, and he was elected there very soon to be a member of the City Soviet. That was in Kerensky's regime. He tried to organize the soldiers and peasants in the villages into soviets, and he was elected chairman of the soviets.

Q. Did Kerensky's regime encourage the formation of the soviets?

A. Oh, no. There were soviets while Kerensky's regime was in existence, but they didn't have any power.

Q. When you were forming these soviets, was that consciously with the purpose of another revolution?

A. Yes. We all knew that the time would come when the workers would get the power through these organizations. My husband was a member of the City Soviet about four months, I guess, and then the crash came. The Kerensky regime fell in Russia, just as soon as it fell in Russia, naturally it fell in Siberia without any revolution and without any fighting or bloodshed. The Soviets simply took over the power.

Q. He was Mayor and Chairman of the Soviets, both, wasn't he?

A. Yes. Then immediately they called a conference in Habarovsk of all the soviets of the Far East. That was in January 1918, and he was sent as a delegate to that conference. He was elected chairman of the conference—temporary chairman, and afterwards, chairman of the State Soviet.

Q. Of the whole Far East—and how much does that include?

A. Well, Louis Edgar Brown of the Chicago *Daily News* staff wrote in a newspaper that he found Tobinson [Krasnochokov] the dictator of a territory one-third as large as the United States. Of course, the population isn't as large. We had in Vladivostok about 100,000, and Habarovsk about 50,000. Brown called him "dictator" only because he had a great influence over the people, over the peasants and workingmen. They loved him; he was a teacher and comrade. He would sometimes work for eighteen hours a day with the Soviets. In the evenings he would go out and teach the people, eat with them, and sleep with them.

Q. Is he back in America?

A. No, he is not back; I don't know where he is.

Q. Up to the time when this great change took place all over Russia, when the soviets got in power, the industries and the land and the various economic enterprises of Vladivostok were still in private hands and were still private property?

A. Yes.

Q. Had the workers made any attempt to control or to appropriate them under the Kerensky regime?

A. No, they were just organizing towards change.

Q. Your husband, while he was mayor under the Kerensky regime, functioned exactly as a socialist mayor would function here in America?

A. Yes—only at the same time he educated and taught the people.

Q. But there was no form whatever of nationalization or municipalization of industry?

A. No, the soviets were simply educating and organizing against the Kerensky power all the time.

Q. Now, I would like you to describe as accurately as you can just what happened as soon as the soviets got control of the situation there.

A. Well, they went very slowly. First, they organized the State Soviet—the central power—the State Soviet of the Far East. Next they went quietly to work and nationalized the fleet. You know the Far East is surrounded by the Amur River; there are many sailors and many boats that belong to private people, and they nationalized these first. Then they nationalized the mines. First, of course, they would call a conference of the peasants and miners, and these would pass resolutions favoring the nationalizing of the mines, and then they would proceed to take them over. In Blagovieschensk a big fight was put up by the White Guards and the Cossacks. While this conference was in session, and after the resolutions were passed, they surrounded the building and arrested 400 peasants and workers and all the members of the conference. My husband was arrested among them, and kept in prison for six days.

When the peasants of the district learned that the members of their conference were arrested, they came running from all the villages and all the cities around, not organizing at all but just pouring out, about 10,000 of them a day, with hammers and hatchets and wood and whatever they had in their hands, to free the members of the conference. It happened just in one day—the minute they learned that the conference was arrested. Everybody came—women with wagons bringing bread and meat, cooking right there in the open air for the fighters. It took them about a week to recapture the city. They had to put up a hard fight because the White Guards and the Cossacks got the help of the Chinese [troops], who were just over the frontier.

When the Red Guards had captured the depot, and the White Guards saw that they were coming back strong and would soon take the prison, they issued an order to shoot Krasnochokov. But just at the same time the keys of the prison were given over to the Red Guard. They came, opened the doors and took out all the prisoners. They took him out and carried him almost all day on their shoulders in the streets. Afterwards he stayed there for six weeks, organizing the city, putting the soviets on a solid footing, and nationalizing the fleet and the gold mines and coal mines.

Blagovieschensk is a big city, and there is plenty of white flour and plenty of food there [ . . . ] so the bakeries also were nationalized, and things were sold at half the price [as when] they had been in private hands. And the hotels were also nationalized, and the moving pictures, etc. [ . . . ]

Q. Were such popular demonstrations organized in any?

A. Usually it was spontaneous.

Q. Did you say they came across the country in wagons or in trains?

A. They walked and came in wagons from the surrounding villages. Many times they walked a whole day, or a day and a night, to the front. They kept on this way for four or five days—coming more and more—until there were enough to get back the city.

Q. These mines that were nationalized, were they owned by Russian capital?

A. Yes, Russian. I met the wife of a former owner of the mines. She didn't know who I was, and she just went on telling me about her hard luck, and how now they had to live quietly on a farm. "Of course we did get away with some money," she said, "and so we live quietly, and wait until the soviet power is abolished again, and we hope we will get back our mines." I said: "What does your husband do now?" And she said: "Well, he has to work; he works in the mines and gets wages."

Q. Now those mines that were nationalized by an edict of the soviet, the titles were thereby transferred from the hands of the capitalist class, so to speak, into the hands of the Russian Republic, but what happened after that? Who ran those mines? How did they organize the work in those mines, and to what organization was given the power to regulate all the internal affairs, and who employed the men?

A. First of all, they organized unions, industrial unions. There were no unions there before—or if there were, they didn't have any power. Now only the unions have control over the shops and factories

Q. And these unions were responsible only to the soviet?

A. Every union had a representative in the soviet—every industry. If a union consisted of more than 300 it had two representatives. If it consisted of 300 it had one representative, who knew all the inner affairs and protected the union. Everyone—the manager and the common [workers]—received the same wages, 400 to 500 rubles a month. [A]nd the commissars also received 400 rubles a month. The President of the State Soviet received 400 rubles a month.

Q. Now those managers, those engineers and the highly technical experts that manage industries, you know, are generally selected by the capitalist class, and they don't come out of the working class. Were those men, the same old managers belonging to the bourgeoisie, employed by the workers, or did the miners themselves develop . . .

A. Well, many of the experts didn't want to work. The managers would sabotage against the Soviet and the unions and [would] simply fold their hands and say, "We won't work with you." And they finally would go to Shanghai or Japan and join some counter-revolutionary plot. But many of them rolled up their sleeves, and helped us in the work. They remained on the job at our salary.

Q. And in other cases the workmen would select someone from among themselves to be the manager?

A. That is exactly how it was in case they didn't get an expert. The Soviets also tried to organize the unemployed—tried to give them work so that they should produce something. All the unemployed were put in one big building, and everyone had to work. They produced clothing and hats and shoes and everything in that building. It was called by a Russian name which means "Work for the Commune."

Q. And they were paid regular wages?

A. Paid regular wages.

Q. Could you tell us something about schools? Did your children go to school under the Soviet regime?

A. Yes, my children went to school. We organized the schools. The teachers also formed a union and called a conference and laid out their program—how they wanted to teach the children and what was best for the children. Of course, this was probably abolished when the reactionary power took control again. I spoke to many teachers before I left, and asked if they would continue teaching under the old laws again, and they said: "No, we are going to quit teaching in the cities and go to the farmers and villages and teach quietly, where nobody can interfere with us."

Q. When the teachers organized a union and took over the schools themselves, did they improve them?

A. Yes, they improved them greatly. [They] tried to bring the free spirit into the schools. They tried to learn to know every individual child, and they would go home to the mothers and learn their life at home and they would find out the child's position and the child's background, and would act accordingly with the child. In the classes every morning the children would elect their own chairman for the day, and the teacher would just sit aside and watch them. Then if anybody had to be punished they wouldn't come to the teacher, but would call a meeting—a revolutionary tribunal—and decide what to do. Of course it was somewhat comical, but the children would rarely do any mischief because they would be ashamed before each other. I spoke to many young teachers and asked them if they had ever heard the name of [education reformers Maria] Montessori or [Francisco] Ferrer, and they said, "No." But they had the same ideas. It just came natural to them.

Q. Did you stay there long enough to see whether the people in general seemed more healthy and happy or were they worried and was there a great deal of trouble?

A. No, they were not worried or troubled. The people were very happy because of the fact that they lived better, economically, under the Soviet Government than they had lived before. The wages were higher, bread was cheaper, and the theatres and moving pictures were better and cheaper. We had a Soviet Theatre. Of course the workingmen and the peasants could hardly reach the theatres at all before, and they all enjoyed them under the Soviet Government.

Q. Was it a free theatre?

A. Not free, but cheaper. It was a cooperative theatre.

Q. What about the priests and the ministers of religion and all that?

A. They all opposed the soviets.

Q. What is the relation of the people to the church? Do they neglect the church?

A. Yes. You see before they really didn't have any other enjoyment or any other amusement but going to church. Under the soviet there were more meetings and more lectures and theatres and moving pictures, and they would go to the churches more rarely. The priests didn't like that. [ . . . ] There were many days that the White Guards and the reactionary power would try to rise against the soviets, but they had very small power because the people wouldn't back them. They didn't have any ammunition or arms, and so they just did their howling in the streets and then went home to sleep.

Q. Did you have to keep a lot in prison?

A. Yes, but we never kept them for long because the soviets in Siberia felt strong and they were not afraid of the counter-revolutionists. They knew that they didn't have any power at all. The people and the soldiers were all with the Soviet Government. They really loved the Soviet Government and they wanted to fight for it.

Q. The bourgeoisie—the few that there were around—they were living merely on the actual cash that they had, were they?

A. Yes, most of them lived on what they had before. Many of them, though, went to work, because we invited anyone that wanted to work to become a member of the union and take a job, and they could become managers or select any work that fitted them.

Q. Were there any executions of counter-revolutionists in Siberia?

A. No, not a single one during the nine months—of course we had fights. While the Soviet Government was in power, it always had an army standing guard on two fronts. One was in the central part of Siberia; the other near the Chinese frontiers.

Q. What did you start to say about nine months?

A. I said during the nine months that the soviet was in power there wasn't a single execution. Not a single death-sentence imposed by the Revolutionary Tribunal. We were most all of us against capital punishment. We had them in prison, those that were dangerous.

Q. How long were [the] sentences of conspirators?

A. They were indeterminate—just until we felt strong enough to let them free.

Q. Say that again.

A. Well, the tribunal decided that they would not give or issue any sentence. We kept them in prison as long as felt that they were dangerous. As soon as the soviet felt that they wouldn't do any harm, they let them free. We had many counter-revolutionists that became sympathetic to the soviet afterward, some from necessity and others from understanding.

Q. Will you tell us your viewpoint about the Czecho-Slovaks [a volunteer legion fighting against the Austro-Hungarian Empire alongside the Allies that happened to be in Russia at the time of the October Revolution]?

A. At first the Czecho-Slovaks came through Siberia with the intention of going to the French front. Many regiments stopped in Vladivostok, and of course the soviets gave them the best reception and the best buildings, thinking of them as guests and trying to accommodate them. But then many regiments arrived in Central Siberia carrying Russian arms with them, and the Central Siberia Soviet became a little suspicious, because the Russian arms could not be any good in France. So they asked them to leave the arms in Siberia—the rifles and the guns. They refused to do that and the Red Guards surrounded the trains and wouldn't let them proceed to Vladivostok. A good deal of trouble followed, but finally we tried to come to an understanding with the Czecho-Slovaks. We organized a peace conference in Central Siberia, to which all the cities should send delegates and the Czecho-Slovaks should send delegates. The conference took place in Irkutsk.

While the peace conference was in session a shot was heard outside the depot where the trains were—the Czecho-Slovak trains. Of course, we don't know by whom that shot was fired. Supposedly it was fired by some of the counter-revolutionists trying to make trouble. Well, anyway, one Czecho-Slovak was wounded and then the fight began. The Czecho-Slovaks fired from the trains and the Red Guards fired back. It was a two-day fight. Very many wounded Czecho-Slovaks came to us in Habarovsk and we shipped them to Vladivostok. The Czecho-Slovaks heard the news in Vladivostok and with the help of the Japanese and the English they arrested the soviet in Vladivostok, without giving them time or helping them to investigate by whom that shot was fired or who started the trouble. They just simply jailed the members of the Soviet. While they were being arrested, one member [of the Bolsheviks Party] shot himself in the Soviet. He didn't want to give in. He knew what was coming. It came so suddenly they weren't prepared for a fight. The shops were busy and the sailors were at work. After the Soviet was arrested there were about three or four days of fighting. Many factories wouldn't give in until they killed out everyone.

Q. What did they do with the leaders of the Soviet?

A. In Vladivostok they are keeping them in prison. When they took Habarovsk, however, they put out sixteen people in a row and shot them, many of them teachers. Some of them were the most intelligent people we had.

Q. What had become of your Government—the commissars, had they gone farther away?

A. When Nikolsk and Vladivostok were taken we organized a strong army and tried to put up a fight. We held the front four weeks until the English and Americans came. The Czecho-Slovaks and Japanese could not take Habarovsk; for four weeks they were put back. During that time a special conference was called in Habarovsk of the remaining Soviets to decide what to do—whether to retreat or fight on. The people would not listen to giving up the power. They wanted to fight. Of course they couldn't see the uselessness of it as the leaders could, but the leaders urged them to retreat and wait until the Allies should come to their senses. The commissars and leaders retreated in two boats to the wilderness alongside the Amur. I left them about two weeks before they retreated, taking my children to Nicolaievsk and waiting there for a boat to take me to Vladivostok. It took me six weeks to get to Vladivostok. During that time I was recognized once, and arrested, and my cabin was searched, but I was allowed to go on. When I came to Vladivostok I read in the newspapers that some of the Commissars had been caught and among them my husband, and they were—the news was that he had been shot.

The last time I spoke to him was when I was waiting in Nicolaievsk for the boat. The day they were to leave I spoke to him over the long-distance, and he said: "We are leaving at six o'clock in the evening." He just told me that they were leaving "for business," and I understood that they had given up.

Q. You didn't tell us about the nationalization of the land, I wish you would describe how that was done. Were there any fights about the allotment of it?

A. No, there were no fights. Of course, there were some small misunderstandings, but they called meetings, and people would explain to each other what was being done, and they always came to an understanding. They didn't want any fights. I think they are very good-natured people.

Q. Were there large estates there?

A. No, in Siberia there aren't. They are just settlers, you see. I think they had it harder in Russia—in Central Russia—than in Siberia, because there were great landowners.

Q. And during the summer when you were there all the peasants went to work and tilled the land?

A. Yes. Many soldiers that were set free went back to their homes and farms and cultivated the land, and they were really expecting to have a very good crop. They had most of them tried to put in an eight-hour day's work, and they expected to have enough bread this winter to feed Russia—to feed Central Russia. And they would have if it hadn't been for the counter-revolutionary uprisings and for the attacks of the Czecho-Slovaks and the armies of the Allies. They would no sooner start to work than they would have to leave their tools and take a rifle in their hands and go out and defend themselves. And so it was whenever we wanted to do any constructive work. Even in the State Soviet they would have a meeting about organizing some important work, and then a telegram would come of an uprising, and they would have to leave the meeting and raise an army. We never had two months of quiet to show what the Soviet could do. [ . . . ]

Q. How close connection did you have with the government at Petrograd and Moscow?

A. In the beginning all the decrees that they had in Russia we had in Siberia, and telegrams came every week. My husband once spoke on the long-distance phone to Lenine in Moscow. But later, about four months before the Allies came, we didn't have any communication whatever with Russia, and we didn't know whether the Soviets there were dead or what had happened. We had to work independently. We issued our own money in the Far East.

Q. Is there a bitterer feeling against the Allies than against their own reactionaries in Russia?

A. It is the same feeling; they feel that it is just one company. They don't discriminate between them.

Q. They haven't any admiration for Mr. Wilson there, have they?

A. Well, they heard of Mr. Wilson, and they had faith in him, and really the people in Siberia thought that the Americans would not send in their troops. They hoped and believed that the Americans would not send in troops, and they were surprised when they did. I was surprised, too.

Q. How did you manage to get away?

A. I got a passport under a false name and went to Yokohama. While I was there I bought a copy of the Japanese *Advertiser*, published in English, and I found there a paragraph about my husband. I will read it to you:

The most important personage in Siberia at present is Krasnochokov, the leader of the Siberian Bolsheviks. No one now knows his whereabouts, but he is really an admirably strong man, while being in possession of a large sum of money with which he can easily start disturbances in either Mongolia or Manchuria. Four of his colleagues are now imprisoned in Vladivostok, and the Allied authorities are exerting themselves for the arrest of Krasnochokov. He may, perhaps, have the intention to go to America.

That makes me hope that my husband was not executed, after all. But, of course, I do not know. If he is alive he will communicate with me as soon as he can.

# 33.

# The Red Convicts of Cherm

*This selection from **Albert Rhys Williams** shows how the revolution spread even to the most desolate corner of Siberia and points to the redemptive power of mass social struggles. It is especially poignant for exposing the myth of irredeemable criminality, instead pointing out the brutality inherent in mass incarceration under capitalism. It takes place in the Chermkhovo penal colony in Siberia.[1]*

Their clothes were black from the mines and tied up with strings, their faces grim and grimy. Some were ox-like hulks of man. Some were gnarled and knotted, warped by a thousand gales. Here were the cannibal-convicts of Tolstoy, slant-browed and brutal-jawed. Here was Dostoyevsky's *House of the Dead*. With limping steps, cheeks slashed and eyes gouged out they came, marked by bullet, knife and mine disaster, some cursed by an evil birth. But few, if any, weaklings.

By a long, grueling process the weak had been killed off. These thousands were the survivors of tens of thousands, driven out on the gray highroad to Cherm. Through sleet and snow, winter blast and summer blaze they had staggered along. Torture chambers had racked their limbs. Gendarmes' sabers had cracked their skulls. Iron fetters had cut their flesh. Cossacks' whips had gashed their backs, and Cossacks' hooves had pounded them to earth.

Like their bodies, their souls, too, had been knouted [flogged with a whip made of leather thongs twisted with wire]. Like a bloodhound the law had hung on their trail, driving them into dungeons, driving them to this dismal outpost of Siberia, driving them off the face of the earth into its caverns, to

193

strain like beasts, digging the coal in the dark, and handing it up to those who live in the light.

Now out of the mines they come marching up into the light. Guns in hand, flying red flags of revolt, they are loose in the highways, moving forward like a great herd, the incarnation of brute strength. In their path lies a warm, luxurious parlor car—another universe, a million miles removed. Now it is just a few inches away, within their grasp. Three minutes, and they could leave this train sacked from end to end as though gutted by a cyclone. How sweet for once to glut themselves! And how easy! One swift lunge forward. One furious onset.

But their actions show neither haste nor frenzy. Stretching their banners on the ground they range themselves in a crescent, massed in the center, facing the train. Now we can scan those faces. Sullen, defiant, blind with deep hate, brutalized by toil. On all of them the ravages of vice and terror. In all of them an infinitude of pain and torment, the poignant sorrow of the world. But in their eyes is a strange light—a look of exultation. Or is that a glitter of revenge? A blow for blow. The law has given them a thousand blows. Is it their turn? Will they avenge the long years of bitterness?

A hand touches our shoulder. We turn to look at the faces of two burly miners. They tell us that they are the Commissars of Cherm. At the same time they signal the banner-bearers, and the red standards rise up before our eyes. On one in large letters is the old familiar slogan: *Proletarians, arise! You have nothing to lose but your chains.* On another: *We stretch out our hands to the miners in all lands. Greetings to our comrades throughout the world.*

"Hats off!" shouts the commissar. Awkwardly they bare their heads and stand, Caps in hand. Then slowly begins the hymn of the International:

> *Arise, ye prisoners of starvation!*
> *Arise, ye wretched of the earth!*
> *For justice thunders condemnation,*
> *A better world's in birth.*
> *No more tradition's chains shall bind you;*
> *Arise, ye slaves! No more in thrall.*
> *The world shall rise on new foundations.*
> *You have been naught: you shall be all.*

I have heard the streets of cities around the world ringing to the International, ringing from mast columns of the marchers. I have heard rebel students send it floating through college halls. I have heard the International on the voices of 2,000 Soviet delegates, blending with military bands, or rolling through the pillars of the Tauride Palace. But none of the singers looked the "wretched of the earth." They were sympathizers or representatives of the wretched. These miner-convicts of Cherm where the wretched themselves, most wretched of all. Wretched in garments and looks, and even in voice.

With broken voices, and out of tune they sang, but in their singing one felt the pain and protest of the broken of all ages: a sigh of the captive, the moan of the galley slave lashed to the oar, the groan of the serf stretched on the wheel, the cries from the cross, the anguish of myriads of the condemned, welling up out of the long reaches of the past.

These convicts were in apostolic succession to the suffering of the centuries. They were the excommunicated of society, mangled, crushed by its heavy hand, and hurled down into the darkness of this pit. Now out of the pit rises this victory hymn of the vanquished. Long bludgeoned into silence, they break into song—a song not of complaint, but of conquest. No longer are they social outcasts, but citizens. More than that—makers of a new society!

Their limbs are numb with cold. But their hearts are on fire. Harsh and rugged faces are touched with a sunrise glow. Dull eyes grow bright. Defiant ones grow soft. In them lies the transfiguring vision of the toilers of all nations found together in one big fraternity—the International.

"Long live the International! Long live the American workers!" they shout. Then opening their ranks, they thrust forward one of their number. He is of giant stature, a veritable Jean Valjean of a man. With a Jean Valjean of a heart.

"In the name of the miners of Cherm," he says, "we greet the comrades on this train! In the old days how different it was! Day after day, trains roll through here, but we dared not come near them. Some of us did wrong, we know. But many of us were brutally wronged. Has there been justice, some would be on this train and some on the train be in the mines.

"But most of the passengers didn't know there were any mines. In their warm beds, they didn't know that way down below were thousands of moles, digging coal for heat in the cars and steam in the engine. They didn't know that hundreds of us were starved to death, flogged to death or killed by falling rock. If they did know, they didn't care. To them we were dregs and outcasts. To them we were nothing at all.

"Now we are everything! We have joined International. We fall in today for the armies of labor in all lands. We are in the vanguard of them all. We, who were slaves, have been made freest of all.

"Not our freedom alone we want, comrades, but freedom for the workers throughout the world. Unless they, too, are free, we cannot keep the freedom we have to own the mines and run them ourselves.

"Already the greedy hands of the imperialists of the world are reaching out across the seas. Only the hands of the workers of the world can tear those clutches from our throats."

The range and insight of the man's mind was amazing. So amazed was Kuntz that his own speech in reply faltered. My hold on Russian quite collapsed. Our part in this affair was wan and pallid. But these miners did not feel so. They came into the breach with a cheer for the International, and another for the International Orchestra.

The "Orchestra" comprised four violins played by four prisoners of war; a Czech, a Hungarian, an Austrian, and a German. Captured on the Eastern front, from camp to camp they had been relayed along to these convict-miners in Siberia. Thousands of miles from home! Still farther in race and breeding from these Russian masses drawn from the soil. But cast and creed and race had fallen before the Revolution. To their convict-miner comrades here in this dark cold they played, as in happier days they might have played at a music festival under the garden lights of Berlin or Budapest. The flaming passion in their veins cracked into the strings of their violins and out into the heart strings of their hearers.

The whole conclave—miners, musicians and visitors, Teutons, Slavs and Americans—became one. All barriers were down as the commissars came pressing up to greet us. One huge hulking fellow, with fists like pile-drivers, took our hands in his. Twice he tried to speak and twice he choked. Unable to put sentiments of brotherhood into words, he put them into a sudden terrific grip of his hand. I can feel that great hand today.

# 34.

# The Origins of Workers' Control in Russia

*John Reed arrived in Sweden February last, on his way from Russia, in answer to false stories being circulated by the capitalist press about the management of Russian industries. Owing to a variety of circumstances, it has not hitherto been published and now appears for the first time.*
— *The Revolutionary Age*, November 23, 1918[1]

The capitalist press has diligently spread abroad all sorts of stories about the foolish conduct of the Russian industrial workers during the Revolution; of their extravagant demands, their ignorance and the brutality with which they have treated manufacturers and technical experts. The outside world has received the impression that the Russian workingman gets enormous wages, refuses to work, and that in short he has ruined Russian industry.

It is true that in Russia industry is at a low ebb. In the first place, coal was impossible to procure for a long time, because Kaledine and his Cossacks had control of the Donetz Basin, and after them the Germans; machinery has deteriorated, owing to the fact that no new parts have come from abroad for two long years and more, and the technical experts, engineers, etc., faithful to the capitalist class, at first refused to submit to the direction of the workmen's committees; and last of all, the working class itself has been too hotly absorbed in politics, and in fighting the enemies of the Revolution—from Kornilov to Kerensky, Kaledine, the Ukrainian Rada, Germany, the Czecho-Slovaks and the Allies. But on the technical side, if Russian industry was ruined, it is the manufacturers and owners who are to blame—they who tried to starve the Revolution by shutting down the factories and mines, by ruining organization,

197

wrecking the railroads, deliberately destroying the machinery of industry, and flooding the mines.

Many of the tales about extravagant demands, of workmen's control committees which broke down, etc., are of course true. But the important thing is that until the November Revolution, the Russian workmen as a whole were still over-worked, underpaid, (except in certain special factories), and that at the same time there was growing up all over Russia a spontaneous industrial organization capable of being at least the promising frame-work of a new industrial order.

The three cardinal demands of the November Revolution were Peace, Land to the Peasants, and Workers' Control of Industry, and of these three the last point of Workers' Control was perhaps the most important, because the tendency of new Russia is more and more toward the abolition of the political state, and the evolution of industrial democracy.

The history of labor organization in Russia is very brief. Before the 1905 Revolution no labor unions, in the strict sense of the word, existed. The only recognized workmen's representation was the election of a *starosta*, or "elder," much as the *starostas* are elected in Russian villages, and even in Russian prisons, and with about as much power. In 1905, some 200,000 workmen joined the unions. Stolypin suppressed them. Some little unions persisted, but they were finally crushed, their funds seized, their leaders sent to Siberia. After that the unions existed half-secretly, with a membership over all Russia of about 10,000. During the war, however, all attempts at labor organization were ruthlessly stamped out, and workmen discovered in any connection with labor organizations were sent to the front.

The Revolution released the workers partly from this bondage, and pushed toward rapid organization. After four months of the Revolution the first conference of the Professional Union of All Russia was held—200 delegates representing more than 1,400,000 workers. Two months later the membership was calculated at more than 3,000,000, according to the report of Riazanov; it is now more than double that number.

Now these Professional Unions (Professiollalne Soyuse) were modeled on the French syndicates, with the addition of government cooperation suggested by the German labor union system. They were mainly concerned with the fight for shorter hours, higher wages—in short, the routine business of labor unions everywhere. For instance, they established a system of Conciliation Chambers for the hearing of industrial disputes for industrial arbitration under government supervision. But their important work was the organization of all the workers into great industrial unions, in the dissolution of all the petty craft organizations, merging them into the big unions. Thus in the government-run factory at Sestroretzk, for example, all those who worked upon the manufacture of rifles—the men who forged barrels, the machinists who fitted the mechanism, the carpenters who made the stock—all were members of Metal Workers' Union.

But the Professional Unions, in spite of their importance, occupied a secondary position in the workers' minds. In the first place, the Soviets, half-political, half-economic, absorbed their energies; in the second place, those unique organizations, spontaneously created by the Russian Revolution, the Factory Shop Committees (Fabritchnoe Zavodski Comitiet) required their attention. These latter are the real foundation of the Workers' Control of Industry.

The Factory Committees originated in the government munitions factories. At the outbreak of the Revolution, most of the administrators of the government factories, chiefly military officers who brutalized the workers with all the privilege of military law, ran away. Unlike the private manufacturers, these government officials had no interest in the business. The workers, in order to prevent the closing down of the factory, had to take charge of the administration. In some places, as at Sestroretzk, this meant taking charge of the town also. And these government plants were run with such inefficiency, so much corruption, that the Workers' Committee, although it raised wages, shortened hours, and hired more hands, actually increased production and reduced expenses—at the same time completing new buildings begun by dishonest contractors, constructing a fine new hospital, and giving the town its first sewerage system. With these government plants the Factory Shop Committees had a comparatively easy time. For a long time after the Revolution there was no authority to question the authority of the workers, and finally when the Kerensky government began to interfere, the workers had complete control.

Working as they were on munitions, with standing orders, there was no excuse for closing down, and in fuel and raw materials the government itself supplied them. Although many times under the inefficient Kerensky government the government shops were in danger of closing down, and the Shop Committees had to send their delegates to Baku to buy oil, to Kharkov for coal, and to Siberia for iron.

From Sestroretzk the Shop Committee spread like wildfire to other government shops—then to private establishments working on government orders, then to private industries, and finally to the factories which were closed down at the beginning of the Revolution. First the movement was confined to Petrograd, but soon it began to spread over all Russia, and just before the October Revolution the first All-Russian Congress of Factory Shop Committees took place. At the present time, representatives of the Factory Shop Committees and representatives of the Professional Unions make up the Department of Labor of the new government, and compose the Council of Workers' Control.

The first Committees in the private factories were vainly engaged in keeping the industry going, in the face of lack of coal, of raw material, and especially, the sabotage of the owners and the administrative force, who wanted to shut down. It was a question of life and death to the workers. The newly formed Shop Committees were forced to find out how many orders the factory had, how much fuel and raw material were on hand, what was the income from the business—in order to determine the wages to be paid—and to control—itself—discipline of the workers, and the hiring and discharging of men. In factories which the owners insisted they could not keep open, the workers were forced to take charge themselves, and run the business as well as they could.

Some of the experiments were very interesting. For example, there was a cotton factory in Novgorod which was abandoned by its owners. The workers—inexperienced in administration—took charge. The first thing they did was to manufacture enough cloth for their own needs, and then for the needs of the other workers in Novgorod. After that the Shop Committee sent men out to factories in other cities, offering to exchange cotton cloth for other articles they needed—shoes, implements; they exchanged cloth for bread with the peasants; and finally they began to take orders from commercial houses. For their raw material they had to send men south to the cotton-growing country, and then with the railroad employees' union they had to pay with cloth for the transportation of the cotton. So with fuel from the coal mines of the Don.

In the great private industries which remained open, the Factory Shop Committees appointed delegates to confer with the administration about getting fuel, raw material, and even orders. They had to keep account of all that came into the factory, and all that went out. They made a valuation of the entire plant, so as to find out how much the factory was worth, how much stock was held, what the profits were. Everywhere the workers' greatest difficulty was with the owners, who concealed profits, refused orders, and tried in every way to destroy the efficiency of the plant, so as to discredit the workers' organizations. All counter-revolutionary or anti-democratic engineers, clerks, foremen, etc. were discharged by the Factory Shop Committees, nor could they enter any other factory without the recommendation of the Factory Shop Committee of their preceding place of employment. Workers were required to join the union before they were hired, and the Factory Shop Committee supervised the carrying out of all union scales and regulations.

The fight by the capitalists against these Factory Shop Committees was extremely bitter. Their work was hindered at every step. The most extravagant lies have been published in the capitalist press about "lazy workmen" who spent all their time in talking when they should be working—while as a matter of fact the Factory Shop Committees usually had to work eighteen hours a day; about the enormous size of the Committees—while for example at Putilov Works, the largest factory in Petrograd, employing about 40,000 men, the Central Factory Shop Committee, representing eleven departments and 46 shops, consisted of twenty-two men. Even Skobelev, "Socialist" Minister of Labor under the Kerensky government, issued an order in the first part of September that the Factory Shop Committees should only meet "after working-hours," and no longer receive wages for their time on Committee business. As a matter of fact, the Factory Shop Committees were all that kept Russian industry from complete disintegration during the days of the Coalition Government. Thus the new Russian industrial order was born of necessity.

Each Factory Shop Committee has five departments: Production and Distribution, Fuel, Raw Materials, Technical Organization of the Industry, and Demobilization (or changing from a war to peace basis). In each district, all the factories of one industry combined to send two delegates to a district council, and each district council sent one delegate to the city council—which in turn had its delegates in the All-Russian Council, in the Central Committee of the Professional Unions and in the Soviet.

Not all workmen are union workmen in Russia; but every factory worker must be represented in the Factory Shop Committee. And the Factory Shop Committee supplements and completes the work of the Professional Unions, and absolutely controls production at its very source.

This method of controlling production by the workers, sprung spontaneously from the Russian revolution, has just been legalized by the new Workmen's and Peasants' Government of the Russian Republic. Also it has become possible, through the power of the government, for workmen themselves to take over and operate all plants whose owners cannot keep them open. With unlimited credit behind them, and the huge, organized force of the government, there is no reason why the workers cannot hire engineers and technical staff, or why, with such training, they may not be able, in a few years, to take over the greater part of Russian industrial enterprise. With the control of the means of production and in the hands of the popular government, the main obstacle to the achievement of industrial democracy has vanished.

# 35.

# Ministry of Social Welfare

*Here **Louise Bryant** reviews the work of Alexandra Kollontai as the People's Commissar of Welfare, as she took charge of creating a welfare state from scratch in wartime conditions. This meant enacting revolutionary laws aimed at liberating women and scrambling to care for millions of disabled veterans and orphaned children, all the while overcoming opposition from staff of the old capitalist state machine.[1]*

When Kollontay took over her department she found a terrific chaos, and millions of lives depended on her sanity in dealing with the situation and pulling herself out of a carefully planned political intrigue. Countess [Sofia] Panina, who had been in charge of the department before Kollontay [under the Kerensky government], true to the principles of the bourgeoisie, had persuaded the higher employees to go on strike. It is amazing how quickly the bourgeoisie of Russia learned from the working class how to sabotage. The employees hid the keys of the safes and secreted the books and resorted to all manner of underhanded acts. Kollontay called them together and quite calmly ordered them to be locked up. As a matter of fact it was only her long practice in self-control that made it possible for Kollontay to appear calm. She was really deeply disturbed, and told me afterward that she had a terrific struggle with herself before she was able to give the command for the arrests.

"I kept saying to myself: 'Is this you, Alexandra Kollontay, ordering arrests?' Afterwards I used to lie awake nights and wonder how I did it."

Nevertheless the strikers must have been unaware of her struggle, for they returned the keys and the books early the next morning. The entire strike [of the Ministry staff] was broken in three days. Kollontay called another meeting, which even the lowest servants were asked to attend. She was very frank with them at this meeting. Russia, she explained, was bankrupt; there were little funds to carry on charitable work; no one was to receive even a "good" salary; she herself was to get $50 a month [300 or 400 rubles], which is the salary of every commissar.

This came as a great blow to the professional social workers, who up to this time had received as much as 25,000 rubles a year. Kollontay shocked them even more by announcing that thereafter all employees should continue to be present at meetings, which would be held frequently, and that the same consideration would be given to suggestions from scrubwomen as from professional philanthropists. Everyone was to have an equal chance of promotion.

I used to go up to Kollontay's office on the Kazanskaya and she explained many of her problems to me. She was very much touched by the way some of her lower employees had responded to her appeal in this crisis. It really was astonishing how much many of these simple and uneducated old servants understood about the work. And when they once realized that they were a part of the larger plan they gladly worked for sixteen hours a day to help Kollontay, whom they all called "Little Comrade."

The work of her department covered a vast field, touching all Russia. "One of my greatest tasks," said Kollontay, "is to change the whole system which takes care of the two and a half million maimed soldiers, who are absolutely destitute." [ . . . ]

One way by which Kollontay secured money for immediate needs was by placing an exorbitant tax on playing cards, which had to be purchased through her department. Playing cards in Russia, as in most continental countries, have always been a government monopoly, and the profits go to charity. Kollontay increased the price from 30 rubles for a dozen decks to 360 rubles.

One of her dearest ambitions for years has been to establish a home for convalescent mothers known as the Palace of Motherhood. This work is actually being carried out, and what few physicians remain in Petrograd are keenly interested in it.

On Kollontay's suggestion, the Bolshevik Government passed a measure providing free care for sixteen weeks for women before, during, and after confinement [childbirth]. When they leave the home they can go back if they are not well, and they are required to work only four hours a day in the factories for the first month after returning. This applies to all women, whether married or single. The Bolsheviki believe that this care of mothers is one of the first debts of the state.

The foundling homes are a terrible problem. Russia has long been famous for the slaughter of her infants, mostly through starvation or neglect. Kollontay arranged a plan whereby children are taken care of by peasant women in their own homes, where they are treated as members of the family. Every child in Russia now attends public school. All private institutions are officially abolished. Not only the children in prisons, in reform schools and in orphan asylums now must go to public schools, but also the children of the aristocracy must attend these same schools.

"In free Russia," said Kollontay, "there will be neither segregation nor aristocracy in children's education."

One day when I went to see Kollontay a long line of sweet-faced old people was standing outside her door. They had come as a delegation from one of the old people's homes. Kollontay explained their presence. "I have removed the people who used to be over them and turned their institutions into little republics. They come in every day now and express their gratitude. They elect their own officers and have their own political fights; choose their own menus—"

I interrupted her. "What would that consist of in the present day?" I asked.

Kollontay burst out laughing. "Surely," she said, "you must understand that there is a great deal of moral satisfaction in deciding whether you want thick cabbage soup or thin cabbage soup!" And this was the whole secret of Kollontay's success, that she allowed other people to make their own decisions.

Kollontay spoke to me about American assistance only two days before I left Russia. She hoped, she said, that trained people interested in her work would come to her aid. There is such a pitiful lack of everything in Russia today. Surgical dressings for example, have to be used over and over again and good doctors are almost impossible to find.

# 36.

# The First Woman Commissar

*Kollontai herself reviews her challenges as the People's Commissar of Welfare, paying special attention to efforts to provide health and child care, education, and employment equality for women in the new Soviet state.*[1]

The Soviet Government was formed. I was appointed People's Commissar of Social Welfare. I was the only woman in the cabinet and the first woman in history who had ever been recognized as a member of a government. When one recalls the first months of the Workers' Government, months which were so rich in magnificent illusions, plans, ardent initiatives to improve life, to organize the world anew, months of the real romanticism of the Revolution, one would in fact like to write about all else save about one's self. I occupied the post of Minister of Social Welfare from October of 1917 to March of 1918. It was not without opposition that I was received by the former officials of the Ministry. Most of them sabotaged us openly and simply did not show up for work. But precisely this office could not interrupt its work, come what may, since in itself it was an extraordinarily complicated operation. It included the whole welfare program for the war-disabled, hence for hundreds of thousands of crippled soldiers and officers, the pension system in general, foundling homes, homes for the aged, orphanages, hospitals for the needy, the workshops making artificial limbs, the administration of playing-card factories (the manufacture of playing cards was a state monopoly), the educational system, clinical hospitals for women. In addition a whole series of educational institutes for young girls were also under the direction of this Ministry.

207

One can easily imagine the enormous demands these tasks made upon a small group of people who, at the same time, were novices in state administration. In a clear awareness of these difficulties I formed, immediately, an auxiliary council in which experts such as physicians, jurists, pedagogues were represented alongside the workers and the minor officials of the Ministry. The sacrifice, the energy with which the minor employees bore the burden of this difficult task was truly exemplary. It was not only a matter of keeping the work of the Ministry going, but also of initiating reforms and improvements. New, fresh forces replaced the sabotaging officers of the old regime. A new life stirred in the offices of the formerly highly conservative Ministry. Days of grueling work! And at night the sessions of the councils of the People's Commissar (of the cabinet) under Lenin's chairmanship. A small, modest room and only one secretary who recorded the resolutions which changed Russia's life to its bottommost foundations.

My first act as a People's Commissar was to compensate a small peasant for his requisitioned horse. Actually, by no stretch of the imagination did this belong to the functions of my office. But the man was determined to receive compensation for his horse. He had travelled from his distant village to the capital and had knocked patiently on the doors of all the ministries. Always with no results! Then the Bolshevik Revolution broke out. The man had heard that the Bolsheviks were in favor of the workers and peasants. So he went to the Smolny Institute, to Lenin, who had to pay out the compensation. I do not know how the conversation between Lenin and the small peasant went. As a result of it, however, the man came to me with a small page torn from Lenin's notebook on which I was requested to settle the matter somehow since at the moment the People's Commissariat for Social Welfare had the greatest amount of cash at its disposal. The small peasant received his compensation.

My main work as People's Commissar consisted in the following: by decree to improve the situation of the war-disabled, to abolish religious instruction in the schools for young girls, which were under the Ministry (this was still before the general separation of church and state) and to transfer priests to the civil service, to introduce the right of self-administration for pupils in the schools for girls, to reorganize the former orphanages into government Children's Homes (no distinction was to be made between orphaned children and those who still had fathers and mothers), to set up the first hostels for the needy and street urchins, to convene a committee, composed only of doctors, which was to be commissioned to elaborate the free public health system for the whole country.

In my opinion, the most important accomplishment of the People's Commissariat, however, was the legal foundation of a Central Office for Maternity and Infant Welfare. The draft of the bill relating to this Central Office was signed by me in January of 1918. A second decree followed in which I changed all maternity hospitals into free Homes for Maternity and Infant Care, in order thereby to set the groundwork for a comprehensive government system of prenatal care. I was greatly assisted in coping with these tasks by Dr. Korolef. We also planned a "Prenatal Care Palace," a model home with an exhibition room in which courses for mothers would be held and, among many other things, model day nurseries were also to be established. We were just about completing preparations for such a facility in the building of a girls' boarding school at which formerly young girls of the nobility had been educated and which was still under the direction of a countess, when a fire destroyed our work, which had barely begun! Had the fire been set deliberately? I was dragged out of bed in the middle of the night. I rushed to the scene of the fire; the beautiful exhibition room was totally ruined, as were all the other rooms. Only the huge nameplate "Prenatal Care Palace" still hung over the entrance door.

My efforts to nationalize maternity and infant care set off a new wave of insane attacks against me. All kinds of lies were related about the "nationalization of women," about my legislative proposals, which assertedly ordained that little girls of twelve were to become mothers. A special fury gripped the religious followers of the old regime when, on my own authority (the cabinet later criticized me for this action), I transformed the famous Alexander Nevsky monastery into a home for war invalids. The monks resisted and a shooting fray ensued. The press again raised a loud hue and cry against me. The church organized street demonstrations against my action and also pronounced "anathema" against me.

I received countless threatening letters, but I never requested military protection. I always went out alone, unarmed and without any kind of a bodyguard. In fact I never gave a thought to any kind of danger, being all too engrossed in matters of an utterly different character. In February of 1918 a first state delegation of the Soviets was sent to Sweden in order to clarify different economic and political questions. As People's Commissar I headed this delegation. But our vessel was shipwrecked; we were saved by landing on the Aland Islands, which belonged to Finland. At this very time the struggle between the Whites and the Reds in the country had reached its most crucial moment, and the German Army was also making ready to wage war against Finland.

The White troops occupied the Aland Islands on the very evening of our shipwreck, as we were seated at dinner in an inn of the city of Marieham, rejoicing over our rescue. We managed to escape thanks to the greatest determination and cunning, yet one of our group, a young Finn, was captured and shot. We returned to Petrograd, where the evacuation of the capital was being prepared with feverish haste: German troops already stood before the gates of the city.

# 37.

# Women Workers and Soviet Russia

*Inessa Armand was one of the central Bolshevik underground organizers prior to the Revolution, returning to revolutionary Russia on the sealed train with Zinoviev and Lenin. In the aftermath of the Revolution, alongside Kollontai, she took charge of Zhenotdel, the Women's Department of the Bolshevik Party, mandated with implementing Soviet laws regarding women's equality in spheres of education, childcare, divorce, and workplace rights for both women and children. Zhenotdel also helped secure the right to free, legal abortion for the first time in any country. Armand explains why privatized domestic labor and childcare are at the root of women's oppression and describes the concrete steps women took to link their own liberation with socialism.[1]*

Soviet power is the first to create the conditions in which women may, at long last, begin the work of their full emancipation. Throughout the centuries, she [woman] was a slave. At first, under the reign of small-scale production, she was a slave to the family; then, during the rise of capitalism, she suffered under three different masters: the state, the factory and, still, the family. This was so not only under the backward and barbaric Tsarist regime, but also true in the most "civilized democracies" of Western Europe and America.

Under the bourgeois regime, woman workers were stripped of even the meager rights afforded to the male worker. In the workshop, in the factory, she was even more oppressed, more exploited than the male worker because the boss used his power to oppress her not only as a worker, but also to inflict on her all sorts of outrages and violence as a woman. Furthermore, in no place

211

212 | Eyewitnesses to the Russian Revolution

and at no time has prostitution, the ugliest phenomenon, the most heinous form of proletarian wage slavery, more lavishly flourished than under the reign of capitalism.

Women workers and peasants are slaves in the family, not only because of the power of the husband but also because the factory tears women workers from the family home without providing for childcare or the needs of the domestic economy, thus transforming motherhood into a heavy, unbearable cross. So long as the power of the bourgeoisie existed, women workers and peasants could not overcome this triple bondage, which is the basis upon which the bourgeois regime rests and without which it cannot exist.

Soviet power, the power of the proletariat, opens the doors wide to women and provides them with the possibility of absolute liberation. The Soviet constitution extended all political and civil rights to women, and now women workers and peasants enjoy the same voting rights as their male counterparts. Just like men, women can cast a vote and be elected; they can take any job suited to them in the factory committees in Soviet institutions, including becoming a People's Commissar.

The socialization of production, the expropriation of the capitalists and the large landowners has led to the complete elimination of all exploitation and all economic inequality. In Soviet Russia, a woman worker in the factory is no longer a paid servant, but a woman in full possession of all her rights who, on equal footing with her male workers, organizes, manages, and directs all production and distribution through her Soviet institutions and unions. It is likewise within the family and with respect to marriage. Soviet power has already granted complete equality between the rights of husband and wife. The power of the husband, of the father, no longer exists. The formalities of marriage and divorce have been reduced to a minimum: just a simple declaration on the part of the interested persons in the corresponding commissariat office.

Soviet power has eradicated all differences in terms of rights between "legitimate" and "illegitimate" children, thus eliminating one of the worst instances of bourgeois inequality. In Soviet Russia, there are no more "illegitimate children." Because of this, all children are in equal measure future citizens who may exercise their rights and expect to be cared for. Soviet power takes responsibility for children's education and instruction, from their birth until the age of sixteen or seventeen and provides them with all necessary nurturing. Under the reign of capitalism, working-class children had to work at a young age and were therefore deprived by the workshop, by the factory, of maternal care, while the bourgeois government worried little on their behalf.

As a consequence, proletarian children atrophied physically and morally, they languished and died.

Even now, Soviet power, despite the disorganization caused by the blockade, uninterrupted aggressions of White Guards, and untold hardships, already partially ensures public support for children (for example, it has created free child-care centers, free dining halls, school canteens, etc.). Educational instruction is free everywhere, from elementary schools to universities and colleges. Nurseries and kindergartens have been created. Children are provided shoes and clothing at school. Social welfare is consistently growing, including provisions for maternal and child care, homes for mothers and children, daycare centers, etc.

Children are forbidden to work until their sixteenth birthday and children between the ages of sixteen and eighteen years old can only work six hours per day. Women are relieved of all work duties eight weeks prior to giving birth and for eight weeks after as well, and during this period they are provided support equivalent to their daily salary. In addition, a series of decrees have been enacted that protect women during pregnancy as well as extending general labor protections. And, I repeat, even accounting for the hitherto unknown difficulties we are suffering, one can say with certainty that care for mothers and children is better organized in Soviet Russia than elsewhere. And these are only the first steps.

In addition, through the creation of public dining rooms, the private family kitchen will gradually disappear from the domestic economy. The home-cooked family dinner is much touted by the bourgeoisie, but from the point of view of the economy, it is not at all consistent with the goal of women's emancipation; for women peasants, and especially for women workers, this unbearable burden absorbs any time for leisure, depriving them of the opportunity to go to meetings, to read, and to take part in the class struggle. The home-cooked family dinner, under the bourgeois regime, promotes ignorance and backwardness and, in this way, is one of the best tools in the capitalist's hands in his fight against the worker.

The Soviet system is in transition from capitalism to communism, it is impossible to achieve this without the absolute liberation of all the exploited and, therefore, of women. That is why the Soviet system broke all the chains which had for centuries oppressed the women workers and the peasants. From the first days after the October Revolution, women workers understood perfectly that they were entering a new era of full emancipation.

At their first conferences (including May 1918 in the city of Moscow, in June 1918 for the province of Moscow, and November 1918 when more than a thousand delegates attended a national conference representing more than a million women workers), women workers took note of this fact. In the resolution on the question of the family, the Moscow province conference resolved that, with the passage of power into the hands of the Soviets, not only was the complete political and civic emancipation of women becoming possible, but the absolute suppression of sex slavery in the family was possible as well. Thus it was necessary to elucidate and elaborate the conditions for this emancipation. In the resolution passed at the National Congress of Women, with respect to the roles of women workers, it stated, among other things:

> Soviet power, after having achieved full emancipation for the whole working class, after having established equal rights between men and women, after granting women workers absolute mastery over their own lives alongside their male counterparts, grants them the power to organize, by any means necessary, the working class and the poor in cities and in the countryside in order to secure it.
>
> Following the October Revolution, following the transfer of power to the Soviets, the complete liberation of women workers, by eliminating all the old forms of the family and of the domestic economy, becomes not only possible but is a necessary condition for the establishment of socialism.

# V

# BY WAY OF AN ASSESSMENT

# 38.

# Retrospective

*Albert Rhys Williams concludes his remarkable book* Through the Russian Revolution *with a critical retrospective of the state of the revolution just as the darkest days of the civil war were coming to a close in 1921.*[1]

It was not the revolutionists who made the Russian Revolution. This in spite of hosts of revolutionists—who tried their best to make it. For a century gifted men and women of Russia had been agitated over the cruel oppression of the people. So they became agitators. Into the villages, the shops and the slums they went crying:

> *Shake to earth your chains like dew,*
> *Which in sleep have fallen on you.*
> *Ye are many, they are few.*

But the people did not rise. They did not even seem to hear. Then came that supreme agitator—hunger. Hunger, rising out of economic collapse and war, goaded the sluggish masses into action. Moving out against the old worm-eaten structure they brought it down. Elemental impersonal forces did what human agencies found impossible. The revolutionists, however, had their part. They did not make the Revolution. But they made the Revolution a success. By their efforts they had prepared a body of men and women with minds trained to see facts, with a program to fit the facts and with fighting energy to drive it through. There were a million of them—perhaps more, possibly less. The important thing is not their number, but the fact that they were organized to act as receivers of the bankrupt, old order, as a salvage-corps of the Revolution.

217

At the core of this were the Communists. H.G. Wells says, "In the vast disorganization an emergency government supported by a disciplined party of perhaps 150,000 adherents—the Communist Party—took control. [ . . . ] It suppressed brigandage, established a sort of order and security in the exhausted towns and set up a crude rationing system, the only possible government [ . . . ] the only idea, the only solidarity."

For four years the Communists have had control of Russia. What are the fruits of their stewardship? "Repressions, tyranny, violence," cry the enemies. "They have abolished free speech, free press, free assembly. They have imposed drastic military conscription and compulsory labor. They have been incompetent in government, inefficient in industry. They have subordinated the Soviets to the Communist Party. They have lowered their Communist ideals, changed and shifted their program and compromised with the capitalists." Some of these charges are exaggerated. Many can be explained. But they cannot all be explained away. Friends of the Soviet grieve over them. Their enemies have summoned the world to shudder and protest against them.

When I am tempted to join the wailers and the mud-slingers my mind goes back to a conversation on the docks of Vladivostok in June 1918. Colonel Robins, of the American Red Cross, was talking to Constantin Sukhanov, President of the Soviet.

"If no help comes from the Allies, how long can the Soviet last?"

Sukhanov shook his head ruefully.

"Six weeks?" queried Robins.

"It will be hard to hold on longer," said Sukhanov.

Robins turned to me with the same question. I, too, was dubious about the outlook. We were sympathizers. We knew the might and the vitality of the Soviet. But we saw also the tremendous obstacles it confronted. And the odds seemed against it.

In the first place, the Soviet faced the same conditions that had overwhelmed the Czar['s] and Kerensky government, i.e., the dislocation of industry, the paralysis of transport, the hunger and misery of the masses. In the second place the Soviet had to cope with a hundred new obstacles—desertion of the intelligentsia, strike of the old officials, sabotage of the technicians, excommunication by the church, the blockade by the Allies. It was cut off from the grain fields of the Ukraine, the oil fields of Baku, the coal mines of the Don, the cotton of Turkestan—fuel and food reserves were gone. "Now," said their enemies, "the bony hand of hunger will clutch the people by their throat and bring them to their senses." To prevent supply trains reaching the cities, agents of the imperialists dynamited the railway bridges and put emery into the locomotive bearings.

Here were troubles enough to break the strongest souls. But still more were coming. The capitalist press of the world was mobilized against the Bolsheviks. They were pictured as "hirelings of the Kaiser," "red-eyed fanatics," "cold-blooded assassins," "long bearded ruffians running amuck by day, carousing in the Kremlin at night," "profaners of art and culture," "despoilers of women." As a crowning infamy, the "Decree for the Nationalization of Women" was forged and broadcasted through the world. The public was called upon to transfer their hate from the Huns to the Bolsheviks. While abroad hatred against the Bolsheviks as the new "enemies of civilization" mounted from day to day, these selfsame Bolsheviks were straining brains and sinews to rescue civilization in Russia from total collapse. Watching them at their heartbreaking, back-breaking tasks, Ransome wrote:

> No one contends that the Bolsheviks are angels. I only ask that men shall look through the fog of libel that surrounds them and see the ideal for which these young men, are struggling in the only way in which they can struggle. If they fail they will fail with clean shields and clean hearts, having striven for an ideal which will live beyond them. Even if they fail, they will none the less have written a page more daring than any other I can remember in the story of the human race. [ . . . ] When in after years men read that page they will judge your country and my country by the help or hindrance they gave to the writing of it.

This appeal was in vain. As the monarchists of Europe combined to crush the idea loosed on the world by the French Revolution, so the capitalists of Europe and America combined to crush the idea loosed on the world by the Russian Revolution. To these famished, frozen, typhus-stricken Russians sailed no ships of good will laden with books, tools, teachers and engineers but grim ships of war and transports laden with troops and officers, guns and poison gas. Landings were made at strategic points on the coast of Russia. Monarchists, landlords, and Black Hundreds flocked to these rallying centers. New White armies were conscripted, drilled and equipped with hundreds of millions of dollars of supplies. The Interventionists started their drive on Moscow, seeking to plunge the sword into the heart of the Revolution.

Out of the East rolled the hordes of Kolchak following the trail of the Czechs across Siberia. Out of the West struck the armies of Finland, the Letts and Lithuanians. Down from the forests and snowfields of the North moved the British, French and Americans. Up from the seaports of the South plunged the tanks, aeroplanes and Death Battalions of Denikin. From all points of the compass they came. Out of the Estonian marshes—Yudenich. Out of Poland—the veteran legions of Peltura. Out of Crimea—the cavalry of Baron Wrangel. A million-bayonetted ring of steel closed in upon the Revolution. The Revolution staggered under the blows rained upon it, but its heart was undaunted. If it must die—we would die fighting.

Once more in the war weary villages and destitute towns throbbed the drums beating the call to arms. Once more the worn-out lathes and looms were ordered to produce uniforms and rifles. Once more the crippled railways were freighted with soldiers and cannon. Out of the almost exhausted resources of Russia the Revolution armed, uniformed and officered 5 million men and the Red Armies took the field. Only 400 miles from Moscow they hurled themselves against Kolchak and pushed his panic-stricken forces back the 4,000 miles they had advanced across Siberia. In the pine forests of the North, clad in uniforms of white, sliding through the snow on skis, they met the Allies and pushed them back on Archangel, forcing them to ship for home across the waters of the White Sea. They stopped the headlong rush of Denikin at Tula [ . . . ] "in whose red fires the red steel is welded into the bayonets of the invincible Red Army." Driven back to the Black Sea's shores, he escaped on a British cruiser.

Budenny's Cavalry racing day and night across the Ukrainian steppes flung themselves suddenly on the Polish flanks, turned the victorious advance of the legionaries into a disastrous retreat and harried them up to the gates of Warsaw. Wrangel was beaten and bottled up in the Crimea, and while the shock troops of the Soviet hurled themselves against his concrete forts, the main Red Army hurried across the frozen Sea of Azov and the Baron fled to Turkey. In the outskirts of Petrograd, under its very domes, Yudenich was cut to pieces, the armies of the Baltic States were beaten back behind their borders, and the Whites annihilated in Siberia. The Revolution triumphed all around the circle. The Counter-Revolutionists were broken not only by the heavy battalions of the Soviet, but by the Idea incarnated in these armies of the Revolution.

They were armies with banners, red banners emblazoned with the watchwords of a new world. They advanced into battle singing the songs of justice and fraternity. They treated their captured enemies as misguided brothers. They fed them, bound up their wounds and sent them back to tell in their own ranks stories of Bolshevik hospitality. They bombarded the Allied camp with questions: "Why did you come to Russia, Allied Soldiers?" "Why should workmen of France and England murder their fellow-workers of Russia?" "Do you want to destroy our Workmen's Republic?" "Do you want to restore the Czar?" "You are fighting for the bond holders of France, the land grabbers of England, the imperialists of America. Why shed blood for them?" "Why don't you go home?"

Red soldiers rose up to shout these questions across the trenches. Red sentries with hands uplifted rushed forward crying them out. Red aeroplanes dropped them circling down from the skies. The Allied troops pondered over these queries and were shaken. Their morale broke down. They fought half-heartedly. They mutinied. The Whites, in tens of thousands—whole battalions and ambulance corps—came over to the Revolution. One after another the armies of the Counter-Revolution crumpled up or melted away like snow in a Russian spring. The great steel cordon tightening around the Revolution was smashed to bits.

The Revolution was triumphant. The Soviets were saved. But with what appalling sacrifices! "For three years," says Lenin, "our whole energy was devoted to the tasks of war." The wealth of the nation was poured into the army. Fields were untilled, machines untended. Lack of fuel shut down the factories. Green wood under the boilers ruined the locomotives. The retreating armies tore up railway tracks, blew up bridges and depots and fired the grain fields and the villages. The Poles not only destroyed the water works and electric station of Kiev, but in sheer malice dynamited the Cathedral of St. Vladimir.

The Counter-Revolutionists turned their retreat into an orgy of destruction. With torch and dynamite they laid waste the land leaving behind a black wake of ruins and ashes. A host of other evils came out of the war—drastic censorship, arbitrary arrests, drum-head court-martials. The high-handed measures charged against the Communists were to a large extent measures of war—none the less they were casualties to the ideals of the Revolution.

Then the human casualties! The death toll at the front was large. The death lists from the hospitals were appalling. Medicines, gauze and surgical instruments could not come through the blockade. So limbs were amputated without anesthetics. Wounds were bandaged with newspapers. Gangrene and blood poisoning, typhus and cholera swept through the armies unchecked. The Revolution could have sustained the further loss in man-power—for Russia is vast. But it could not afford the loss in brain-power and soul-power, the wholesale massacre of its directing energizing spirits—the Communists. It was these Communists who bore the brunt of the fighting. They were formed into shock battalions. They were rushed into gaps to stiffen the wavering lines. Captured they were always killed. In the three years' war half the young Communists of Russia were slaughtered.

A mere recital of casualties means nothing, for statistics are only unemotional symbols. Let the reader recall the young men he has met in the pages of this book. They were at once dreamers and hard workers, idealists and stern realists—the flower of the Revolution, the incarnation of its dynamic spirit. It seems incredible for the Revolution to go on without them. But it does go on. For they are dead. Nearly everyone in this book is now in his grave. Here is the way some of them died:

Volodarsky—assassinated in the general plot to kill all Soviet leaders.
Neibut—executed on the Kolchak Front.
Yanishev—bayonetted by a White Guard on the Wrangel Front.
Woskov—died of typhus on the Denikin Front.
Tunganogi—shot at his desk by White Guards.
Utkin—dragged from motor car and shot.
Sukhanov—led into the woods in the early morning and clubbed to death with rifle butts.
Melnikov—taken out of prison, shot and bludgeoned.

"They were tortured, they were stoned, they were sawn asunder, they were set wandering in deserts and in mountains, in caves and in dens of the earth."

It was a cold selective killing of the keymen of the revolution, a massacre of its future builders. An incalculable loss to Russia—for these were men who could withstand the corruption of office and the poison of power. Men who could live as valorously as they died. They went to their death in order that the Revolution might live. And it does live. Though crippled and compromised, out of the long ordeal of famine, pestilence, blockade and war, the Russian Revolution emerges victorious.

Is the Revolution worth these sacrifices? These are its assured results:

One. It has destroyed root and branch the State apparatus of Czarism.
Two. It has transferred the great estates of the crown, the landlords and the monastic orders into the hands of the people.
Three. It has nationalized the basic industries and begun the electrification of Russia. It has fenced off Russia from the unlimited exploitation of free booting capitalists.
Four. It has brought into the Soviets 1 million workers and peasants and given them direct experience in government. It has organized 8 million workers into trade unions. It has taught 40 million peasants to read and write. It has opened the doors of tens of thousands of new

schools, libraries and theatres and roused the masses to the wonders of science and art.

Five. It has broken the spell of the past over a great people. Their potential forces have become kinetic. Their fatalistic: "It was so, and it will be so," is changed to "It was so, but it will not be so."

Six. It has assured self-determination to a score of subject races formerly held in vassalage to the Russian Empire. It has given them free hand to develop their own language, literature and institutions. Persia, China, Afghanistan and other backward countries—that is, "countries with great natural resources and small navies"—it has treated as equals.

Seven. It has not paid lip-service to "open diplomacy," but has made it a reality. "It has swept the secret treaties into the ash-barrel of history."

Eight. It has pioneered the way to a new society and made invaluable laboratory experiments in socialism on a colossal scale. It has quickened the faith and increased the morale of the working classes of the world in their battle for the new social order.

The wise men rise up to point out that these results might have been obtained in a better way. Likewise, the Reformation, the Independence of America, the Abolition of Slavery might have been achieved in a more gracious, less violent manner. But history did not move that way. And only the foolish quarrel with history.

# Chronology: The 1917 Russian Revolution

*Note that in 1917 Russia used the Julian calendar that runs 13 days behind the Gregorian calendar in use today. Thus, what was called the February Revolution by the Julian calendar actually occurred in March, according to the Gregorian calendar; likewise, the "October Revolution" took place in November. These dates are designated in the text at various points, with the Julian calendar listed first and the Gregorian date afterwards (in parentheses). This chronology is based on the Julian calendar in use in Russia at the time of the revolution.*

## January 1, 1917

Russia faces a series of devastating defeats on fronts stretching across thousands of miles. Over 1.5 million soldiers desert over the course of 1916. The Bolshevik Party grows to around 24,000 members.

## January 9

Bolsheviks and other antiwar socialists organize demonstrations in honor of Bloody Sunday, when tsarist troops shot down hundreds of peaceful protesters in 1905. Thirty thousand workers in Moscow and up to 145,000 strike in St. Petersburg in response.

## January 31

Petrograd is starving. The city stockpile for flour will last only ten more days; meat supplies are completely depleted. Massive queues for food form, despite subzero temperatures. Crowds of women sporadically break into stores.

## February 10

The Duma (National Assembly) Councilor of State, Mikhail Rodzianko, meets with Tsar Nicholas II in Tsarskoye Selo at the imperial residency, warning him

225

of massive upheaval. Rodzianko insists that tumultuous events can be avoided by strengthening the Duma. Nicholas II ignores this advice.

Meanwhile, Bolsheviks call a strike in Petrograd to protest the arrest of their Duma members in 1915 for opposing the war.

## February 14

The strike called by the Bolsheviks continues, while a Menshevik-initiated strike shows support for the Duma (in opposition to the Tsar) while it opens a new session at the Tauride Palace. Altogether, 90,000 workers from fifty-eight different factories are on strike in St. Petersburg. Police attempt to arrest demonstrators, but they fight back.

## February 22

The Tsar leaves for the General Staff's headquarters in Mogilev. Meanwhile, the bosses at the Putilov iron works lock out striking workers.

## February 23

The February Revolution begins. In honor of International Women's Day, militant women textile workers, many of them soldiers' wives, initiate a massive strike in St. Petersburg, despite calls for restraint by their own union leadership. About 128,000 workers take to the streets; among their chief demands are an end to the war and an increase in food supplies.

## February 24

The strike nearly doubles to around 200,000 workers. Nearly half of all industrial workers in Petrograd are on strike. Strike demands now include overthrowing the autocracy and putting an end to the war. Striking workers fraternize with soldiers and Cossacks.

## February 25

Vyborg District workers break into police stations and cut the telephones to government offices. Armed clashes with the police occur, with many killed and wounded. Meanwhile, Empress Alexandra writes to Nicholas II: "This is a hooligan campaign, with boys and girls running about shouting that they have no bread . . . all this will surely pass." General Khabalov (Commander of the Petrograd District), acting under the Tsar's orders, bans all demonstrations.

## February 26

Early Sunday morning, the police arrest more than a hundred leaders of revolutionary organizations. General Khabalov's soldiers open fire on striking workers. One hundred sixty-nine workers are killed and more than a thousand people are injured. By four that afternoon, the Fourth Company of the Pavlovsky Regiment, outraged that part of their regiment fired on workers, revolt. On the way, police try to detain the company and a firefight ensues.

## February 27

Bolshevik agitators visit with soldiers of the Volynsky Regiment. Before noon, the soldiers decide to kill the commander of the company that had fired on demonstrators the previous day. The soldiers arm themselves and agitate throughout their entire regiment. By afternoon, the Litovsky and Preobrazhensky Regiments join the mutiny, storming the Main Arsenal to secure its 40,000 rifles. Fully armed, they move on to liberate political prisoners from Kresty prison.

By nightfall, 66,000 men of the Petrograd garrison have joined the striking workers. Bolsheviks continue agitating for a new government.

Approximately 200 delegates elected by workers, peasants, and soldiers converge on the Tauride Palace to reconstitute the St. Petersburg Soviet. The Mensheviks and Socialist Revolutionaries win the most votes and elect Menshevik N.S. Chkheidze as chair of the Soviet. Within two weeks, 3,000 delegates are elected to the Soviet.

Meanwhile, Rodzianko asks the Duma to create a Provisional Committee, which asks the Tsar to agree to share power with a prime minister. The Tsar refuses.

## February 28

The revolutionary masses revolt in Moscow. The Tsar's ministers are arrested. The Provisional Committee assumes control of the army, while the Kronstadt sailors mutiny against their officers. The first issue of the Soviet newspaper *Izvestia* is published.

## March 1

The first Joint Plenum of the Soviet of Workers' and Soldiers' Deputies issues Soviet Order No. 1: All soldiers' units will elect Soldiers' Committees. The decree stipulates that soldiers will now accept orders from the Soldiers' Soviet and their locally elected committees. The Soviet also forbids its members from joining the Provisional Government (then in formation), but recognizes the authority of the Duma.

## March 2

The Soviet and Duma continue discussions on the formation of a new government. At the Soviet Plenum, the Bolsheviks criticize the lack of focus on questions of land, peace, and the eight-hour day. At the request of the Provisional Committee, Nicholas II abdicates power to his brother Mikhail, who refuses power, ending the 300-year Romanov dynasty.

The Provisional Government, headed by Georgy Lvov, takes power. It is dominated by conservative (Octobrist) and liberal (Cadet) politicians, but also seats Trudovik/Socialist Revolutionary Alexander Kerensky as Minister of Justice (although as an individual without party authorization).

Workers, soldiers, and young people take to the streets, tearing down statues of the Tsar. Loyalist police ambush and shoot the revelers, but armed Soviet soldiers hunt the police down and arrest them.

## March 3

The Executive Committee of the St. Petersburg Soviet orders the arrest of Tsar Nicholas II.

## March 5

The Bolshevik newspaper *Pravda* restarts publication after being suppressed during the war for its revolutionary opposition.

## March 6

The Provisional Government declares a general amnesty for all political prisoners. A flood of returning exiles begins in earnest.

## March 8

The Petrograd Soviet creates the Contact Commission as an organ of communication between itself and the Provisional Government. Meanwhile, the Provisional Government refuses to grant Finland independence.

## March 9

The United States is the first government in the world to recognize the new Provisional Government formally. Two days later, France, England, and Italy follow suit, after receiving assurances Russia will continue to wage war against Germany and Austria.

## March 12

Stalin arrives in Petrograd after being released from prison. Three days later, he is appointed to the editorial board of *Pravda*, along with Lev Kamenev, replacing the more anti-Provisional-Government Vyacheslav Molotov and Alexander Shlyapnikov.

The Provisional Government repeals the death penalty.

## March 14

The St. Petersburg Soviet addresses "the people of the whole world," declaring an earnest desire to end World War I without annexations or indemnities.

## March 17

Poland appeals for independence. The Provisional Government refuses.

## March 19

The Provisional Government refuses to pass land reform. Instead, the Government condemns looters and spontaneous seizures of the land by poor peasants.

## March 20

The Provisional Government abolishes all religious and ethnic restrictions put in place by the Tsar targeting Jews and other oppressed nationalities. Non-Russian languages are now allowed at private educational institutions and for record-keeping.

## March 21–22

Lenin's "Letters from Afar" are published in *Pravda*, though significantly abridged by the editors.

## March 27

Trotsky leaves exile in New York to return to Russia. Meanwhile, the Provisional Government declares that its sole purpose for continuing the war is the defense of revolutionary Russia. This serves as a compromise with the Petrograd Soviet, which accepts this new formulation.

## March 31

Georgi Plekhanov, the founder of Russian Marxism but now a strongly pro-war Menshevik, arrives in Petrograd after nearly forty years in exile.

## April 3

Lenin, Zinoviev, Armand, and other Bolsheviks arrive in Petrograd from exile in Switzerland. They are met at the train station by a large contingent of workers, soldiers, sailors, and party members. Lenin declares, "Long live the socialist revolution."

## April 4

Lenin delivers his "April Theses," calling for "all power to the soviets" and refusing support for the Provisional Government. Meanwhile, Trotsky is detained in Nova Scotia by British authorities while trying to return to Russia.

## April 12

The Provisional Government grants freedom of assembly and legalizes unions.

## April 18

Massive May Day celebrations occur in Russia. At the same time, Cadet foreign minister Pavel Miliukov secretly promises the Allies that Russia will continue the war until complete victory and declares that Russia intends to annex new territory.

## April 20–21

April Days mass protests begin after Miliukov's secret note is leaked promising to continue the war in alliance with the Allies. The Bolsheviks resolve that the resignation of Miliukov is not enough and adopt Lenin's "all power to the soviets" demand.

## May 1

The Petrograd Soviet votes in favor of forming a new Coalition Government: that is, a Provisional Government with more socialist ministers.

## May 4

Trotsky arrives in Russia.

## May 5

The first Coalition Government forms as the SR and Menshevik parties send official representatives into the Provisional Government alongside Kerensky, who joined the government without party authorization.

## May 17

The Kronstadt Soviet declares itself the sole governing power of Kronstadt Island, a military fortress and base guarding St. Petersburg from the sea.

## May 31

Octobrist war minister Guchkov resigns after street demonstrations against him. Kerensky replaces him, accumulating more power in the Provisional Government and embarking on a speaking tour of the army alongside the General Staff to rally support for a new Russian military offensive.

## June 3

The First All-Russian Congress of Soviets begins in St. Petersburg. The Congress almost unanimously agrees to end World War I, but also pledges to support the Provisional Government, despite (minority) Bolshevik opposition.

## June 5

The parliament of Finland (a territory of Russia) declares independence, except on questions of foreign policy and war. The Provisional Government sends troops to crush the parliament, which soon wavers and votes in favor of its own dissolution.

## June 10

The Central Rada (formed in Kiev on March 4) proclaims independence for the Ukraine. The ongoing Congress of Soviets unanimously supports this declaration of independence.

Meanwhile, an anti-government protest planned by the Bolsheviks is banned by the Soviet Menshevik and SR majority. Menshevik speakers tour factories, telling workers not to stage a demonstration, but they receive a hostile reception. The Bolshevik Central Committee, fearing a trap, calls off the protest.

## June 11

Mensheviks and SRs pass their own motion to hold pro-Soviet demonstrations on June 18 as a way to prove they have more support than the Bolsheviks.

## June 18

Kerensky launches a fresh offensive on the Eastern front despite incredibly low morale and poor supplies and logistics. German counterattacks bring devastating losses: 150,000 Russians are killed, with nearly 250,000 wounded.

The pro-peace Bolsheviks show their massive support with an enormous antiwar demonstration of 400,000 workers and soldiers in St. Petersburg, Moscow, Kiev, Kharkov, Ekaterinoslav, and other cities. Nearly all protestors carry banners echoing Bolshevik slogans such as "All power to the soviets" and "Down with the Ten Capitalist Ministers."

Under the cover of the demonstrations, St. Petersburg anarchists attack the prisons and free 460 prisoners. The Provisional Government turns this into propaganda, charging that the Bolsheviks are responsible. Many St. Petersburg anarchists are arrested.

## June 21

After the demonstration of June 18, workers at the Putilov iron works go on strike. The Bolsheviks, together with workers from seventy other factories, meet with the Putilov workers and sympathize with their grievances but call for restraint. Workers are starving. Soldiers demand to be sent home to plow the fields, while the First Machine Gun Regiment declares that "detachments shall be sent to the front only when the war has a revolutionary character." Entire divisions of soldiers are arrested for disobedience.

## June 23

The Kronstadt anarchists demand the liberation of the St. Petersburg anarchists and threaten to liberate them by force.

## June 24

*Izvestia* reports that the Provisional Government plans to close a series of factories in St. Petersburg, potentially leaving thousands jobless. Meanwhile, the Oranienbaum Palace garrisons inform the government that they support the Kronstadt Soviet.

## June 26

The Grenadier Guard Regiment returns from the front and joins the Kronstadt anarchists.

## July 2

The Russian offensive collapses in retreat.

## July 3–7

The July Days revolt in St. Petersburg.
Trotsky and the Mehzraiontsy join the Bolshevik Party.

## July 7

The Provisional Government orders the arrest of Lenin, Trotksy, Kollontai, Sokolnikov, Zinoviev, and many other Bolshevik leaders. *Pravda* is banned.

Prince Lvov resigns as premier of the Provisional Government and asks Kerensky to form a new cabinet.

## July 11

Lenin goes into hiding.

## July 12

The Provisional Government authorizes military trials at the front, including the death penalty.

## July 18

General Kornilov becomes the Supreme Commander-in-Chief.

## July 22

Trotsky and Lunacharsky are arrested and imprisoned in the Peter and Paul Fortress.

## July 24

The Second Coalition Government is formed of SRs, Mensheviks, and Cadets; Kerensky assumes the position of Minister President.

## July 26–August 3

The Sixth Congress of the RSDLP (Bolsheviks) convenes, representing 240,000 party members.

## August 12–15

The Provisional Government holds a State Conference in Moscow. The Workers'

Soviets overwhelmingly vote for a general strike in opposition to the conference, but the Petrograd Soviet votes 364 to 304 not to strike.

## August 14

Political polarization in the State Conference sharpens when General Kornilov arrives and speaks in ominous tones about the need for order.

## August 18

The St. Petersburg Soviet, despite the objection of Menshevik president Chkheidze, resolves, 900 to 4, to abolish the death penalty. Only the top leaders of the Menshevik party vote against.

## August 19

Kornilov demands that Kerensky allow him to reassign his army to St. Petersburg. Kerensky refuses.

## August 21

The Germans occupy Riga, Latvia. The Russian army does not attempt to defend it and simply retreats, allowing the Germans to occupy this "nest of Bolshevism." Kornilov summons 4,000 of his most loyal officers.

## August 22

Kerensky, thinking he has reached an agreement for a dictatorship, asks Kornilov to send a cavalry corps to Petrograd in order to introduce martial law.

## August 27

Kornilov sends three cavalry divisions to capture St. Petersburg. Kerensky orders them to halt and declares Kornilov a traitor. Meanwhile, the Bolsheviks begin organizing the arming of the St. Petersburg workers for self-defense.

## August 29

Nearly every district in Petrograd has organized Red Guards, now totaling 40,000 armed workers, with thousands of support personnel. Rail workers tear up tracks to prevent Kornilov's advance.

## August 30

The Soviet announces that Kornilov has been defeated and his army completely demoralized.

## August 31

A majority of the St. Petersburg Soviet votes in favor of a new government composed exclusively of socialist parties, with no representatives of the bourgeoisie.

## September 1

The St. Petersburg Soviet adopts a resolution to support the Bolsheviks. The Mensheviks and SRs try to filibuster, but the resulting vote is still devastating: 279 to 115. This demonstrates Bolshevik support to four major cities: St. Petersburg, Ivanovo-Voznesensk, Kronstadt, and Krasnoyarsk. The number of land seizures by the peasants increases to 958 incidents.

## September 2

A joint session of all Soviets in Finland (a territory of Russia) vote on a Soviet government: 700 to 13.

## September 4

Trotsky and other Bolshevik leaders are released from prison after massive public pressure. Kerensky attempts to disband the Military Revolutionary Committee; it refuses.

## September 5

Bolsheviks win majority of delegates in the St. Petersburg and Moscow Soviets.

## September 8

The sailors of the Baltic Fleet, through their elected organs, declare that they will not recognize the authority of the Provisional Government.

## September 14

Lenin also sends a series of letters to the Central Committee in both Moscow and Petrograd, including "Marxism and Insurrection" and "The Bolsheviks Must Assume Power."

## September 14–22

The Provisional Government convenes a Democratic Conference, with 1,200 delegates in attendance, in hopes of buttressing its democratic legitimacy. The Bolsheviks agree to participate in a so-called Pre-Parliament scheduled for October, despite the objections of Lenin and others on the Central Committee.

## September 18

Kerensky orders the dissolution of the Central Committee of the Baltic Fleet. The fleet refuses. In Tashkent, Uzbekistan, the Soviet overthrows the local government. Kerensky sends troops to take back the city.

## September 19

The Moscow Soviet elects Bolshevik Victor Nogin chairman.

## September 23

The parties prepare lists of candidates for the Constituent Assembly elections.

## September 25

Trotsky is elected chairman of the Petrograd Soviet.

Kerensky forms the Third Coalition Government with support from Right Menshevik and SR party leaders, keeping the Foreign Ministry in the hands of the pro-war Mikhail Tereshchenko, a large landowner and sugar baron.

## October

Trade-union membership rises to nearly 2 million workers throughout Russia.

## October 5

The Bolshevik Central Committee reverses its decision to participate in the Pre-Parliament.

## October 6

The Petrograd Soldiers' Soviet declares that it no longer reports to the Provisional Government.

## October 7

The Pre-Parliament begins its first session. When the Bolsheviks' time slot arrives, Trotsky delivers a scathing speech and leads a Bolshevik walkout.

## October 10

The Bolshevik Central Committee debates and approves the decision to overthrow the Provisional Government. Kamenev and Zinoviev strongly disagree with the majority decision to overthrow the government.

## October 12

The Petrograd Soviet creates its own Military Revolutionary Committee, which will lead the insurrection.

## October 18

Kamenev and Zinoviev announce the Bolshevik plan for revolution in a Menshevik newspaper. Lenin demands that both be expelled from the party, but no decision is made.

## October 19

The All-Russian Conference of Factory and Shop Committees votes for "all power to the soviets."

## October 10–23

The Bolsheviks carry on extensive agitation throughout the country to prepare insurrection, including mass meetings in St. Petersburg.

## October 24

The Provisional Government attempts to close the Bolshevik newspaper.

The October Revolution begins. By nightfall, Red Guards and Soviet workers control most bridges and key positions throughout the city, including all roads into the city. Lenin arrives at Smolny.

## October 25

By morning, the Red Guards have seized the General Post Office; the Nikolaevsky, Varshaysky, and Baltiisky train stations; the power stations; the State Bank; the central telephone exchange; and the main government buildings. The Winter Palace, General Staff headquarters, the Marinsky Palace, and a few other buildings remain in the hands of the Provisional Government.

At 10:40 P.M., the Second All-Russian Congress of the Soviets opens at Smolny and the Mensheviks and SRs walk out. Kerensky flees to the north.

## October 26

The Winter Palace is captured at two in the morning.

The Soviet Congress reconvenes in the afternoon and issues decrees on land reform and peace, as well as forming a Bolshevik-led government composed of a Council of People's Commissars (initially all Bolsheviks) and a broader All-Russian Executive Committee consisting of sixty-two Bolsheviks, twenty-nine Social-Revolutionaries, and ten Mensheviks.

## October 27

Kerensky's troops approach St. Petersburg. Soviet power is successfully established in Minsk, Kronstadt, Ivanovo-Voznesensk, Lugansk, Kazan, Rostov-on-Don, Ekaterinburg, Revel, Samara, and Saratov.

## October 29

The Junkers launch an insurrectionary attempt within St. Petersburg but are quickly defeated by the Red Guard on the same day. Meanwhile, the Vikzhel (Executive Committee of Railwaymen) demand a "United Socialist Government" composed of Mensheviks, SRs, and Bolsheviks.

## October 31

The Soviet Revolution wins in Baku, Azerbaijan, and now holds a total of seventeen provincial capitals. Red Guards confront General Krasnov's troops and take back the Pulkovo Hills outside of Petrograd; the opposition dissolves.

## November 1

The Soviet revolution gains control in Tashkent. In the north, General Krasnov is taken prisoner, but Kerensky again escapes.

## November 2

The Soviet Government proclaims the Declaration of Rights of the Peoples of Russia, permitting the nationalities of Russia to break away and have full independence.

## November 3

The Kremlin in Moscow is secured, ending the battle for Moscow. Meanwhile, amid strife inside the Bolshevik party, a minority refuses to cooperate with the new government. Kamenev, Zinoviev, Rykov, Nogin, and others, citing the Vikzhel issue (among others), decide to leave the party. Sverdlov is elected chairman of the All-Russian Central Executive Committee of the Soviet, replacing Kamenev.

## Mid-November

Constituent Assembly elections begin.

The Left Socialist Revolutionary Party formally constitutes itself as an independent party.

## November 18

A Soviet government is established in Vladivostok.

## November 20

The Ukrainian Rada declares itself an independent nation. Meanwhile, General Dukhonin is defeated by the Red Guards at Mogilev.

## November 21

The Soviet government publishes a decree allowing citizens to recall politicians from office.

## November 23

The Soviet government publishes a decree limiting the salaries of highly paid officials.

## November 26

The Soviet government begins peace talks with the Axis powers in Brest-Litovsk.

## November 28

The Soviet government controls twenty-eight provincial capitals, in addition to every major industrial center of the country. It orders the arrest of the leadership of the Cadet party.

Meanwhile, the eight-hour day is introduced for railway workers and the Commissariat of Public Education is created, removing the monopoly on education formerly held by the Russian Orthodox Church.

## December 3

The Soviet Union recognizes the right of the Ukraine to secede, unconditionally and without reservations. The Ukrainian Rada, however, refuses to allow Ukrainian soviets to meet and hold a congress.

## December 6

Russian women win the right to divorce.

## December 7

The Cheka is created to combat counterrevolution and sabotage; Dzerzhinsky is appointed its chairman.

## December 10

Seven members of the Left SRs join the Council of People's Commissars.

## December 14

Nationalization of the banks is proclaimed.

## December 15

The Soviet government offers its first armistice to the Central Powers in an attempt to end the war. Demobilization of the army begins.

## December 17

Results from the Constituent Assembly elections show 36 million votes cast, with 58 percent going to the Socialist Revolutionaries; 25 percent to the Bolsheviks; 13 percent to the Cadets; and 4 percent to the Mensheviks. However, the Right SRs are unfairly represented over the Left SRs, because the candidate lists had been established before the SRs' division into two separate parties.

## December 19

Finland announces its independence from Russia.

## December 25

The First All-Ukraine Congress of Soviets declares Ukraine a Soviet Socialist Republic, still independent from Russia, and disavows the Rada.

## December 31

The Soviet Union accepts Finnish independence.

## January 6, 1918

The Bolsheviks and Left SRs dissolve the Constituent Assembly.

## February 18

Germany resumes its offensive, seizing the Ukraine, Poland, and the Baltic states, and threatens St. Petersburg.

## March 3

The Brest-Litovsk Treaty is signed.

# Biographical and Organizational Glossary

**Alexiev (also Alexeief, Alexeyeff), Mikhail** (1856–1918). High-ranking tsarist general. Commander-in-Chief after the February Revolution. Joined White Army after October Revolution.

**Anet, Claude** (1868–1931). French military officer on assignment in Russia. He sympathized with the anti-tsarist revolution of February, enjoyed easy access to the Russian officer corps, despised the Bolsheviks, and became an ardent admirer of Socialist Revolutionary leader Alexander Kerensky.

**Antonov-Ovseyenko, Vladimir** (1883–1938). Joined the Mensheviks in 1903, sided with the Menshevik Internationalists during World War I, and joined the Bolsheviks prior to the Revolution. Named People's Commissar of Military Affairs after the October Revolution. Executed by Stalin in 1938.

**Armand, Inessa** (1874–1920). Joined the RSDLP in 1903, soon becoming a key Bolshevik underground organizer in Russia. The tsarist secret police considered her one of the Bolsheviks' most important operatives. Returned from exile in a sealed train across Germany with Lenin and Zinoviev in April 1917. After the October Revolution, headed the Moscow Economic Council and then Zhenotdel, the Women's Department of the Bolshevik Party, until her death from typhus in 1920.

**Bakunin, Mikhail** (1814–76). Russian anarchist and ideological foe of Marx and Engels. Advocated secret plots by armed minorities as a means of sparking revolutions, but criticized the Paris Commune for being overly centralized. Became Marx and Engels's chief rival in the International Workingmen's Association, from which he was expelled in 1872.

**Bebel, August** (1840–1913). Cabinet maker and founder of the Social Democratic Workers' Party of Germany in 1869. Led the German Social Democratic Party (SPD) from its founding in 1875, after merging with the Lassallean

243

General German Workers' Association. Close confidant of Marx and Engels. Elected to the Reichstag in 1867. Imprisoned for two years in 1872 for opposing the Franco-Prussian War. An outspoken opponent of German colonialism in Africa and author of many books and articles, including *Women and Socialism* (1879).

**Bernstein, Eduard** (1850–1932). Engels's close associate and literary executor and a leading intellectual in the SPD. After Engels's death in 1895, published a series of attacks arguing that Marx and Engels had been wrong to believe that capitalism could not outgrow economic crisis and that the working class needed to make a revolution in order to achieve socialism. Author of *Evolutionary Socialism* (originally titled *The Premises of Socialism and the Tasks of the Social Democrats*) (1899).

**Bismarck, Otto von** (1815–98). German aristocratic politician who campaigned for the unification of non-Austrian Germany through a series of wars in the 1860s. Appointed First Chancellor of the united German state by King Wilhelm I in 1871 after victory in the Franco-Prussian War. Authored the Anti-Socialist Laws (1878–90), but also instituted a series of social welfare reforms designed to placate socialist demands, such as accident, sickness, and old-age insurance benefits. Held the post of chancellor until 1890.

**Black Hundreds.** Extreme reactionary Russian monarchist gangs organized to carry out extrajudicial attacks on political opponents and ethnic minorities, especially Jews.

**Blanqui, Louis Auguste (August)** (1805–81). French revolutionary greatly admired by Marx for his audacity and leadership qualities. Advocated armed revolution led by secretly organized societies. It was in opposition to Blanqui's conception of a revolutionary dictatorship *over* the proletariat that Marx counterposed his notion of the dictatorship *of* the proletariat. Blanqui was arrested and escaped or was granted amnesty several times between 1848 and 1870. Detained on the eve of the Paris Commune, he was elected its president from his prison cell, where he remained until 1879 when he was elected, again from prison, to the National Assembly. He died shortly thereafter, his health broken by incarceration.

**Bogdanov, Alexander Aleksandrovich** (1873–1928). Major cultural and scientific figure in Russia and close collaborator of Lenin during the early years of the Bolshevik Party. After the defeat of the 1905 Revolution, Bogdanov led a faction of "Ultimatists" who demanded that revolutionary socialists withdraw from the Tsar's Duma, a position that brought him into sharp conflict with Lenin and led to his expulsion from the main Bolshevik organization in 1909. Played only a minor role in politics after that, but emerged after 1917 as a professor of economics at the University of Moscow and cofounder of the Proletkult movement of radical Soviet artists. Died in 1928 from the effects of multiple blood transfusions, which he believed would slow the effects of aging.

**Bolsheviks.** A faction of the Russian Social Democratic Labor Party led by Lenin after the split in the 1903 at the Second Party Congress. Named after the Russian word for "majority," it was founded based on the support of a majority of delegates at that congress. After periods of semi-unity with the Mensheviks ("minority") during and after the 1905 Russian Revolution, the Bolsheviks emerged after 1912 as an independent party based on the belief that the Russian working class must play the leading role in any revolution. Intransigently opposed to World War I, the party gained the support of a small but significant minority of the working class after the February Revolution of 1917. It gained majority support in the working class by the fall of 1917 by advocating an immediate end to the war and the transfer of all power to the Soviets of Workers', Soldiers', and Peasants' Deputies. Led the 1917 October Revolution and organized the first successful workers' state in history.

**Bryant, Louise** (1885–1936). Journalist for *The Masses* and *The Liberator*, feminist, labor activist. Traveled to Russia in 1917 with John Reed. Author of *Six Red Months in Russia: An Observer's Account of Russia Before and During the Proletarian Dictatorship* (1921).

**Bubnov, Andrei** (1883–1938). Bolshevik from 1903. Elected to the Bolshevik Central Committee in 1917. Leader in the Red Army after the October Revolution. Shot by Stalin in 1938.

**Bukharin, Nikolai** (1888–1938). Joined the Bolshevik faction in 1906 as a student leader in Moscow. Became a close collaborator of Lenin and a leading Bolshevik theorist on questions of economy and imperialism. Elected to the Central Committee and Politburo after the October Revolution. Clashed with Lenin over questions of the state and national self-determination during World War I and over the Brest-Litovsk Treaty in 1918. Considered one of the most popular figures in the Communist Party leadership after the revolution. Championed the Soviet New Economic Policy in 1921 and, after Lenin's death, encouraged an "enrich yourselves" policy to peasants in the hope of spurring rapid agricultural growth and moderate industrialization. Served as president of the Communist International from 1926 to

1929 before running afoul of Stalin's consolidation of power. Executed by Stalin in 1938 during the Great Purge.

**Bund, Jewish.** Mass Jewish workers' organization that advocated civil rights and socialism. Refused to join the Russian Social Democratic Labor Party because of conditions put forward by a majority of delegates at the 1903 Congress, but subsequently joined at the 1906 Unification Congress of the RSDLP after the 1905 Revolution.

**Cadets.** Russian political party representing industrial and commercial bourgeoisie along with urban middle classes. After the February Revolution, the Cadets became the main political representatives of anti-Soviet class forces, forming bourgeois allies for Kerensky and Right SRs and Mensheviks in the Provisional Government throughout 1917. Opposed the October Revolution and were suppressed as a party after 1918. Sometimes Kadets.

**Chkheidze, Nikolay** (1864–1926). Georgian Social Democrat (Menshevik) who was elected president of the Executive Committee of the St. Petersburg Soviet in March 1917 before being replaced in September by Trotsky. After the October Revolution, became president of the anti-Soviet Republic of Georgia and attempted to secure an alliance with Great Britain before the Red Army took over in 1921.

**Chernov, Victor** (1873–1952). Founding member of the Socialist Revolutionary Party. Elected to the Second Duma after the 1905 Revolution and was a leader of the SR parliamentary group. Acted as an outspoken opponent of Lenin and the October Revolution from his post as the appointed Minister of Agriculture in Provisional Government. Elected chairman of the Russian Constituent Assembly in January 1918 before its dissolution by the Soviet government. Fled to the United States during the Russian civil war.

**Dan (Gurvich), Fyodor Ilyich** (1871–1947). Joined the socialist movement in 1896; after 1903 became a prominent Menshevik. Elected to the Praesidium of the St. Petersburg Soviet after February Revolution. Hostile to the October Revolution. Sent into exile in 1921.

**Debs, Eugene V.** (1855–1926). Trade-union leader, journalist, cofounder of Socialist Party of America, and five-time presidential candidate. Imprisoned in Leavenworth Penitentiary for antiwar agitation between 1919 and 1921, receiving 900,000 votes for president from his cell in 1920. A proponent of the Bolshevik Revolution, although critical of the Communists later on.

**Defensism; defensist.** During World War I, many European socialists adopted defensism, meaning they were for the defense of their own country. Lenin and the left argued that this position was tantamount to renouncing the struggle against their national ruling classes and was a cover for patriotism. After the February Revolution, many previously antiwar (or "Zimmerwald") socialists became defensists, arguing that the gains of the February Revolution had to be defended from German imperialism. Lenin argued that Marxists would only become defensists after the ruling class was overthrown and the working class was in power.

**Duma**. Elected legislative assembly with limited power, conceded by the Tsar after the 1905 Revolution. Four successive Duma elections featured progressively restrictive and undemocratic voting procedures, each dissolved by royal decree. Bolshevik, Menshevik and Socialist Revolutionary deputies were elected to various Dumas.

**Dubenko, Pavel Dybenko** *(1889–1938)*. Revolutionary activist from 1907 on; joined the Bolsheviks in 1912. In 1915, helped organize a mutiny on the battleship *Emperor Paul I*. Key figure among Bolshevik sailors in 1917; appointed to the Commissariat of Naval Affairs after the October Revolution. Executed by Stalin in 1938.

**Engels, Friedrich** (1821–95). Close friend, benefactor, and collaborator of Marx for forty years; cofounder of the theory that became known as Marxism. Prolific author and journalist. Participated in the German Revolution of 1848, for which he was exiled from Germany for the rest of his life. Leader in the International Workingmen's Association from 1864 to 1872. Served as a practical advisor to the SPD for more than two decades, during its rise from illegality to prominence in Germany, and helped engineer the unification of European socialism in the Second International in 1891. Increasingly vocal critic of the opportunist trend in the SPD in the years before his death.

**First International** (1864–76). Originally named the International Workingmen's Association, it was a loose coalition of socialist organizations and trade unions founded in 1864. Karl Marx and Friedrich Engels played prominent roles in developing the International's program and developing its practical work. Collapsed in wake of the Paris Commune because of repression in France and disputes between socialists and anarchists, represented chiefly by Marx and Bakunin, respectively. Formally dissolved in 1876.

**Fraternization.** The practice of troops from opposing armies communicating and expressing sympathy or solidarity with one another.

**Gotha Program**. Program adopted by the German SPD in 1875.

**Guchkov, Alexander Ivanovich** (1862–1936). Leader of the pro-monarchy Octobrist Party and a Moscow industrialist. Negotiated Tsar Nicholas II's abdication. Served in the Provisional Government as first Minister of War and Navy until being forced out by mass protests during the April Days.

**Gorky, Maxim** (1868–1936). World-famous Russian author. Five times nominated for the Nobel Prize for Literature. Socialist and critic; publisher of the revolutionary *Novaya Zhizn (New Life)* newspaper in 1917; close to Lenin and the Bolsheviks through the October Revolution but critical of them during the civil war.

**Kaledin, Alexey** (1861–1918). Tsarist Cossack cavalry general. Took part in the Kornilov coup. Committed suicide in February 1918 as the Red Army advanced.

**Kamenev (Rosenfeld), Lev Borisovich** (1883–1936). Joined the socialist movement in 1901 and became a prominent Bolshevik organizer beginning in 1903. Returned from Siberian exile after February 1917 and took over editorship of the Bolshevik newspaper *Pravda*. As a member of Central Committee, opposed the October Revolution, but resumed party posts and was elected chairman of the All-Russian Executive Committee of the Soviets. Executed by Stalin in 1936.

**Kerensky, Alexander** (1881–1970). Member of the Trudovik faction of the Socialist Revolution Party. Defended workers and socialists from repression as a lawyer before World War I. Entered the Provisional Government as Minister of Justice in February 1917, then became minister of the Army and Navy and finally, in July, premier. Narrowly escaped from the Soviet government after the Provisional Government's overthrow in October 1917. Emigrated to the United States.

**Kollontai, Alexandra Mikhailovna** (1872–1952). Daughter of an aristocratic family; became a revolutionary in 1896, subsequently joining the Mensheviks until adopting a revolutionary antiwar position in 1915. Joined the Bolsheviks upon returning to Russia from exile in 1917 and was elected to the Central Committee. Served as Commissar of Social Welfare after the Bolshevik Revolution.

**Kornilov, Lavr** (1870–1918). High-ranking tsarist general. Appointed commander-in-chief by Kerensky after the collapse of the Russian offensive in June 1917. Launched a coup attempt against the Provisional Government and Soviets on August 27, 1917; defeated by mass working-class resistance. Killed in battle with the Red Army in April 1918.

**Krupskaya, Nadezhda** (1869–1939). Early convert to Russian Marxism and leader of St. Petersburg's underground movement. Arrested and exiled to Siberia in 1896, where she married Lenin. Helped lead the Bolshevik faction after the 1903 split in the Russian Social Democratic Labor Party; served as the Central Committee's secretary from 1905. Returned from exile with Lenin in 1917 and joined the Central Committee of the Russian Communist Party after Lenin's death in 1924. Criticized some of Stalin's repressive acts in the late 1920s, but served as a Soviet functionary until her death.

**Krylenko, Nikolai Vasilyevich** (1885–1938). Bolshevik from 1904. Imprisoned and exiled for revolutionary activity. Returned to Russia in 1915 to build the Bolshevik underground; arrested and sent to the front in 1916. Elected head of his Army division's soldiers' committee after the February Revolution. Leader in the Military Revolutionary Committee in October 1917 and then the Red Army. Executed by Stalin in 1938.

**Lenin, Vladimir Ilyich** (1871–1924). Brilliant law student turned underground Marxist organizer, prolific author, and revolutionary journalist. His older brother Alexander was executed for taking part in a failed plot to assassinate the Tsar in 1887. Exiled to Siberia in 1897 for political activity, where he married Nadezdha Krupskaya. Escaped to Western Europe, where he became the leading advocate of the 1903 Second Congress of the Russian Social Democratic Labor Party; led the Bolshevik faction during and after the Congress. Returned to Russia during the 1905 Revolution but was exiled after its defeat. Initiated the independent Bolshevik Party in 1912 and helped establish a significant working-class following through publishing the daily newspaper *Pravda*. With the outbreak of World War I, he adopted an extreme antiwar position, insisting that socialists should advocate the overthrow of capitalism as the only means to end the war. Returned from exile in April 1917 after the Tsar's abdication. Advocated "all power to the soviets" as an alternative to the reformist Provisional Government. Elected chairman of the Council of People's Commissars by the Second All-Russian Congress of Soviets on October 27, 1917, after the overthrow of the Provisional Government in Saint Petersburg. Initiated the Third (Communist) International in 1919. Shot by a Socialist Revolutionary leader in the summer of 1918. In May 1922, suffered the first of three strokes that progressively disabled him until his death in January 1924.

**Lunacharsky, Anatol Vasilyevich** (1875–1933). Bolshevik from 1903, but sided with Bogdanov in the split with Lenin in 1908. Rejoined the Bolsheviks in 1917 and became Commissar of Education after the October Revolution.

**Luxemburg, Rosa** (1871–1919). Jewish revolutionary socialist from Poland. Cofounder of the Polish Social Democratic Party and a prominent leader on the extreme left of the German SPD. A prolific writer, organizer, and educator in the workers' movement and the most vocal opponent of Eduard Bernstein. Split with Karl Kautsky over World War I and advocated revolutionary action against the German state, for which she was imprisoned in 1914. The November 1918 revolution freed her from prison and she soon cofounded the German Communist Party (KPD) with Karl Liebknecht in late 1918. Arrested by government troops during the January 1919 uprising and assassinated along with Liebknecht.

**Lvov (also Lvof, Lvoff), Prince Georgy** (1861–1925). Aristocrat and monarchist. Appointed first minister-chairman of the Provisional Government after the February Revolution. Forced out by Kerensky after the July Days. Escaped into exile after the October Revolution.

**Martov, Julius** (1873–1923). Founder of the Russian Social Democratic Labor Party and intellectual leader of its Menshevik faction from 1903 and through his exile after 1905 until the October Revolution. Opposed World War I and broke with the pro-war right wing of the Menshevik party to form an Internationalist faction. Returned to Russia from exile in a sealed train through Germany in May 1917 to support the formation of the Soviet government, but opposed the October Revolution. Supported the Red Army against the White Army. Left Russia in 1920 legally and debated Zinoviev during the Independent Socialist Democratic Party congress that same year, opposing its affiliation to the pro-Bolshevik Third International. Intended to return to Russia, but the Menshevik Party was banned in 1921. Died in Schömberg, Germany.

**Marx, Karl** (1818–1883). With Friedrich Engels, cofounder of the revolutionary theory subsequently known as Marxism, defining socialism as the self-emancipation of the working class. Prolific author and organizer.

**McKay, Claude** (1889–1948). Jamaican American author; rose to national prominence during the Harlem Renaissance. Editor of *The Masses* and *The Liberator*. Worked closely with Communists in early 1920s, including speaking at the Communist International in Moscow, where he delivered a "Report on the Negro Question" that served to transform US Communists' approach to Black liberation.

**Mensheviks.** A faction of the Russian Social Democratic Labor Party led by Martov and Plekhanov after the split in 1903 at the Second Party Congress. Named after the Russian word for "minority." After periods of semi-unity with the Bolsheviks during and after the 1905 Russian Revolution, the Mensheviks were split between left-wing and right-wing trends, exemplified by Martov and Plekhanov respectively, largely based on their attitude toward the tasks of the working class in the anti-tsarist revolution. Many opposed World War I and joined the Zimmerwald antiwar movement. After the February Revolution of 1917, the party's more conservative wing came to lead the First All-Russian Congress of Soviets in alliance with the Socialist Revolutionaries. Martov's Menshevik Internationalists moved sharply to the left but opposed the October uprising, although many left-wing Mensheviks joined the Bolsheviks before and after October.

**Mezhraiontsy.** Committee of revolutionary socialists based in St. Petersburg, independent of the Bolsheviks until their merger in July 1917. Leading figures included Trotsky, Joffe, Lunacharsky, Uritsky, Riazanov, and Volodarsky.

**Miliukov, Pavel** (1859–1943). Cadet politician in the Dumas under the Tsar. Foreign Minister in the first Provisional Government after the February Revolution. Forced to resign by protests during the April Days after promising to continue the war. Supported the Kornilov coup. Opposed the October Revolution and negotiated with the German high command in an attempt to overturn the revolution; subsequently supported the White Army.

**Nogin, Viktor** (1878–1924). Joined the socialist movement in the 1890s and the Bolshevik faction in 1903. Leader of the Moscow Bolsheviks during 1917.

**Oppokov (Lomov), Georgy** (1888–1938). Bolshevik. Early advocate of "all power to the soviets" before Lenin's "April Theses." Candidate member of the Bolshevik Central Committee in 1917. Appointed People's Commissar of Justice after the October Revolution.

**Paris Commune** (March 18–May 28, 1871). After the defeat of French forces under Emperor Louis Napoleon Bonaparte at the hands of the Germans, workers in Paris revolted against the central government and established the first working-class state in history, the Paris Commune. The government was based on direct democracy, radical labor reforms, and the armed power of the working class. See Marx's account in *The Civil War in France*.

**Plekhanov, Georgi** (1856–1918). Brilliant writer of whom Engels thought highly. Considered the founder of Russian Marxism; central to the organization of the Russian Social Democratic Labor Party. Maintained an uneasy alliance with Lenin and the Bolsheviks until the failed 1905 Revolution, after which he drifted steadily to the right, joining the Menshevik camp. Strong supporter of Russia in World War I and opponent of the October Revolution.

**Potresov, Alexander** (1869–1934). Influential early Russian Marxist and one of the initial six editors of *Iskra*, the socialist newspaper Lenin organized in order to build the RSDLP. At the 1903 Party Congress, Potresov was removed from the editorial board by the majority of voting delegates, hardening the split between the Bolsheviks and the Mensheviks. Prominent leader of the Menshevik faction from this time, becoming an outspoken supporter of Russia in World War I.

**Price, Morgan Philips** (1885–1973). Covered the Eastern front as a reporter for the *Manchester Guardian* during World War I. He learned Russian at Cambridge University and, although not a socialist before the revolution, soon became one of the Bolsheviks' most important English-language information outlets. Liberal, then Labor Party Member of Parliament off and on in the 1920s and 1930s.

**Provisional Government.** Ad hoc government of Russia established in the wake of Tsar Nicholas II's abdication in February 1917. Composed of royal ministers and liberal politicians as well as a minority of Socialist Revolutionary and Menshevik representatives. Formed the center of the Russian capitalist state, as opposed to the embryonic working-class state represented by the soviets. Overthrown by the 1917 October Revolution.

**Radek, Karl** (1835–1939). Polish revolutionary socialist, active in the German Communist Party as an ally of Lenin. Leading personality in the founding of the German Communist Party (KPD) and the Third (Communist) International in 1919. Died in a Stalinist concentration camp in 1939.

**Ransome, Arthur** (1884–1967). English gentleman sent to Russia to cover World War I for the *Daily News*, a left-leaning English publication. Best known as a naturalist and children's book author, Ransome had no strong political commitments and viewed his relationship to the Bolsheviks as that of an objective, if sympathetic, reporter.

**Raskolnikov, Fyodor** (1892–1939). Bolshevik sailor and leader of the Kronstadt garrison in 1917. Leader of the Red Navy Caspian Fleet during the civil war. Published an open letter attacking Stalin in 1939. Died under mysterious circumstances.

**Reed, John** (1887–1920). US journalist, labor activist, member of Socialist Party left wing and Industrial Workers of the World. Traveled to Russia in fall of 1917. Author of *Ten Days That Shook the World* (1919). Cofounder of the Communist Labor Party in 1919.

**Riazanov (Goldenbach), David Borisovich** (1870–1938). Well-known socialist historian and activist; returned with Martov from exile in a sealed train through Germany in May 1917. Joined the Mezhraiontsy and then the Bolsheviks in July 1917.

**Rodzianko, Mikhail Vladimirovich** (1859–1923). Prominent tsarist politician and large landowner. Negotiated Tsar Nicholas II's abdication. Passed over for premiership of the Provisional Government because he was too closely associated with the monarchy for popular opinion. Supported the White Army during the civil war before emigrating.

**Russian Social Democratic Labor Party (RSDLP).** Party officially formed in 1898 as a section of the Second International, but immediately broken by the arrests of most of its leading members. Held its second official Congress in 1903, where the party split into competing Bolshevik and Menshevik factions. These factions temporarily reunited in the wake of the 1905 Revolution, but split into irreconcilable parties after 1912.

**Rykov, Alexei** (1881–1938). Joined the RSDLP in 1898 and Bolsheviks in 1903. Long exile and imprisonment. Elected to Bolshevik Central Committee in July 1917 and served on Moscow Military Revolutionary Committee. People's Commissar of Internal Affairs after October Revolution. Shot by Stalin in 1938.

**Scheidemann, Philipp** (1865–1939). Leader of the right wing of the German Social Democratic Party. Proclaimed the end of monarchy and the birth of the German Republic from a balcony on November 9, 1918, in opposition to Karl Liebknecht's proclamation of the German Socialist Republic later that day. Elected to the Council of People's Deputies from the German Workers' and Soldiers' Councils between November 1918 and February 1919, but opposed the Councils assuming state power. Briefly headed the national government in wake of the November 1918 revolution.

**Second International** (1899–present). Coalition of mass socialist parties that sought to coordinate communication and action for the international workers' movement. Proclaimed May Day an international workers' holiday in 1889 and International Women's Day in 1910. Split between pro-war, pacifist, and revolutionary anti-imperialist factions during World War I. After its left wing split to form the revolutionary Third International in 1919 in the wake of the Russian Revolution, the Second International moved sharply to the right. Today it remains the official organization of reformist socialist parties such as the French Socialist Party, the British Labor Party, and the German Social Democratic Party.

**Shulgin, Vasilii Vitalyevich** (1878–1945). Prominent tsarist politician. Opposed the February Revolution. Supported the Provisional Government against the soviets; backed the Kornilov coup and subsequently the White Army.

**Shliapnikov, Alexander Gavrilovich** (1875–1937). Joined the Bolsheviks in 1903. Prominent industrial workers' leader and Bolshevik representative on the Executive Committee of the St. Petersburg Soviet after the February Revolution. Served as People's Commissar of Labor after the October Revolution.

**Skobelev, Matvey** (1885–1938). Joined the RSDLP in 1903, aligning with the Menshevik faction. Collaborated closely with Leon Trotsky, editing *Pravda* between 1908 and 1912 (not to be confused with Lenin's paper of the same name launched in 1912 in St. Petersburg) before being elected to the Fourth Duma in 1912. Central leader of the St. Petersburg Soviet from February 1917, then minister of labor in the Provisional Government. Opposed the October Revolution and returned home to Baku, then under occupation by British troops. After Red Army's victory in the civil war, emigrated to Paris but returned to the Soviet Union, joining the Communist Party in 1922 as a foreign trade specialist. Executed during Stalin's 1938 Great Purge.

**Slutskaya, Vera** (1874–1917). Joined revolutionary movement through Jewish Bund in 1898, but joined Bolsheviks in 1903. Returned from exile in 1917 to organize and agitate among poor working-class women. Worked as secretary of the Bolshevik Vassilievsky Island district committee. Took part in the October Revolution in St. Petersburg. Killed by Kerensky's counterrevolutionary troops on the outskirts of St. Petersburg on October 30, 1917.

**Social Democratic Party (SPD).** Formed in 1875 in Gotha, Germany, from a merger of the General German Workers' Association (organized by Ferdinand Lassalle in 1863) and the German Social Democratic Workers' Party (founded by Wilhelm Liebknecht and August Bebel in Eisenach, Germany, in 1869). Despite the Anti-Socialist Laws in force between 1878 and 1890, the SPD grew significantly and emerged with 20 percent of the popular vote by the time it was legalized in 1890, adopting a new program at Erfurt, Germany, in 1891. It became the largest and most influential party in the Second International. In the years before World War I, it grew to nearly a million members, including right, center, and left factions. In August 1914, SPD Reichstag deputies voted unanimously to support war credits, abiding by party discipline. Under the shadow of World War I, the majority of the party radicalized and was expelled by the SPD leadership, forming the United Social Democratic Party (USPD) in 1917. A small minority left the USPD after the November 1918 revolution to form the German Communist Party (KPD) that December.

**Socialist Revolutionary Party.** Founded in 1902 by Victor Chernov, Yekaterina Breshko-Breshkovskaya, Maria Spiridonova, and other heirs of the Russian populist tradition. Advocated land reform and democracy, but a majority of the party supported Russia in World War I. Along with the Mensheviks, won majority support in the soviets in early 1917 before the workers and soldiers shifted to the Bolshevik Party. The party split between right-wing and left-wing Socialist Revolutionaries during the revolution, with the right wing led by Provisional Government Minister of Agriculture Chernov and the Left SRs led by Spiridonova.

**Soviets.** Russian word for *council*, referring to democratically elected representative organizations of the working class. Soviets first formed in Russia during the 1905 Revolution and were revived in February 1917 in St. Petersburg, rapidly spreading across all Russian cities, rural areas, and the army and navy. Coordinated by the All-Russian Congress of Soviets. Lenin argued that soviets served as a working-class alternative to the capitalist Provisional Government and should be understood as the potential basis for a revolutionary workers' state, as elaborated in his slogan "all power to the soviets." The Second All-Russian Congress of Soviets assumed state power after the October Revolution.

**Stalin, Josef** (1878–1953). Early member of the Bolshevik faction and a consistent supporter of Lenin. Played an important role in the Bolshevik Party during the repression in the summer of 1917. After the devastation of the Russian civil war, international isolation, and Lenin's death in the early 1920s, Stalin personified the bureaucratic turn in the Bolshevik Party. By the late 1920s, he had consolidated control over the party's apparatus and launched a series of Five-Year Plans aimed at smashing all internal political opposition and forcing rapid industrialization in order to compete with Western European capitalist states. By the early 1930s Stalin had initiated brutal purges of almost the entire past leadership of the Bolshevik Party.

**Stassova, Elana** (1873–1966). Joined the RSDLP in 1900 and worked as an underground Bolshevik organizer in St. Petersburg. Candidate member and secretary of the Bolshevik Central Committee in 1917.

**Steinberg, Isaac Nachman** (1888–1957). Lawyer and activist. Joined the Socialist Revolution Party after the 1905 Revolution. Gave critical support to the October Revolution, becoming People's Commissar of Justice between

December 1917 and March 1918 before resigning in protest of the Brest-Litovsk Treaty.

**Sukhanov, N.N.** (1882–1940). Prominent revolutionary writer and independent Marxist. Served on the Executive Committee of the St. Petersburg Soviet throughout 1917 and eventually joined Martov's Menshevik Internationalist party. Editor of the St. Petersburg revolutionary newspaper *Novaya Zhizn* (*New Life*). Opposed the Bolshevik Revolution, but argued it was necessary to remain in the Soviet government after October. Wrote *The Russian Revolution: A Personal Account*, considered one of the most important historical texts of 1917.

**Sverdlov, Yakov Mikhailovich** (1885–1919). Joined the Russian Social Democratic Labor Party in 1902 and sided with the Bolshevik faction in 1903. After 1905, spent the next eleven years in prison and Siberian exile. Granted amnesty during the February Revolution. Member of the Bolshevik Central Committee and key organizer of the October Revolution. Elected chair of the Executive of the All-Russian Congress of Soviets. Died of typhus or influenza in March 1919.

**Tereshchenko, Mikhail Ivanovich** (1888–1956). Tsarist statesman, sugar magnate, and banker. Emigrated after the October Revolution.

**Third International** (1919–43). Popularly called the Communist International or Comintern. Initiated by the revolutionary left wing of the Second International, principally the Bolshevik Party. By 1920, majorities or large minorities of the most important socialist parties had joined the Third International, forming mass parties in France, Italy, Germany, and Bulgaria and smaller parties of thousands or tens of thousands in the United States, Britain, and China. By the 1930s, large parties had taken root in India, Indonesia, and various countries in Latin America and other parts of the world. Stalin's bureaucratic counterrevolution in Russia transformed the Comintern into a tool of Soviet foreign policy, destroying the member parties' commitment to working-class self-emancipation. Dissolved by Stalin in 1943 as a gesture of unity with the Allies during World War II.

**Tobinson, Gertrude M.** (ca. 1880–unknown). Participant in the Vladivostok Far Eastern Soviet in Siberia. Wife of Krasnochokov, leader of local Soviet.

**Trotsky, Leon** (1879–1940). Early member of the RSDLP and leader in the Menshevik faction after the 1903 Second Congress. Elected president of the St. Petersburg Soviet in the 1905 Revolution. Opposed Lenin's Bolshevik faction before World War I, but opposed the war alongside the revolutionary left. Trotsky and his supporters joined the Bolshevik Party in May and June of 1917. Elected Commissar of Foreign Affairs after the October Revolution. Leader of the Red Army in the Russian civil war. Stalin's chief political opponent in the 1920s and 1930s; exiled from the Soviet Union in 1929 and assassinated on Stalin's orders in Mexico in 1940.

**Tsereteli, Irakli** (1881–1952). Founding member of the RSDLP. Joined the Menshevik faction at the 1903 conference. Elected to the Second Duma after the 1905 Revolution; exiled to Siberia in 1913. Minister of post and telegraph and of the interior under the Provisional Government. Opposed the October Revolution, returning home to support the British-backed Democratic Republic of Georgia in 1918. Emigrated to Paris after the Red Army took Tbilisi in 1921, then eventually to the United States.

**Uritsky, Moisei Solomonovich** (1873–1918). Menshevik organizer after 1903. Joined the Mezhraiontsy Committee and then the Bolsheviks in July 1917. Became leader in Cheka after the October Revolution and was assassinated by an SR in August 1918.

**Wild Division.** Also known as the Savage Division. A group of Muslim volunteers from Chechnya, Azerbaijan, and elsewhere who fought for the Russian Empire under the command of the Tsar's brother.

**Williams, Albert Rhys** (1883–1962). Congregational minister and journalist. Traveled to Europe to do relief work during World War I. Acquaintance of Reed and Bryant. Toured Russia throughout 1917 and 1918 and wrote *Through the Russian Revolution* (1921), among other pro-Soviet books, over the ensuing decades.

**Yakovleva, Varvara Nikolaevna** (1884–1941 or 1944). Joined the Bolsheviks in 1904; injured during the 1905 Revolution. Candidate member of the Bolshevik Central Committee in 1917. Worked in the Cheka in Moscow after October Revolution. In 1922 became People's Commissar of Education and in 1929 People's Commissar of Finance. Executed by Stalin in 1941 or 1944.

**Zimmerwald Conference**, 1915. Antiwar gathering of revolutionary socialists in Zimmerwald, Switzerland. Followed by the Kienthal Conference in 1916. Served as the basis for a united, antiwar revolutionary left during World War I.

**Zinoviev (Radomyslsky), Grigory Evseyevich** (1883–1936). One of original Bolsheviks and Lenin's closest collaborator, returning with him from exile on the sealed German train in April 1917. As a member of Bolshevik Central Committee, he opposed the October Revolution, but assumed party posts afterward, including as chairman of the Third International. Executed by Stalin in 1936.

# Further Reading

## From Haymarket Books

Tariq Ali, *Leon Trotsky: An Illustrated Introduction*, 2013.

Anthony Arnove, ed., *Russia: From Workers' State to State Capitalism*, 2003.

Tony Cliff, *All Power to the Soviets: Lenin 1914–1917 (Vol. 2)*, 2004.

Duncan Hallas, *Trotsky's Marxism and Other Essays*, 2005.

Neil Harding, *Lenin's Political Thought: Theory and Practice in the Democratic and Socialist Revolutions*, 2009.

Paul LeBlanc, *Lenin and the Revolutionary Party*, 2015.

V.I. Lenin, *State and Revolution*, introduced and annotated by Todd Chretien, 2014.

Kevin Murphy, *Revolution and Counterrevolution: Class Struggle in a Moscow Metal Factory*, 2007.

Alexander Rabinowitch, *The Bolsheviks Come to Power: The Revolution of 1917 in Petrograd*, 2009.

Natalia Sedova and Victor Serge, *The Life and Death of Leon Trotsky*, 2015.

Victor Serge, *Revolution in Danger: Writings from Russia, 1919–1921*, translated and introduced by Ian Birchall, 2011.

Victor Serge, *Year One of the Russian Revolution*, translated and introduced by Peter Sedgwick, 2015.

Alexander Shlyapnikov, *1885–1937: Life of an Old Bolshevik*, 2015.

Leon Trotsky, *History of the Russian Revolution*, 2007.

## Plus

Jane McDermid and Anna Hillyar, *Midwives of Revolution: Female Bolsheviks and Women Workers in 1917* (Athens: Ohio University Press, 1999).

China Miéville, *October: The Story of the Russian Revolution* (London: Verso: 2017).

*Socialist Worker,* ten-part series, *The Making of the Russian Revolution*, 2015, https://socialistworker.org/2015/11/05/making-of-the-russian-revolution.

Ahmed Shawki, "80 Years Since the Russian Revolution," *International Socialist Review* 3 (Winter 1997).

John Reed, *Ten Days that Shook the World* (New York: Penguin Classics, 2007). Also available online at the Marxist Internet Archive.

# Notes

## Introduction

1. Julius Martov, cited in Chris Harman, "Russia: How the Revolution Was Lost," *International Socialism Journal*, Autumn 1967.
2. Leon Trotsky, "Stalinism and Bolshevism," *Socialist Appeal* 1, no. 7, September 25, 1937, 4–5.
3. Karl Marx, "Letter from the International Workingmen's Association to Abraham Lincoln on the Occasion of his Second Inauguration," The General Council of the First International 1866-1868, Minutes (Moscow: Progress Publishers, Moscow, 1964), 266.
4. Karl Marx, *The Eighteenth Brumaire of Louis Bonaparte* (Chicago: Charles Kerr, 1907), 5.
5. See Richard B. Day and Daniel F Gaido, eds. and trans., *Witnesses to Permanent Revolution: The Documentary Record* (Chicago: Haymarket Books, 2011).
6. V.I. Lenin, "Letters from Afar, First Letter," in *Collected Works*, vol. 23 (Moscow: Progress Publishers, 1964), 304.
7. Leon Trotsky, *Results and Prospects*, 1906, chapter 4.
8. Lenin, "What Is to Be Done?" in *Collected Works*, vol. 5 (Moscow: Progress Publishers, 1960), 412.
9. Albert Rhys Williams, *Through the Russian Revolution* (New York: Boni and Liveright, 1921), 177.
10. Victor Serge, *Year One of the Russian Revolution*, translated by Peter Sedgwick (New York: Writers and Readers, 1992), 328.
11. Anthony Arnove, "The Fall of Stalinism Ten Years On," *International Socialist Review* 10 (Winter 2000).
12. Ibid.
13. Eugene V. Debs, "The Day of the People," *Class Struggle* III, no. 10 (February 1919).

## 1. Storm Bursts

1. Claude Anet, *Through the Russian Revolution: Notes of an Eye-Witness, from 12th March to 30th May* (London: Hutchinson & Co., 1917), 13–50.

## 2. Five Days: Scenes from the February Revolution
1. Leon Trotsky, *The History of the Russian Revolution* (Chicago: Haymarket Books, 2007), 75–99.

## 3. Political Parties in Russia
1. V.I. Lenin, "Political Parties in Russia and the Tasks of the Proletariat," *Collected Works*, vol. 24 (Moscow: Progress Publishers, 1964), 93–106.

## 4. The Provisional Government Prevaricates
1. Anet, *Through the Russian Revolution*, 107–13.

## 5. Lenin Returns to Russia
1. F.F. Raskolnikov, *Kronstadt and Petrograd in 1917* (London: New Park, 1982), 76–77.

## 6. Horrible Socialist Jargon
1. Anet, *Through the Russian Revolution*, 134–47.

## 7. Lenin's April Theses
1. V.I. Lenin, in *Pravda*, April 7, 1917, in *Collected Works*, vol. 24, 19–26.

## 8. Tsereteli's April Anti-Theses
1. Anet, *Through the Russian Revolution*, 188–89.

## 9. Kerensky's First Visit to the Army
1. Alexander Kerensky, *The Catastrophe* (New York: Periodicals Service Co., 1927), chapter VIII.

## 10. June 18 Soviet Demonstration
1. Nikolai Nikolaevich Sukhanov and Joel Carmichael, *The Russian Revolution of 1917: A Personal Record* (Princeton, NJ: Princeton University Press, 1984), 415–18.

## 11. Bolsheviks on Battleships
1. Raskolnikov, *Kronstadt and Petrograd*, 124–28.

## 12. The July Days
1. Trotsky, *History of the Russian Revolution*, 378–417.

## 13. The Kornilov Coup
1. Kerensky, *Catastrophe*, chapters 26 and 27.

## 14. Fight Kornilov, but Don't Support Kerensky

1. V.I. Lenin, *Collected Works*, vol. 25 (Moscow: Progress Publishers, 1977), 289–93.

## 15. Use Kerensky as a Gun-Rest to Shoot at Kornilov

1. Trotsky, *History of the Russian Revolution*, chapters 33 and 34.

## 16. A Peaceful Road to All Power to the Soviets?

1. Lenin, *Collected Works*, vol. 25, 308–14.

## 17. Overview of the Situation in September 1917

1. Morgan Philips Price, *Capitalist Europe and Socialist Russia* November 1918, published in May 1919 by the British Socialist Party, http://www.marxistsfr.org/archive/price/1918/europe-russia.htm.

## 18. The Provisional Government and the Soviet

1. Arthur Ransome, *The Truth about Russia*, pamphlet published by the Workers' Socialist Federation, 1918, https://www.marxists.org/history/archive/ransome/1918/truth-russia.htm.

## 19. Marxism and Insurrection

1. Lenin, "Marxism and Insurrection," *Collected Works*, vol. 26, 22–27.

## 20. The Bolsheviks Vote on Insurrection

1. Ann Bone, trans., *The Bolsheviks and the October Revolution: Minutes of the Central Committee of the Russian Social Democratic Labor Party (Bolsheviks) August 1917–February 1918* (London: Pluto Press, 1974), 87–109.

## 21. Preparing October

1. Albert Rhys Williams, *Through the Russian Revolution* (New York: Boni and Liveright, 1921), 89–97.

## 22. Smolny and the Winter Palace

1. Louise Bryant, *Six Red Months in Russia* (New York: George H. Doran Company, 1918), chapters 4 and 8.

## 23. Women Fighters in the October Revolution

1. Alexandra Kollontai, *Selected Articles and Speeches* (Moscow: Progress Publishers, 1984; first published in *Zhensky Zhurnal* (*Women's Journal*) 11, November 1927.

## 24. The Soviets Take Power
1. John Reed, *Ten Days That Shook the World* (New York: Boni and Liveright, 1919).

## 25. The Intelligentsia Desert
1. Williams, *Through the Russian Revolution*, 100–103.

## 26. The Mensheviks Walk Out and Split
1. Sukhanov and Carmichael, *Russian Revolution*, 631–46.

## 27. The October Days
1. N.K. Krupskaya, *Reminiscences of Lenin*, translated by Bernard Isaacs (New York: International Publishers, 1970), "The October Days" chapter.

## 28. A New Power
1. Trotsky, *History of the Russian Revolution*, chapters 47 and 48.

## 29. Kerensky Is Coming!
1. John Reed, "Kerensky Is Coming!" *Liberator*, July 1918, 23–27.

## 30. The Fall of the Constituent Assembly
1. Isaac Nachman Steinberg, *In the Workshop of Revolution* (London: Victor Gollancz, Ltd.: 1955), 52–56.

## 31. Radek at Brest-Litovsk
1. William Hard, *Raymond Robins' Own Story* (New York: Harper & Brothers Publishers, 1920), 123–125.

## 32. The Far Eastern Soviet in Siberia
1. Interview with Gertrude M. Tobinson, *Liberator*, April 1919, 31–36.

## 33. The Red Convicts of Cherm
1. Williams, *Through the Russian Revolution*, 207–15.

## 34. The Origins of Workers' Control in Russia
1. John Reed, "The Origins of Workers' Control in Russia," *Revolutionary Age* 1, no. 3, November 23, 1918.

## 35. The Ministry of Social Welfare
1. Louise Bryant, *Six Red Months in Russia*, chapter 12.

## 36. The First Woman Commissar

1. Alexandra Kollontai, *The Autobiography of a Sexually Emancipated Communist Woman*, translated by Salvator Attansio, https://www.marxists.org/archive/kollonta/1926/autobiography.htm.

## 37. Women Workers and Soviet Russia

1. Inessa Armand, "Women Workers and Soviet Russia," first published in *Stat'i*, 1920, 68, in Russian as "Zadachi rabotnits v Sovetskoi Rossii"; translated from French by Todd Chretien from https://www.marxists.org/francais/armand/works/1920/07/ouvriere.htm.

## 38. Retrospective

1. Williams, *Through the Russian Revolution*, 275–86.

# Index

# About Haymarket Books

Haymarket Books is a radical, independent, nonprofit book publisher based in Chicago.

Our mission is to publish books that contribute to struggles for social and economic justice. We strive to make our books a vibrant and organic part of social movements and the education and development of a critical, engaged, international left.

We take inspiration and courage from our namesakes, the Haymarket martyrs, who gave their lives fighting for a better world. Their 1886 struggle for the eight-hour day—which gave us May Day, the international workers' holiday—reminds workers around the world that ordinary people can organize and struggle for their own liberation. These struggles continue today across the globe—struggles against oppression, exploitation, poverty, and war.

Since our founding in 2001, Haymarket Books has published more than five hundred titles. Radically independent, we seek to drive a wedge into the risk-averse world of corporate book publishing. Our authors include Noam Chomsky, Arundhati Roy, Rebecca Solnit, Angela Davis, Howard Zinn, Amy Goodman, Wallace Shawn, Mike Davis, Winona LaDuke, Ilan Pappé, Richard Wolff, Dave Zirin, Keeanga-Yamahtta Taylor, Nick Turse, Dahr Jamail, David Barsamian, Elizabeth Laird, Amira Hass, Mark Steel, Avi Lewis, Naomi Klein, and Neil Davidson. We are also the trade publishers of the acclaimed Historical Materialism Book Series and of Dispatch Books.

# Also Available from Haymarket Books

*In Celebration of the Centenary of the Russian Revolution*

*1905*
  Leon Trotsky

*Alexander Shlyapnikov, 1885–1937*
  Barbara C. Allen

*Alexandra Kollontai: A Biography*
  Cathy Porter

*All Power to the Soviets: Lenin 1914–1917 (Vol. 2)*
  Tony Cliff

*The Bolsheviks Come to Power*
  Alexander Rabinowitch

*Building the Party: Lenin 1893–1914 (Vol. 1)*
  by Tony Cliff

*Clara Zetkin: Selected Writings*
Clara Zetkin, edited by Philip S.
Foner, Foreword by Angela Y. Davis
and Rosalyn Baxandall

*Eyewitnesses to the Russian Revolution*
Edited by Todd Chretien

*History of the Russian Revolution*
Leon Trotsky

*Lenin and the Revolutionary Party*
Paul Le Blanc

*Lenin Rediscovered*
Lars T. Lih

*Lenin's Moscow*
by Alfred Rosmer, translated by Ian
Birchall

*Lenin's Political Thought*
Neil Harding

*Leon Trotsky and the Organizational
Principles of the Revolutionary Party*
Dianne Feeley, Paul Le Blanc and
Thomas Twiss, Introduction by
George Breitman

*Leon Trotsky: An Illustrated Introduction*
Tariq Ali, Illustrated by Phil Evans

*Lessons of October*
Leon Trotsky

*The Life and Death of Leon Trotsky*
Natalia Sedova and Victor Serge

*The October Revolution in Prospect
and Retrospect*
John E. Marot

*October Song: Bolshevik Triumph,
Communist Tragedy, 1917–1924*
Paul Le Blanc

*Red Petrograd: Revolution
in the Factories, 1917–1918*
S. A. Smith

*Reminiscences of Lenin*
Nadezhda K. Krupskaya

*Revolution Besieged: Lenin
1917–1923 (Vol. 3)*
Tony Cliff

*Revolution and Counterrevolution:
Class Struggle in a Moscow Metal Factory*
Kevin Murphy

*Revolution in Danger*
Victor Serge

*The Russian Social-Democratic Labour
Party: 1889–1904*
Edited by Richard Mullin

*Russia: From Workers' State
to State Capitalism*
Anthony Arnove, Tony Cliff,
Chris Harman and Ahmed Shawki

*State and Revolution*
V. I. Lenin, annotated and
introduced by Todd Chretien

*To the Masses: Proceedings of the Third
Congress of the Communist International,
1921*
Edited by John Riddell

*Toward the United Front: Proceedings
of the Fourth Congress of the Communist
International, 1922*
Edited by John Riddell

*Trotsky and the Problem
of Soviet Bureaucracy*
Thomas Twiss

*Unfinished Leninism: The Rise and
Return of a Revolutionary Doctrine*
by Paul Le Blanc

*Year One of the Russian Revolution*
Victor Serge

# About the Editor

Todd Chretien is a member of the International Socialist Organization, a frequent contributor to *Socialist Worker* and the *International Socialist Review*, and editor of Haymarket Books' edition of *State and Revolution* by V. I. Lenin (2014).